GUIDANCE DEPT.

THE COMPASSIONATE SCHOOL

A Practical Guide to Educating Abused and Traumatized Children

Gertrude Morrow

Prentice-Hall, Inc.
Englewood Cliffs, New Jersey

Prentice-Hall International, Inc., *London*
Prentice-Hall of Australia, Pty. Ltd., *Sydney*
Prentice-Hall Canada, Inc., *Toronto*
Prentice-Hall of India Private Ltd., *New Delhi*
Prentice-Hall of Japan, Inc., *Tokyo*
Prentice-Hall of Southeast Asia Pte. Ltd., *Singapore*
Editora Prentice-Hall do Brasil Ltda., *Rio de Janeiro*
Prentice-Hall Hispanoamericana, S.A., *Mexico*

© 1987 *by*

PRENTICE-HALL, INC.

Englewood Cliffs, N.J.

10 9 8 7 6 5 4

*For retired teachers, especially my aunt, Mary R. Riggs,
who give continued service through volunteer tutoring
and substitute teaching. Your contributions are appreci-
ated and valued.*

Library of Congress Cataloging-in-Publication Data

Morrow, Gertrude.
    The Compassionate school.

    Includes index.
    1. Teacher participation in personnel service—
United States.   2. Abused children—Education—
United States.   3. Problem children—Education
United States.   4.Teacher and community—
United States.   I. Title.
LB1027.5.M625   1987   371.4'6   86-30597

ISBN 0-13-154742-9

Printed in the United States of America

About This Book

"There is no such thing as a normal classroom anymore. Every teacher has to deal with all kinds of disturbed kids," says Ruth Friedman, Chief of Psycho-Social Therapy at Pritzker Children's Psychiatric Unit of Michael Reese Hospital, in a February 12, 1984 article in the *Chicago Tribune*.

The Compassionate School: A Practical Guide to Educating Abused and Traumatized Children will help classroom teachers, school administrators, counselors, and psychologists identify and work with these disturbed children who have been abused and neglected, distressed by parental divorce, and affected by the loss of a significant attachment figure through death or abandonment.

Children and adolescents can also be traumatized when they witness acts of violence or accidents in which people are killed. This also happens in response to hearing that a classmate has committed suicide, or that children in their own community or elsewhere have been kidnapped, brutally killed, or held hostage.

Traumas make children extremely anxious and create obstacles to learning and mastering normal fears that come with growing up. Withdrawing, acting out aggressively, and regressing to the behavior of a younger child are among the ways children react to trauma. Teachers confronted with students who wear a hurt or lost look, who do not talk, do not remember what is said, or who wander aimlessly about the room, wonder how to reach and teach them. This book tells how, by becoming a *compassionate school*.

A compassionate school is more than the sum of the compassionate individuals found in every school. First and foremost, it embraces the philosophy of community education. This means that the community and school must not only cooperate in the education of the children, but also that the school must be concerned about the education of *all* members of the community. Second, a compassionate school promotes social development as well as intellectual development, instills altruistic attitudes, and demands social acceptance of and respect for *all* students. Third, in a compassionate school the classroom will be organized for cooperative learning. Students of varying abilities will work together on a team, supporting and helping each other to accomplish the goals of the learning project. Competition will not be between one student and another, but between teams or classes that are balanced in terms of skills and learning expertise.

This book offers step-by-step procedures and strategies for becoming a compassionate school so that you can meet the challenge posed by traumatized children.

Consider the following:

- It is estimated that one million children are abused every year. At least half, and perhaps as many as two-thirds, are school-aged.

- One million adolescents run away from home every year. Most are victims of abuse, and a majority of these adolescents become prostitutes or delinquents.

- Researchers have concluded that one out of four girls and at least one out of seven boys will be sexually abused before age eighteen. (It is possible that these estimates are too conservative.)

- At least two thousand children die each year as a result of neglect or physical abuse.

- Twenty percent of children live in families whose income is below the poverty level. Neglect of children in these families may be related to their condition of poverty.

- Each year, over one million new children below the age of eighteen experience the divorce of their parents. As many as half of all children have now experienced family disruption through divorce.

- Over a quarter of a million women are in prison, a majority of whom are mothers of young children.

- Fifty to sixty percent of mothers are in the work force. Thirty to fifty percent of children who are currently entering school have spent their earliest years in a child care center or under the care of a person other than their mother. There is an enormous number of latchkey children.

- Suicides among teenagers have been increasing at an alarming rate.

- At least five percent of all children experience the death of a parent before age eighteen.

We can serve these children and their families more effectively than we have been by striving to be a compassionate school. Even if the ideal of the compassionate school cannot be fully realized, every school can at least fully participate in the strenuous efforts to reduce child abuse in all its forms, reduce alcohol and drug abuse in adults as well as children, prevent child and adolescent suicide, and ameliorate the effects of divorce, death, and separation on the developmental progress of children and adolescents.

With its straightforward, easy-to-understand explanations and ready-to-use checklists and forms, *The Compassionate School* will help you reach every child in your classroom.

Gertrude Morrow

About the Author

Gertrude Morrow, M.A. (University of Michigan), has been a practicing psychologist for over twenty-five years, including nine years as a school psychologist for the Evanston and Northbrook (Illinois) school districts. Her professional experience also includes service as a psychologist at the Lansing Children's Center and school diagnostician for the Mason County Schools in Michigan, and psychologist for the Evanston Hospital Evaluation Center for Learning.

Also the author of *Helping Chronically Ill Children in School: A Practical Guide for Teachers, Counselors, and Administrators* (Parker, 1985), Mrs. Morrow is listed in the National Register of Health Service Providers in Psychology and belongs to the Michigan and National Associations of School Psychologists.

Contents

PART I

PROTECTING CHILDREN

Schools have a moral and legal obligation to see that children are protected from harm while in school, as well as enroute to and from school. The school must also be concerned about protecting children outside of school hours because millions of children have no adult available to them for several hours a day. Chapter 1 describes school policies, procedures, and programs that are needed to protect children from abuse and make them feel safe in a world full of danger and terror.

Chapter **1**

Expanding the
Protective Function
of the School

Being a child in today's world is not easy. With the American family under stress, with so many adults busy and burdened, there is little doubt that basic nurture, and protection by adults, both so necessary for healthy development, are lacking for many children.

Some experts tell us that children can truly feel safe only if there are several adults whom they know well and who are interested in their development, and one or more of them is available at all times. Yet millions of children are alone before and after school because of their parents' work schedules. To an extent, this fact implicates the school: "Schools have a legal, moral, and historical mandate to ensure that there are many adults who are interested in a particular child's welfare."[1]

This chapter will suggest ways in which the school can provide a protective umbrella for children outside of school, as well as while they are attending class. First, we will consider the plight of latchkey children.

LATCHKEY CHILDREN

Children who take care of themselves without an adult present have come to be known as latchkey children. They are so called because they often wear a key around the neck and let themselves into an empty house when they return from school. The dramatic increase in single-parent families and families with two working parents has produced

3

sixteen million children between the ages of five and thirteen whose mothers work.[2] Some of these children are in day care homes or centers, or have the other parent at home before and after school, but there are probably between five and ten million, some as young as five or six, who are left by themselves.[3] As we might expect, the largest number of latchkey children live in low-income areas, while high-income suburban areas have the fewest number. If your school is in a low-income area, it is possible that one child out of every three goes home to an empty house. Many of these children are also alone for one hour or more in the mornings before school starts. Children who are alone in the mornings have special stresses that impact directly on getting to school and being suitably clothed and fed. Let's take a look at Jason:

> Jason, a third grader, lives alone with his mother who leaves for work at 7:30, an hour before Jason starts out for school. His conscientious mother gets Jason up early enough to see that he is dressed and groomed properly and eats a good breakfast. She fixes his lunch and reminds him of the rules he must follow in her absence. When she leaves, Jason turns on the TV and becomes mesmerized. He does not notice the time until school has started. Rushing because he is late, he forgets his lunch and school papers, and on the way to school begins to dread the scornful look he has learned to expect from his teacher.

Not all children who are alone in the morning are up, dressed, and fed before parents leave for work. A study of latchkey children revealed that such parents usually telephone their children to wake them up, but do not usually call to tell them it is time to leave for school. These children not only have to get themselves off to school on their own, they must also dress and groom themselves without supervision, and get their own breakfast and lunch.

Some households are similar to Mary's:

> Mary is a nine-year-old fourth grader who has two younger siblings, six-year-old Joey and five-year-old Martha. Mary is very busy from the time both parents leave for work at 7:30. She clears the table and rinses the dishes. Then she reminds Joey and Martha to brush their teeth and wipe their faces. She makes three lunches while her siblings draw at the table. Next, she arranges three piles of coats, lunches, and school things, checks the house to be sure lights and the TV are off, locks the house, and then escorts her brother and sister the four blocks to school.

School Behaviors of Latchkey Children

Jason watches TV to forget he feels scared, sad, and lonely. Mary is too busy to think about or feel anything until she gets to school. At school, Jason drifts into a prolonged reverie about scary things that could happen to him when he is alone, and imagines what he would do to come through these harrowing experiences without harm. This is his way of coping with the fears engendered by being alone so much, a way to rehearse the best actions to take in dangerous situations. He gets little schoolwork done unless another child, his teacher, or an aide works with him. Interacting with another person keeps him from daydreaming.

When Mary is no longer responsible for her younger siblings, she begins to hear an inner voice saying, "It's a lot of work taking care of Joey and Martha. I wish I could be the one being taken care of." Mary's teacher describes her as being disorganized because she can't keep track of where she left her papers, seldom has the correct place in her book, and her desk is usually in disarray. Mary's behavior seems to show that she is unconsciously acting helpless and irresponsible in school so she can be taken care of.

Although their responses are different, both Jason and Mary are feeling burdened and deprived. Their learning is impaired because inner preoccupations and unmet needs interrupt their attention and concentration. These children who are being cheated of their rights to be protected and nurtured are using school time to cope and compensate.

Fortunately for the schools, not all latchkey children have learning problems, but a large number do. Even if latchkey children are good students and well adjusted socially, they may be absent frequently because they miss the bus, are often tardy like Jason, or are poorly clad or unfed. All of these problems cause difficulties for teachers and principals.

Scared, Lonely, Bored, and Sad Children

Educators Lynnette and Thomas Long interviewed hundreds of latchkey children. They found that these children are scared, lonely, and bored; many are sad. Most latchkey children are expected to go directly home and lock themselves in the house. They are not permitted to have friends over or play outside.[4] These requirements place severe restrictions on two important aspects of growth: socialization and physical activity. Their isolation deprives them of the interpersonal experiences that develop social skills, and the physical activity needed for health, well-being, and as an outlet for tension and pent-up emotions.

Locked in, but Still Frightened

Although they are locked in their houses, latchkey children are afraid when they are alone. They hear sounds and imagine that someone is trying to get in. In their boredom, some of them may do forbidden things like playing with matches, cooking on the stove, watching scary movies on TV, or going outside to play. They place themselves in dangerous situations by breaking rules and, knowing this, they are afraid of the possible consequences. Scary movies fascinate children, and when an adult is present they can be helped to master fears by having the movies explained or interpreted by the adult. However, children who are alone are likely to become intensely frightened because no one is present to reassure them or clarify the experience for them.

Because of this aloneness, latchkey children look to pets for comfort and protection. Frightened children want large mean dogs; those who have them admit to feeling less afraid because they believe that the dog will scare away possible intruders. Lonely children want small pets they can talk to and cuddle.[5]

PROTECTING CHILDREN IN SCHOOL

Hundreds of thousands of children are reported missing each year. Although many missing children are runaways, others are abducted and murdered, and still others are kidnapped by a noncustodial parent. If a child is expected at school, we can no longer assume that he is safely at home or with a parent on a trip or an errand.

Phone Check of Absent Children

Protection of children requires that someone at school call home to check on a child who does not show up when expected. Some schools already do this routinely, but many do not. Those that do not should be aware that the Adam Walsh Child Resource Center (Ft. Lauderdale, Florida) actively lobbies for child protection legislation, and among other efforts, it is pressuring state legislatures to pass laws that would require schools to notify parents of a child's absence after the morning roll is taken. It may soon be a legal requirement to make such a phone check.

Protection from Physical Abuse

Reports by school staff of abuse severe enough to cause physical damage and occasionally death, are received regularly by several national organizations. Historically, corporal punishment has been an accepted method of dealing with child misconduct, both at school and at home. However, there is no longer a tenable rationale for its use. Corporal punishment does not work. On the contrary, there is an abundant literature documenting that paddling children *increases* aggressiveness and creates retaliatory hostility in its recipients. Studies have shown that the highest rates of vandalism against schools occur in places where corporal punishment is prevalent or excessive.

Abolishing Corporal Punishment. Corporal punishment has long been banned in most other countries of the world. Yet, despite what is known about the physical and psychological damage done to children who are punished by paddlings and so on, only a few states have enacted laws to prevent the use of corporal punishment. Laws in every state, as well as a national law, provide for the protection of children from physical abuse by their caretakers. However, school personnel are not considered caretakers; children are not protected by law from abuse by teachers and principals. It is a strange paradox that educators are allowed to paddle and inflict severe physical punishment that would be considered child abuse if delivered by parents. In essence, the practice of corporal punishment in schools sanctions child abuse at home.

The Law and Corporal Punishment. Child advocates are pushing for a federal law that would prohibit the use of corporal punishment in schools. Others are suggesting that we must grant children the same constitutional rights of protection from cruel and unusual punishment (Eighth Amendment) and guarantee of due process that adults have. Supreme Court rulings (*Baker v. Owen*, 1975 and *Ingraham v. Wright*, 1977) have made it difficult to challenge corporal punishment in federal court, either on constitutional grounds or on grounds of due process. In *Baker v. Owen*, the Court ruled that reasonable force (most difficult to define) by school officials is permissible. In *Ingraham v. Wright*, the Court ruled that the Eighth Amendment (prohibiting cruel and unusual punishment) does not apply to discipline in schools.

School Board Policy and Corporal Punishment. It is encouraging that Boards of Education in many large urban school systems have established policies forbidding the use of corporal punishment; other smaller systems have followed suit. In some instances, State Boards of Education have created policies that either forbid or restrict the use of corporal punishment.

Abolishing corporal punishment will be more easily accomplished if educators know what kind of disciplinary approaches are more constructive and more effective. Through the National Center for the Study of Corporal Punishment and Alternatives in the Schools (Temple

University, Philadelphia, Pennsylvania), workshops can be arranged to train educators in alternative methods of discipline.

Protection from Psychological Abuse

An insidious form of child mistreatment that teachers and administrators are sometimes guilty of is verbal and emotional abuse. Making fun of children, calling them demeaning nicknames, deprecating or humiliating them, and using bizarre kinds of disciplinary measures are among the many forms this kind of abuse takes.

Use of Teacher Consultants. The public is demanding that schools rid classrooms of incompetent teachers, and peer supervision may be one of the most effective ways to accomplish this. A plan of peer supervision was implemented in 1981 in the Toledo, Ohio public schools through a contractual agreement between the administration and the local union, and has now gained the support of its national organization, the American Federation of Teachers. The Toledo plan provides a system of checks and balances, assuring that the administration and the union will have commensurate powers that allow them to work together compatibly. The peer supervisors, called consulting teachers, are chosen by mutual agreement between the administration and the union. They relinquish their classroom responsibilities and become full-time evaluators.

The consulting teachers observe first-year teachers in class, write evaluations, and hold conferences with them to discuss performance and offer advice. In March, they recommend whether the new teachers should be retained or fired. They have the same responsibilities toward veteran teachers with problems but have no say in deciding any course of action. A nine-member review board, made up of five teachers and four administrators, considers the evaluations submitted by the consulting teachers. Six votes are needed to take action, and decisions of the review board are subject to approval by the superintendent and the school board. Consulting teachers are allowed to serve no more than three years.[6]

PROTECTING CHILDREN IN THE "OUTSIDE WORLD"

Parents do not like to leave their children alone, but do so out of necessity. They invariably feel guilty and do not want others to know their child is home alone for fear of being judged or criticized. They also believe it is a protection for their child if others do not know he or she is alone.[7]

Teachers need to know what hours the mother works, and what arrangements have been made for the child when she is not there. If the mother does not volunteer this information, the school should ask for it. If a teacher has more than one latchkey child in class, it is a good idea to keep a chart handy that lists the plan for each child. (See Figure 1-1.) Lynnette and Thomas Long suggest ways in which parents can alleviate fears, dangers, and undue stress for children who must be alone. Recommend their book, *The Handbook for Latchkey Children and Their Parents*, to parents. Another helpful book is *Alone After School: A Self-Care Guide for Latchkey Children and Their Parents* by Helen L. Swan and Victoria Houston, published by Prentice-Hall.

What Schools Can Do

We may believe that all school-age children should be under the care or supervision of an interested adult, but there are not nearly enough child care spaces to make this possible. Instead of criticizing parents who leave their children alone, we should support and guide them so that they can provide a safe and constructive environment. Approaches to helping children who must be on their own involve reducing their sense of isolation, increasing their sense of being safe, and finding a solution for their boredom and lack of physical activity. In each category there are ways in which schools can help.

Reduce Isolation. Social isolation, the lack of a support network, is a significant aspect of family situations that produce physical child abuse. Children suffer from being isolated even if they are not abused. Garbarino says, "Isolation is the greatest danger facing children."[8]

Social isolation can be lessened by school policies that encourage social events in which parents, children, and staff participate; frequent visiting at school by parents; the use of parent volunteers in offices, library, and classrooms; and the use of school facilities for self-help group meetings.

Our challenge is to find a replacement for the kin network, which in the past was the source of important support functions for families. Aunts, uncles, and grandparents, who are generally no longer available to assist in the nurturing and protecting of children, must be replaced by other adults in the school and neighborhood. Ellen Galinsky and William Hooks refer to day care as "The New Extended Family"[9] while others focus on the development of social networks as replacement of the extended family.

Establish Neighborhood Networks. By recognizing that families need a social support system in order to rear children successfully,

INDIVIDUAL PLANS FOR EACH LATCHKEY CHILD IN CLASS

Child's name _____

Parent(s) are not home from _____ to _____

In case of emergency call (Telephone #) _____

(Person's name) _____

Arrangements for child after school _____

_____

_____

- -

Child's name _____

Parent(s) are not home from _____ to _____

In case of emergency call (Telephone #) _____

(Person's name) _____

Arrangements for child after school _____

_____

_____

Child's name ————————————————————————

Parent(s) are not home from ————————— to —————————

In case of emergency call (Telephone #) ————————————

(Person's name) ————————————

Arrangements for child after school ————————————

————————————————————————————————

————————————————————————————————

Child's name ————————————————————————

Parent(s) are not home from ————————— to —————————

In case of emergency call (Telephone #) ————————————

(Person's name) ————————————

Arrangements for child after school ————————————

————————————————————————————————

————————————————————————————————

Figure 1-1

schools can facilitate the development of neighborhood networks. In large cities there are community organizers, often professionals hired by the city or deployed from nearby universities. These people find leaders within a neighborhood whom they train and assist in developing social networks and needed social programs within the community. In other communities similar services may be provided by child advocate organizations or mental health associations. The school principal or counselor should determine if these services exist and actively cooperate with the leaders.

Another way that schools facilitate the development of social networks is through activities of the P.T.A. Regularly scheduled coffee klatches at school encourage neighbors to meet and get acquainted. Neighborhood chairmen, appointed by the P.T.A. and given names and phone numbers of families on the block, can plan block parties or other social events among neighbors, help mothers make informal child care exchanges, and so on.

Initiate Self-Protection Week. Although some school systems have successfully incorporated units on physical and sexual abuse into the curriculum, most of the educators I have talked to are not ready to do so. However, I think the notion of setting aside a week soon after school begins each fall as Self-Protection Week would be accepted by many educators. The concept of self protection is sufficiently different from the concept of safety to deserve a separate emphasis and special time to publicize its importance. Information about programs such as the Block Parent/Safe Home plan and PhoneFriend (discussed later in this chapter) can be given to the children during Self-Protection Week so these services will be linked in their minds to the concept of self-protection.

During Self-Protection Week, children should receive information about child maltreatment. Thus, they will know that child abuse is something they can talk about. Most physically abused children do not realize that parents or other caretakers are failing in the obligation to protect and nurture them. They think that they are bad and deserve the abuse they receive. Children need to learn to discriminate between adult behavior that is appropriate and that which is not appropriate. It has been found that when children are taught this kind of discrimination, and the words *physical abuse* and *sexual abuse,* they will seek help for themselves from trusted adults. I believe it is feasible to teach these basic ideas in short programs.

One aspect of learning to protect oneself is accepting a degree of dependence on others. We must teach and reinforce the concept of *mutual protection.* Our cultural tradition has prized rugged individualism, and the values of cooperation and group spirit among children have been overlooked. When cooperation among children is emphasized, and acts of benevolence of one group member toward another are rewarded, children learn to stick up for one another, go for help when one is in trouble, or offer help themselves when that is within their capability. Children come to understand that protecting each other is a natural extension of self-protection, and that this is expected of them.

Alleviate Boredom: Provide Innovative After-School Programs

There is little chance of alleviating children's at-home-alone boredom and providing them with needed physical activity unless they are in a child care program or otherwise involved in an organized activity. Not all children are inclined toward competitive sports or music, the usual extracurricular activities provided by schools. After-school clubs, focused on fine arts, homemaking, and recreational interests are suitable for the elementary age group as well as adolescents. Schools can offer art, drama, creative writing, cooking, knitting, sewing, weaving, and inventing (games, machines) clubs. Participation in these clubs will help children discover interests and talents, as well as alleviate boredom. Cooperative sports and games will allow children to have fun, learn to cooperate, and develop social skills. This kind of physical activity enhances self-esteem because everyone is a winner, and no one is a loser. Survival skill classes that teach children how to use household appliances properly, how to handle simple emergencies, how to feed, toilet, and comfort small children, and how to cook are especially appropriate for latchkey youngsters.

If schools routinely provided this diversity of after-school activities, it would automatically be providing child care for children of ages nine, ten, and older. Such programs should be available to all children, thus creating enrichment opportunities for children who have a parent at home but an otherwise barren home life. Children who suffer any form of abuse have a tremendous need to build self-esteem, and to reestablish a sense of trust in adults. Enrichment programs create opportunities for these children to get back on the track of healthy personality development through involvement in worthwhile activities that interest and motivate them.

What Parents Can Do

Parents and parent-school groups can do much to increase their children's sense of safety.

Block Parent Plan. Getting to and from school is dangerous in some areas. Ideally, children should always walk to school in groups. If groupings don't occur spontaneously, parents should try to arrange for their child to walk with others on the block. For the child who must get him- or herself off in the morning, it helps to have a neighbor's child call for him or her. You may need to encourage parents to make such arrangements. Inform the shy mother or one who is new to the neighborhood who nearby children are, and which families might be most cooperative and receptive.

Even if no danger is thought to exist, children will feel less anxious on their way to and from school if a Block Parent plan is in operation. In some areas the program may be called Safe Homes or something similar. Whatever it is called, the goal of protection is implicit in each plan. Adult volunteers whose homes are on the routes that children take to school agree to stand by at school opening and closing times so their home can be a haven for any child who is frightened or in danger. A large orange sign is placed in the front window of the house or apartment, and children are instructed at the beginning of each school year to become aware of the location of these "safe homes." In my school district, the P.T.A. organizes the Block Parent plan. In areas where a majority of mothers work, other "at-home" adults, such as retirees or elderly persons, may need to be recruited for a Safe Home plan. If the P.T.A. cannot set up the program itself, it should take the initiative to find some individual or organization from the community at large to do it.

PhoneFriend. Another support service for latchkey children that is beginning to proliferate is called PhoneFriend (from community to community, the name of the service varies). This service provides a friendly person whom a child can contact by telephone. For a child, this is like having a surrogate parent because the person will listen, reassure, help a child solve a problem, explain something he or she doesn't understand about the homework, or advise the child how to deal with a crisis. As a result, children feel less alone and less frightened. Experience has shown that many children call PhoneFriend for comfort, or just to reassure themselves that someone is there if they need help. If adult volunteers are used, the cost of providing this service is minimal, and can be funded rather easily from one or more charitable organizations within the community. The organizer of such a service can conceivably be the Association of University Women, Mental Health Association, or any church or child welfare organization, as well as the P.T.A.

SCHOOL-AGE CHILD CARE

Prior to 1980, few school-age children were being cared for within the framework of an appropriate care center, but school-age child care plans have increasingly been implemented. It appears that many individuals, government officials, and community agencies are sensing the imperative to provide appropriate kinds of care for children five years of age and older. School-age child care programs vary widely depending on the needs and makeup of individual communities. A manual that is invaluable to anyone wishing to start a day care center is *School-Age Child Care: An Action Manual.*[10] Another which is valuable for its description of a variety of programs that work is *The New Extended Family: Day Care That Works.*[11]

Garbarino poses this challenge to schools: "Latchkey children...frequently exhibit a variety of developmental problems that impair school functioning.... Schools must take the leadership in bringing nurturant control and supervision back into children's lives."[12] If you accept his challenge, two approaches in regard to leadership are possible. One is for schools to call on community agencies to initiate action on behalf of latchkey children; the other is for a school system itself to implement child care programs. The latter is more difficult and demanding, but it is being done successfully in some communities.

School Collaboration

Whichever approach is taken, an implicit premise is that there should be collaboration between the school and the organizations of the community. If the school is establishing child care programs, it should ask for support and assistance from the community; in turn, if parents or community agencies want to start programs, they should know that the school system will collaborate.

Day Care Centers Located in Schools. Without themselves being responsible for the administration of day care programs, there are a number of ways in which schools can collaborate with community efforts to bring all children under adult supervision. The most obvious and perhaps the most important way to collaborate is to allow a day care program operated by others to be housed in the school. The additional utilities and custodial service needed to operate the care center after school hours is only a small financial extra for the school system and can be contributed as another show of interest and support. A number of school boards have established this pattern of involvement.

Bus Routes. A second way that the school and the community can cooperate is to arrange bus routes that allow children to be dropped off at centers located elsewhere in the community. One of the more exciting experiments being tried is attaching day care centers to facilities for the elderly. Transportation to such a combined care center might be too costly for the providers of the program, but costs little extra for the school district. Day care homes are popular in some communities and are usually within the boundaries of the school district. Children can just as easily be dropped off at a day care home as at their own residence.

Referral Source. For parents seeking to solve their child care problems, the school can serve as a referral source. Most schools have counselors or social workers who could easily compile a list of reputable day care programs operating in the community, and make this information available to parents. Where financial help is needed, information about where to seek this can also be offered.

Use of School Facilities by Outside Centers. Administrators of day care centers located in churches or "Y"s may wish to expand program opportunities for children by using school facilities. For example, woodworking, cooking, sewing, and swimming facilities are often desired, and these may be available in a nearby school. In this instance, the school collaborates by allowing the outside child care center to bring children to the school to use these special facilities.

Check-in Plan for Pre-teens. Older elementary and junior high school students, feeling the need for more autonomy and freedom, may be rebellious about the idea of going to a child care center. Yet these youngsters need a sense of centering in their lives, and the protection of someone knowing where they are. A suitable arrangement for pre-adolescents could be to have the center serve merely as a check-in point so that someone would keep track of their whereabouts. Each young person would be officially enrolled at the center, and assigned to a specific staff member whose surrogate parenting job would be to know whether a child was at music, dance, or art class, scouts, soccer practice, and so on.

Youth Centers. Adolescents are adrift in our society. Even though they can and want to take care of themselves, they still need adults to guide and show caring for them. They struggle to come to terms with mixed-up emotions, opposing impulses, loyalty conflicts, severe disappointments, and unexpected disillusionment. Drop-in youth centers are an answer to the needs of adolescents.

Youth centers are staffed by young social workers or youth group workers who dress casually and mix and mingle with the young people, establishing relationships and offering guidance. The youth workers are there to listen, counsel, help youngsters find jobs, help them develop social skills and find friends, or direct them to places where they can get needed services. Young people may need legal or medical help which they do not want their parents to know about; or they may need birth control information or help with a drug or alcohol problem that has not yet been discovered by the parents. Youth centers are typically organized by a coalition of community agencies and budgeted through United Fund monies. Schools should be represented on the boards of youth centers in order to have input into their programming and selection of personnel.

REPORTING CHILD ABUSE

If you are working in a school, you are required *by law* to report to the state child protective agency any child you have sufficient reason to believe is being abused by a parent or caretaker. If this comes as a surprise to you, it is because many school districts do not have a Board-established policy about child abuse, and administrators have not communicated to staff members that they have a legal mandate to report. There are even instances where top administrators appear to be ignorant of the law. *All* states have laws that explicitly name school personnel among those who *must* report suspected child abuse, and thirty-nine states stipulate a penalty for *failing to report*.

Every school system should adopt and issue a child abuse and neglect policy that informs school personnel of their legal obligations and immunities with regard to reporting. The School Board should also inform the local community that school personnel are obligated to report suspected child abuse or neglect.

Any policy regarding child abuse and neglect must comply with state laws, which vary from state to state. The reporting policy should cite the elements listed in Figure 1-2. Most important, the adopted policy must be widely disseminated. Copies of the policy should be distributed to all school employees and parents and throughout the community *every year*.

MODEL FOR CHILD ABUSE POLICY STATEMENT

Element to Be Cited	Sample Wording
A brief rationale for involving school personnel in reporting	Because of their sustained contact with school-age children, school employees are in an excellent position to identify abused or neglected children and to refer them for treatment and protection.
The name and appropriate section numbers of the state reporting statute	To comply with the Mandatory Reporting of Child Abuse Act (Section 350-1 through 350-5), Hawaii Revised Statutes (1968), as amended (Supp. 1975),...
Who specifically is mandated to report and (if applicable) who may report	...it is the policy of the _____ School District that any teacher or other school employee...
Reportable conditions as defined by state law	...who suspects that a child's physical or mental health or welfare may be adversely affected by abuse or neglect...
The person or agency to receive reports	...shall report to the department of social services... *or* ...shall report to the principal, who shall then call the department of social services...
The information required of the reporter	a....and give the following information: name, address, and age of student; name and address of parent or caretaker; nature and extent of injuries or description of neglect; any other information that might help establish the cause of the injuries or condition.

	b. School employees shall not contact the child's family or any other persons to determine the cause of the suspected abuse or neglect.
	c. It is not the responsibility of the school employee to prove that the child has been abused or neglected, or to determine whether the child is in need of protection.
Expected professional conduct by school	Any personal interview or physical inspection of the child should be conducted in a professional manner...
The exact language of the law to define "abuse" and "neglect'; if necessary, explain, clarify or expand	" 'Abuse' means the infliction by other than accidental means, of physical harm upon the body of a child." " 'Neglect' means the failure to provide necessary food, care, clothing, shelter, or medical attention for a child."
The method by which school personnel are to report (if appropriate, list telephone number for reporting) and the time in which to report	An oral report must be made as soon as possible by telephone or otherwise and may be followed by a written report.
Whether or not there is immunity from civil liability and criminal penalty for those who report or participate in an investigation or judicial proceeding; and whether immunity is for "good faith" reporting	In Illinois, anyone making a report in accordance with state law or participating in a resulting judicial proceeding is presumed to be acting in good faith and, in doing so, is immune from any civil or criminal liability that might otherwise be imposed.

	or
	In Maryland, there is no immunity from civil suits for untrue statements made by one citizen against another.
Penalty for failure to report, if established by state law	Failure to report may result in a misdemeanor charge: punishment by a fine of up to $500, imprisonment up to one year or both.
Action taken by school board for failure to report	Failure to report may result in disciplinary action against the employee.
Any provisions of the law regarding the confidentiality of records pertaining to reports of suspected abuse or neglect	All records concerning reports of suspected abuse or neglect are confidential. Anyone who permits, assists, or encourages the release of information from records to a person or agency not legally permitted to have access may be guilty of a misdemeanor.

Figure 1-2

Reprinted with permission, from *Education Policies and Practices Regarding Child Abuse and Neglect and Recommendations for Policy Development* (Denver, CO: Education Commission of the States, 1976).

Endnotes

1. James Garbarino, "The Role of the School in the Human Ecology of Child Maltreatment," *School Review*, 1979, p. 203.
2. Ruth Baden and others, *School-Age Child Care: An Action Manual* (Boston:Auburn House, 1982), p. 2.
3. Lynnette Long and Thomas Long, *The Handbook for Latchkey Children and Their Parents* (New York: Berkley Books, 1983), p. 10.
4. Ibid., p. 4.
5. Ibid., pp. 19,20.
6. Casey Banas, "Teachers Putting Pressure on Peers to Make the Grade," Chicago Tribune, Feb.10, 1985.
7. Long and Long, *Latchkey Children*, p. 4.
8. Garbarino, "Role of the School," p. 203.
9. Ellen Galinsky and William Hooks, *The New Expanded Family: Day Care That Works* (Boston: Houghton-Mifflin, 1977).
10. Ruth Baden and others, *School-Age Child Care.*
11. Ellen Galinsky and William Hooks, *The New Extended Family.*
12. Garbarino, "Role of the School," p. 202.

PART II

CHILD ABUSE IN ITS VARIOUS FORMS

Societal awareness that child abuse is a major problem has been evolving over the past twenty years. In the beginning the term battered child *was coined, because the children who came to attention were seriously injured by being hit, kicked, burned, shaken, or thrown around. As the problem was examined more fully, it became evident that more children were being seriously neglected than were being physically abused. Neglect is just as traumatizing and as deadly as physical abuse, but its dynamics are somewhat different. It is a form of abuse because of the resultant damage to the child. Neglect may be considered to be a passive form of abuse.*

More recently we have been made aware that sexual abuse of children is occurring at a shocking rate. Increasingly, we are facing the fact that psychological abuse, also rampant, is a prime factor in perpetuating the cycle of abuse from one generation to the next. Psychological abuse contributes to underdeveloped potential and is probably the greatest single factor accounting for the high rate of students dropping out of school. The following four chapters will deal with each form of abuse in terms of causes, consequences, roles of professionals, and ways to help.

Chapter 2

Physical
Child Abuse

For many people, the horrifying facts about child abuse are incomprehensible. How can parents burn, lacerate, and bludgeon their children? Why do they torture, blind, or break the bones of their own offspring? As we shall see, only a small proportion of parents who do unthinkable things to their children are mentally ill.

Almost everyone is capable of physically abusing his or her own child *if sufficiently provoked and under excessive stress.* It is important to keep this in mind, because abusing parents need understanding and help, not rejection and condemnation.

The information in this chapter refutes some commonly held beliefs. You may have already assimilated the usual myths; if so, some shifts in your thinking will be necessary. To start that process consider these facts:

- Parents who abuse their children do not really want to hurt them, and they almost always feel guilty and ashamed.
- Physical abuse usually stops once the family has been reported to Protective Services. Reporting is the first step toward getting help for a child.
- In most instances, the family will remain intact while receiving help. However, temporary removal of the child is often necessary. Permanent removal is needed in only ten to fifteen percent of the cases.
- For most abusers, treatment and rehabilitation will produce positive results.

- Teachers and administrators abuse children in the guise of discipline. School staff are the *only* authorities in the country who are allowed to abuse those in their charge. Even guards are not legally permitted to abuse prisoners in jails.

HISTORICAL ROOTS OF CHILD ABUSE

Physical abuse of children did not suddenly erupt in the twentieth century. We all share the historical roots from which it stems. Child abuse survives from one generation to the next, and each one of our families has probably had physical abuse somewhere in its background. The fact that so many families have broken the generational cycle, and diluted or minimized the practice of abusing children, reflects the evolution of a more humane attitude toward children, and parallels the development of universal education. Knowledge and enlightenment, combined with political action, changes in societal attitudes, new educational programs, and expanded treatment programs can lead to a drastic reduction in the incidence of abuse.

Child abuse has existed since ancient times. Historically, infanticide was an accepted method of controlling population size and eliminating babies born with defects. Killing babies or abandoning them to freeze or starve was not only condoned, but sometimes ordered by law. In some ancient societies, babies or children were killed as sacrifices to atone for sins or to appease the gods. In other societies, children were maimed or mutilated in symbolic rites.

Harsh physical punishment also has a long history, sanctioned by the old adage "spare the rod and spoil the child." Severe physical punishments, which today would be considered child abuse, have been justified by parents and educators through the centuries as necessary means of teaching children to behave and obey, and for "driving the devil out of them." It is because of the long-standing acceptance of corporal punishment that it is so hard to eliminate it.

Other forms of child maltreatment accepted until the nineteenth century included forcing children to work at hard labor in dangerous environments, apprenticing them to earn their own living at the age of seven or eight (sometimes earlier), and failing to care for them when they were ill. It was common to turn children out to fend for themselves if apprenticeships could not be found for them. One of the earliest child welfare activities in this country was established in response to the thousands of homeless children roaming the streets of New York in the early 1800s. Concerned adults organized a program to send the children to the midwest to be adopted by families who wanted and valued children.

It is only in the past 100-150 years that we as a society have developed a more humane and protective attitude toward children, and only since 1964 have there been laws to protect children from abuse.

Defining Physical Abuse

No definition of physical abuse has been developed that is acceptable to all professionals. Legal definitions vary from state to state, and these in turn are interpreted in procedural terms by each state's protective service system. Most laws define physical abuse broadly, as nonaccidental injury to a child perpetrated by a parent or person in the caretaker role.

Arriving at a universally acceptable definition is a problem because various groups disagree on the point at which physical punishment becomes excessive and therefore not justifiable as discipline. Although it is generally acknowledged that punishment that leaves marks on a child's body, or results in injury requiring medical attention constitutes abuse, this idea is not accepted by some ethnic groups, particularly in the case of a child who is at or above the "age of reason" (seven years or older).

Most workers in the field agree that physical abuse happens as a result of *recurring loss of self-control* when dealing with a child. This can occur in the course of administering physical punishment, but it also happens when a parent vents rage on a child in an apparent irrational manner.

Abusive episodes are explosive, violent, and intense. The parent as well as the child knows when they begin and end. Most abusing parents know they're out of control when they physically attack their child, and know they're doing wrong. What they don't know is how to keep the abuse from happening.[1]

Temporary loss of self-control on a single occasion does not make a person a child abuser, and usually causes the parent to become aware of the potential to lose control. Almost every parent has experienced raging anger at an offspring on one or more occasions, and has felt the *urge* to act out violent feelings. The important difference between abusing and nonabusing parents is that abusers act out their violent feelings, while nonabusers have *learned to cope with such feelings without attacking* a child.

Dynamics of Child Abuse

The dynamics of child abuse involve the interaction of three variables: the *participants* (a parent and a child), the *context* in which the abuse occurs, and a *crisis event* that precipitates a specific incident of abuse. We must not fool ourselves that thinking only about the abuser or the abused child can solve the problem. Productive approaches to the prevention and treatment of the problem must consider all factors as well as the manner in which they interact. Until recently, context was the most overlooked factor.

The Abusing Parent. The following discussion uses "parent" as meaning the regular, ongoing, live-in caretaker of a child, whether or not there is a blood or legal relationship between adult and child.

In most abusive families, one parent is the active abuser while the other parent, who tacitly condones the abuse by taking no action to stop it, is considered a passive abuser. The parent most likely to be the active abuser is the one who spends the greatest amount of time with the children, and in most instances this is the mother. However, in periods of high unemployment, or where there is a disabled father, or a father who works the night shift and is at home while the mother works during the day, this father has the most contact with the children and is more likely to be the active abuser. When a father is also a violent wife beater, it is probably unfair to consider the mother to be a collaborator in the abuse because she may be terrorized, afraid for her life, and thus unable to take any action to protect the children.

Childhoods of abusers. Almost without exception, parents who abuse their children have suffered one or more forms of abuse during childhood. All abusing parents do not report that they were physically abused as children (although a high percentage do), but virtually all report that they suffered from severe psychological abuse. Many were neglected or sexually abused as well as being physically and verbally abused. The memory of their physical abuse is sometimes repressed by the time they reach adulthood, but, unfortunately, the rage and fear experienced during abusive episodes remain, as does the damage to their self-esteem. Repressed rage is the hidden force that erupts during an abusive episode with a child.

Case histories tell us that as children, physical abusers suffered many losses through death or abandonment; many lived in institutions or experienced repeated changes in foster home placement. Because of the cruelty and abuse experienced during childhood, they grow up believing themselves to be worthless and bad, inadequate and unlovable. As a result of these feelings they tend to find mates who have similar abusive backgrounds and similar low esteem. When two deprived and psychologically damaged people marry, they are destined to have multiple problems.

Damaged childhoods can be compensated for, and we know that not every abused child grows up to be an abusing parent. Those who do not become abusers have found substitute nurturance from a foster parent, teacher, counselor, minister, relative, neighbor, or most probably several of these. New and rewarding attachments with supportive adults can restore an abused child's self-esteem because the caring adults challenge the child's negative view of self received from parents.

Low self-esteem. Abusive parents feel negative about themselves. As children they were told over and over that they were bad, that they could never do anything right. They were called a variety of humiliating and derogatory terms, and these were incorporated into their self-image. They hate just about everything about themselves. Many repeatedly experience suicidal thoughts and feelings, particularly after an abusive episode. Guilt and shame about the abuse reinforces already existing feelings of being worthless and no good.

Another consequence of their low self-esteem is that abusing parents do not expect to have their needs met. They have few friends and are reluctant to ask anyone for help. Lacking friends and unable to ask for help, they have no one to turn to in times of crisis; thus, they do not receive feedback from others who could help them find better ways of coping or help them learn new ways to solve problems.

Lack of social skills. Abusers tend to have poor social perception and ineffective modes of communicating. Their lack of social skills causes them to have difficulties in relationships with spouse, employer, neighbors, their children, and their children's teachers. Their inability to make and keep friends leaves them isolated, without a much-needed support system. They often do not know how to talk to their children, nor how to enjoy them.

Lack of parenting skills. Never having had adequate nurturance during childhood, nor a model of proper parenting, the abused child grown up has little knowledge of how to parent. The abused female child, as an adult, comes to motherhood with such emotional deficits that she has great difficulty meeting the demands of a baby or growing child. Yet, women who have been deprived and rejected by their own mothers grow up wanting children because they believe they can get from a baby the love and approval they never had. They seek parenthood even though they are totally unprepared to meet its requirements.

Ignorance about child development. An aspect of the abusing parent's lack of preparation for parenthood is ignorance about child growth and development. Abusing parents frequently expect a baby or small child to do things he or she is totally incapable of, or attribute to an infant the capacity for motivations he or she can't possibly have. For example, a mother may think a baby who spits up is doing this to annoy her or to get back at her for some imagined neglect. When her baby has a bowel movement at an inconvenient time (and is howling to be changed), the mother may think the baby is doing this to make life difficult for her. Such a parent may expect a child of three to be able to learn to read or write or to dress completely without help. The mother becomes angry at her baby for being mean to her or is displeased because her three-year-old doesn't fulfill expectations. In these cases, severe punishment is likely to result.

Categories of abusers. Physical abusers share most of the characteristics mentioned in the preceding paragraphs, but still they are individuals with unique personalities and temperaments. They hide their abuse out of guilt, shame, and fear, and on the surface it is not always possible to distinguish an abuser from a nonabuser. A person can be an abuser without anyone suspecting it. Suburbia has its share of abusing mothers, but they are rarely reported because no one wants to believe that these affluent (and often well educated) women are capable of physically abusing their children. Should their abuse become known, these women have more at stake to lose than mothers of low socioeconomic status. They are likely to use parental stress hot lines, and seek out Parents Anonymous groups before they are discovered and reported.

Some child abuse researchers have attempted to classify abusers into several types. However, I find it most productive to think in terms of two major categories: treatable and untreatable.

1. The experience of Parents Anonymous self-help groups is that approximately eighty-five to ninety percent of all physical abusers are capable of transforming themselves into nonabusers; that is, they are *treatable abusers.* Through their own determination and effort, and with the help of group members, professionals, and a variety of educational and support services, they are able to find alternatives to abuse, learn ways in which to cope with stress, recognize an impending crisis and ask for help in dealing with it, and develop a positive self-image to replace their sense of worthlessness. All of these skills, as well as a change in

self-image, must be developed and integrated before permanent cessation of abuse can be assured.

Because the parents in this category love their children and want
to stop abusing (though they don't know how), the abused child usually
does not need to be removed from the home. Exceptions are infants
and children under the age of three where the abuse started early and
has been severe. Temporary placement until the mother has been
under treatment for a while is usually necessary for the very young.

2. Of the ten to fifteen percent of abusers who are untreatable, a
majority are mentally ill. Individuals who make up the balance of this
untreatable category are either mentally retarded, belong to a religious
cult that believes in harsh physical punishment or bizarre practices
harmful to children, or, although sane and not mentally retarded, hate
their children so much that they do not respond to therapy and do not
stop abusing.

It is usually imperative that the children of untreatable abusers be
permanently removed from the home. It is generally acknowledged
that laws must be modernized to make it easier in these cases to
terminate parental rights promptly, so a permanent plan can be made
for each of the children. Because the hazards of moving a child through
a series of different foster homes are almost as damaging as the abuse
received, it is important to make such a child available for adoption as
quickly as possible.

One of the problems in making the decision to legally terminate
parental rights is the lack of absolutes in clearly establishing to which
category a particular parent belongs. Some mentally retarded parents
can refrain from abusing if given a lot of supervision and daily help in
caring for their child. Some parents appear to be treatable when they
really aren't. Child advocate groups continue to wrestle with this issue
of identifying the treatable and the untreatable.

Children Vulnerable for Abuse. In families where violence is the
usual way of dealing with problems, all children as well as the mother
are likely to be abused. Mentally ill parents, who are the ones most
likely to deliberately kill their children, also will usually attempt to kill
all the children rather than just one. However, in half or more of
abusing families, the common pattern is for parental rage to be focused
on one child who is vulnerable. This child becomes the target child for
one or more of the reasons discussed here.

Children under the age of three. Infants and young children are
vulnerable to abuse because they have such insistent and persistent
needs for care that any parent can become worn out and frustrated in
attempting to meet those needs. Crying, as well as issues surrounding

feeding and elimination, create stress that can escalate to an intolerable level.

An abuse-prone mother, who has always felt inadequate, is likely to view herself as an even greater failure when she can't stop her baby's crying, can't get him or her fed without a mess, and can't get him or her toilet trained by nine or twelve months of age. In addition, when the baby refuses a bottle offered, pushes food away, or won't cooperate in toilet training, the mother may interpret this as the baby's rejecting her, as she was rejected by her own mother. This combination of unrealistic expectations for herself and her infant, and distorted perceptions of the baby's reactions, can precipitate abuse.

An infant's normal behaviors, such as banging toys, pushing or pulling levers on household machines, tearing up magazines, poking mother's eyes or pulling her hair, may be regarded as actions requiring discipline. Abusing parents are overly concerned that a baby will become spoiled if not promptly disciplined, and it is common for them to start spanking the baby for naughty behavior at six months of age. Spanking can easily get out of hand, as the baby invariably responds with intensified crying that increases parental anger. It hardly needs to be pointed out that infants and young children are the ones at greatest risk for brain damage, crippling, or death from an attack by an adult.

Mothers who discipline their babies for what we know to be normal and healthy development are trying to be proper parents. As long as we allow people to grow up in ignorance about child development, and as long as our society condones physical punishment as an acceptable form of discipline, we all share to some extent the blame for the abuse of infants.

Children who require excessive care. Premature babies and children with special physical problems, such as a chronic illness or a handicap, require a great deal of care and also have medical expenses that cause a financial burden. These children create a lot of stress for mature parents in stable families, so their care and expense may be just too much to bear for parents who are immature and have many family problems. For these reasons, the child may be at risk for abuse if the parents have the characteristics of potential abusers.

Children who are difficult to rear. Hyperactive children, children with negative temperament, and children with special educational needs are difficult to live with and train, and they are another group that is vulnerable to abuse. Likewise, retarded children, children with severe learning disabilities, and those with behavior difficulties severe enough to require special class placement are not only hard to rear, they are also a blow to the family's esteem. As abusing parents already have extremely low self-esteem, they will suffer even more damage to their esteem if they have a child requiring a special class. It is quite possible that the child has become special because of severe abuse early in life, and this makes it even harder to put up with the kinds of problems these special children have.

Children who disappoint parents. Adopted children are often a disappointment to parents, and they are among this group of vulnerables. They are overly represented in the population of abused infants than is warranted by their incidence in the general population.[2] Biological offspring also disappoint their parents for a variety of reasons. A mother can feel disappointed in the sex of her baby, its looks, the way it responds or fails to respond, or simply because she doesn't like the baby. Perhaps the baby comes at a time that is very stressful for the family and is resented for creating further stress. A mother who has many medical problems during and after the pregnancy, or who is deserted by the father at this time, is likely to blame the baby and perceive the baby negatively no matter how attractive the child seems to others.

Sometimes the mother is disappointed and dislikes a particular child because this child reminds the mother of herself: as she hates herself, she hates the child who is a mirror of herself. The child may look or act like a hated brother, father, or spouse, and the mother projects her feelings toward the hated adult onto the child who is his image. School-age children may become the objects of abuse because they get poor marks in school or have trouble getting along with peers. For whatever reason, when a parent has trouble liking a child, that child will become the target of abuse.

The Context of Child Abuse. It is usually the combination of a parent with a potential to abuse, a vulnerable child, and a stressful situation that produces child abuse. The stressful situation is the context, and includes both the personal situation of the parent and the societal factors that impinge on that personal situation.

Isolation. Families in which abuse occurs are socially isolated. They lack meaningful ties to others such as relatives, friends, and church and social organizations. They have no reliable support system to provide corrective feedback about their parenting behavior and offer assistance, guidance, and emotional support at times when the family is stressed or in the midst of crisis. All families require various sources of help throughout the life cycle, because stress and crisis come uninvited and cannot be eliminated. An important aspect of abuse prevention is the establishing of both informal and formal support networks and programs to assist people who are in crisis.

Societal attitudes. Americans are imbued with an individualistic ethos that implies everyone should solve his or her own problems without the help of others. We also accept the idea that children are the property of parents, permitting parents to deal with their children as they see fit, rather than in keeping with a standard of child care that we know will facilitate healthy emotional and physical development. Furthermore, we have a strong emphasis on the right to privacy. Children are conditioned early that what goes on in the family is private business, so they are afraid to reveal to others who could help what goes on at home behind closed doors. Likewise, outside adults are reluctant to confront parents about the way they treat their children because *they* have also been conditioned that it is none of their business. This matter of privacy has been a deterrent, keeping concerned adults from intervening on behalf of an abused child, and we probably won't change the pattern of child abuse unless adults who care dare to get involved.

Stress and Crisis. Abusive episodes occur in the context of stress and crisis. Families in which abuse occurs are highly stressed, and the parents have never learned effective ways of coping with crises. A crisis is a situation loaded with energy, like the eye of a hurricane. The force of the tension that builds up is so great that it makes a person feel as if he or she is going to fall apart or fly to pieces. When this happens to an abuser, the parent attacks the child.

Events that trigger abuse. Multiple or continual stress will ultimately build up to a crisis. In abusing families crisis is often a way of life. However, it doesn't take something as serious as job loss, medical problems, death, or marital separation to create a crisis. The multiple frustrations of daily life can become so overwhelming that inner tension builds up to an explosive level. The event that precipitates abuse can be as minor as a spilled glass of milk, a child walking across a freshly washed and waxed floor with dirty boots, or a small child asking a fatigued mother for a peanut butter sandwich.

The event that precipitates an abusive episode is insignificant in and of itself, unless it provides a clue that will help a parent avoid abusing. If there is a pattern and the mother can learn to identify it, she can learn to get away from her child when that behavior occurs. Often, there is no particular kind of event that triggers the abuse. It is just whatever happens when the mother has reached the peak of her tolerance for the inner tension that has been building for days or weeks.

Even if the triggering event follows no pattern, discussing it can help a parent learn to stop abusing. An abuser must become aware of his or her body tension in order to know when the point of exploding is close. The parent must learn to identify the body sensations that are present just prior to an abusive explosion so he or she can use the parental stress hot line, or some other source of support, or take the rage out by hitting a pillow, kicking, or screaming, instead of attacking the child. The precipitating event thus serves as a marker, a point of reference in recalling the bodily sensations that preceded it.

Consequences of Physical Abuse

Many studies have documented the pervasiveness of neurologic damage/dysfunction, developmental deviations, and personality abnormalities in abused children.[3] Martin considers child abuse to be the major cause of handicapping conditions in the child population.[4]

Basis of Neuro-Psycho-Developmental Deviations. Children incur the most serious physical damage when abuse happens during infancy and the preschool years. These children will become special education legacies to the school, entering as mentally retarded, physically handicapped, or learning disabled. Even if they have not been organically damaged from injuries to the head, children abused from their earliest years will show neuro-psycho-developmental problems and personality deviations as a result of the emotional abuse and aberrant parenting they receive. In other words, neurological function and developmental progress can become impaired as a result of the abusive environment itself.[5]

Neurological dysfunctions also occur as a consequence of physical neglect. Up to thirty percent of abused children are nutritionally deprived or have other signs of physical neglect. There is an increased frequency of illness, and often poor medical care of the abused child when he or she is ill.[6]

Motor and Language Delays. In children who are not otherwise retarded or physically handicapped, delays in motor development and language development are frequently discovered during developmental assessment. The language delays are partly the result of minimal stimulation and little feedback from parents who do not interact verbally to any great extent with the abused child. An additional hypothesis is that abused children may *inhibit* their motor and language functions *in order to survive.* They are likely to get abused or punished for active behavior, running about, or getting into things, and talking also causes trouble because abusive parents hit a child for "sassing," questioning things, complaining, or expressing negative feelings.[7] To avoid abuse, they become passive and inactive, and talk only when necessary.

In these instances, the neurological signs that are noted may not be related to biological damage, but reflect that the nervous system of the child is adapting to the dangers in the environment. Martin stresses that psychological and environmental factors can cause impaired thinking, impaired perception, delayed language abilities, tremors, incoordination, abnormal muscle tone, impaired balance, and so on.[8]

Learning and Competence. The abused child's attitudes toward learning are negatively affected by his or her rearing because from the earliest years, the child has experienced a double bind regarding the development of competence. On the one hand, the parents have unrealistic and distorted expectations for the child, which can't possibly be met. On the other hand, if the child tries to do what the parent wants and comes close, but is not quite able to accomplish the task, he or she will be verbally and physically abused. Even though the parent seems to want the child to be competent, the expectations are so high and any attempts so firmly punished that the child is "damned if he does and damned if he doesn't" try to perform the task the parent sets for him or her.[9]

The outcome of this double bind is that in the classroom, many of these children will want to give up before trying a task, manifesting their fear of failure in an "I can't" attitude. Those who are not so immobilized by fear of failing will show a compulsive effort to get things "just right." They waste time and energy in their anxious perfectionism, which is their way to avoid the criticism or punishment that has always ensued when they failed to measure up. At the end of the day, most of their work is not done. Thus, learning problems that result because of developmental delays are further complicated by self-defeating attitudes and ineffective work habits.

Survival Learning. Abused children may not learn to feel competent, but they do learn a set of "survival strategies" that help them avoid abuse. Avoiding abuse is possible if a child becomes alert to environmental cues that can tell him or her whether he or she is safe or in danger. Not surprisingly, then, we find that abused children use their perception and intelligence to detect and evaluate small changes in movements, tone of voice, facial expressions, moods, and emotional reactions of their parents in order to know whether they are in danger. This hypervigilance serves a survival function for the abused child, but it is another behavior that will impair academic learning. This habit interferes with attending to instruction.

Abused children also learn, often as early as age two, to comfort, placate, and entertain their parents. If they can keep their parents in good humor, abuse is less likely to occur. Attending to their parents in these ways can also earn them the love they want and need, which is only available to them on a conditional basis. Other ways to avoid abuse, learned early on, are to make few demands and to hide when they perceive parental anger intensifying. Generalized to the classroom, these children may be afraid to ask for help or for additional explanations of a new concept, and they may become acutely anxious if the teacher shows anger, even if it is not directed at them.

Psychological Risks. Almost every abused child pays a psychological price for being reared in an abusive family. Studies show that abused children have an impaired capacity to enjoy life, and are at high risk for emotional disturbance. They have low self-esteem as a consequence of their verbal abuse, and have little trust in adults. They spend a great deal of their energy managing their anxieties. Many are unusually aggressive and/or self-abusive. In one report quoted by Martin, 8.3 percent of abused children, with a mean age of 8.5, had attempted suicide, and 20 percent had self-mutilative behavior.[10]

HOW TO DETECT PHYSICAL ABUSE

A heightened awareness of the dynamics of child abuse prepares us to sense abusive situations. We begin to take note of behaviors, and pay attention to comments that formerly would not have had significance. For example, one sentence in a social history, that Allan was threatening his parents to tell his teacher on them, was enough to alert me to any comments Allan might make in my interview with him that would lead to a disclosure of abuse. Once alerted, I realized that bits of accumulated data revealed evidence of child abuse. Then when I talked with Allan I was aware of his dropping cues that led to further documentation of an abusive situation.

In another instance, the social history of a child who was having marked difficulty with oral expression contained the information that parents had been worried about spoiling her during infancy, that she had sustained a number of "accidental injuries" before age three, and that spanking was currently a family issue because Marie became upset to the point of hysteria when spanked. I was prepared to discover physical abuse, but instead got a frank disclosure of family sexual abuse.

Whether a teacher or social worker, you should become particularly alert to parental disclosures that fit the pattern of an abusive family, as well as words and actions of a child that indicate all is not well between him or herself and a parent. When an inner voice is saying, "I wonder if Tommy is being abused," it is time to start making written notes of information gained from conversations with parent or child, and of significant observations. As written notes accumulate, organize them on a form similar to Figure 2-1, and keep it on file to add to from time to time.

Parental Indicators

Physical abuse should be suspected if a parent shows the characteristic traits of abusers previously discussed, as well as others given in Figure 2-2.

If a parent does not mention fear of losing control but speaks about what a difficult time the child is giving her, and her anger about it, it is appropriate to ask if she ever worries that she might abuse the child. The parent's own fear is an indicator of her awareness of the potential to lose control.

If you have regular contact with a parent, her behavior and attitudes may well be as important indicators of an abusive situation as signs in the child. (See Figure 2-3.) Many of the behavior indicators in a child—for example, withdrawal, aggressiveness, or discomfort with physical contact—are also seen in children who are not being abused. Being an astute observer is important, as there are some behaviors that are quite suggestive of physical abuse, and when observations of the child are collated with those of the parent, a picture of probable abuse may emerge. Any symptoms of emotional disturbance, as well as indicators, should be entered on the observational chart.

Indicators in the Child

Abused children get the idea that they are bad and deserve the abuse they receive. They are strongly attached to their parents, and show the same kind of loyalty to them that other children do, so it is uncommon for a child to tell an adult of his or her abuse. However, the child may complain that a parent is always angry, or tell that he or she receives many spankings. A child may come to school early and find reasons to stay after school as long as possible because he or she doesn't want to go home. Young children may role-play their abusive parent in the housekeeping corner or dramatize abusive situations with puppets, toy animals, or in verbal narrations that accompany their paintings or drawings. Older children who abuse younger ones may be reenacting their own abuse. Self-abusive behavior is also strongly suggestive that a child is being abused.

Child's name _____ Age _____ Grade _____

INFORMATION NOTES

Date	Parental Traits/Behavior	Family Problems	Child's Traits/Behavior/ Physical Evidence

Figure 2-1

OBSERVATIONAL CHART OF PARENTAL BEHAVIOR AND INDICATORS OF ABUSE

Parent's Name _____

Child's Name _____

Date _____   Observer's Signature _____

Parent:

_____ feels worthless and inadequate

_____ has negative feelings about him- or herself and has low self-esteem

_____ does not have a lot of friends

_____ has poor social perception

_____ has a lack of parenting skills

_____ is ignorant about child development

_____ shows signs of loss of control or a fear of losing control ("I get so furious at him that I'm afraid I might really hurt him")

_____ is unusually negative about the child

_____ complains about the trouble the child creates or of not being able to handle the child

_____ has an unusually punitive attitude and believes in physical punishment (frequently mentions spanking child)

_____ has brought the child to a variety of doctors or hospital clinics for past injuries (so no one will notice the frequency of injuries)

COMMENTS _____

_____

_____

_____

_____

Figure 2-2

OBSERVATIONAL CHART OF CHILD BEHAVIOR AND INDICATORS OF ABUSE

Child's Name ——————————————————————————

Parent's Name ——————————————————————————

Date ———————————— Observer's Signature ————————————

Child:

———— receives a lot of spankings at home

———— complains that his or her parent is always angry

———— comes to school early and finds reasons to stay after school as long as possible

———— role-plays abusive parents in class or dramatizes abusive situations with puppets and toys or in artwork

———— abuses younger children

———— is frequently absent from school, many times with no explanations

———— wears clothing inappropriate to the weather (usually long sleeves and pants to hide bruises)

———— shows physical evidence of abuse (describe below and on Form 2-4)

———— withdraws from social gatherings and from people

———— shows aggressive behavior

———— is not comfortable with personal contact

———— is self-abusive or expresses suicidal ideas

COMMENTS ——————————————————————————

——————————————————————————

——————————————————————————

Figure 2-3

In order to cover up their abuse, parents may keep children home until bruises become less visible, marks disappear, or to give themselves time to construct a plausible explanation for an injury. Frequent absences from school, and unexplained absences, should arouse suspicion, especially if your observational chart is showing other indicators. If a child is wearing clothing inappropriate to the weather in order to cover the body, it may be to hide evidence of abuse.

Physical Evidence of Abuse. Marks on a child's body that are not typical of accidental injury are usually indicative of an abusive situation. However, unless a child is severely injured, it is important to gather further information and not jump to the conclusion that these must mean he or she is being abused. Bruising easily is characteristic of certain illnesses, such as hemophilia and leukemia. Also, young children often have freak accidents, like falling off the back of a sofa and hitting the face or eye on a table corner or doorknob.

You should always inquire about bruises and injuries, keep a record of anything unusual, and keep track of frequency. (See Figure 2-4.) The kinds of marks that show abuse are human bite marks, fork-tine punctures, patterned bruises, injuries around the mouth or behind the ears, clumps of hair pulled out, rope marks around the wrists or ankles, finger marks around the neck or on the face, burns, and bruises in various stages of healing. (Bruises change color as they heal: under five days, they are red-blue; from five to seven days, green; from seven to ten days, yellow; and from ten to fourteen days, brown.) Cigarette burns are also indicative of abuse or self-abuse.

HOW TO REPORT PHYSICAL ABUSE

All states have laws naming school personnel as mandated reporters of child abuse, which means that anyone working in a school has a legal responsibility to report. Further, most laws stipulate that you should report when you have "reasonable cause to suspect" or "reasonable cause to believe" abuse. However, without clear-cut evidence in the form of marks on a child's body, "reasonable cause to suspect abuse" can create a lot of confusion, conflict, and indecisiveness for the school professional.

Analyses of abuse statistics reveal that, in half of the investigated cases reported by school personnel, insufficient evidence of abuse was found.[11] Although you don't have to have definitive evidence of abuse in order to report, and many child advocates would say, "If in doubt, report," it is a fact that the child protective systems are overtaxed by a

FREQUENCY OF UNUSUAL BRUISES AND INJURIES

Child's Name _____

Observer's Signature _____

Type of Unusual Bruise or Injury	Date Noticed	Child's Explanation

Figure 2-4

marked increase in reporting in the past few years, and valuable resources are used up in investigating cases where abuse is not substantiated. The following guidelines are presented to help you make the decision about reporting *suspected* abuse situations (when physical evidence of excessive punishment is lacking).

Deciding When to Report Suspected Abuse

Substantive evidence for suspecting an abusive situation consists of a *prevalence* of parental and child indicators, the presence of a stressful home situation, and perhaps also some allusion by parent or child to the severity of spankings. When physical evidence of abuse is also present, you should report. When abuse is not clearly indicated, but only suspected, you must first assess whether the child is in any danger of being harmed, then determine the parent's willingness to voluntarily cooperate in obtaining help.

Assessing the Danger of Harm to a Child

If a child is fearful of being harmed by a parent, or if you have any basis for believing that bodily harm is a real possibility (a parent is mentally ill or retarded), always report on the basis of substantive evidence. The following case illustrates the process of assessing the danger of harm and determining parents' openness to help:

> During an interview with Kevin, a nine-year-old boy who had trans-ferred from an out-of-state school, I observed a deep and long scratch on his neck, which he said his mother had inflicted accidentally (children usually try to protect their parents). Kevin described a conflictive family and "out-of-control" episodes by his mother during which she "slapped him up." He alluded to bruises in association with nightmares that had been severe until the year before, when they pretty much stopped after he was taken to a doctor. My impression was that this was an abusive situation that had probably improved somewhat after the medical contact the previous year. On the basis of the following, I concluded Kevin was not in any immediate danger of bodily harm: he said his mother did not hit him with objects; that he ran away when she was about to hit him; that his father, when present, intervened to stop his mother. In addition, his human figure drawing and Rorschach responses did not reflect bodily anxiety.

Physical abuse reflects a dysfunctional family, a family in need of psychological help. When I discussed Kevin's revelations with his parents, they acknowledged that what Kevin had said was true. They were dissatisfied with the high level of family chaos, and expressed a desire for help. They gave permission (in writing) for Kevin to be seen by the school counselor, and asked for referral to a family therapist. The mother was receptive to using the parental stress hot line number I gave her when she became frustrated with Kevin or his younger brothers who were now beginning to be "just like Kevin."

If Kevin's parents had blamed their son for the family stress, justified their behavior as right and necessary, become angry and defensive about the idea of using the parental stress hot line, or refused counseling for Kevin, I would have considered them to be denying their problem and unwilling to do anything without the coercion of legal authority (protective services), and reported them immediately. I felt confident about deferring reporting not only because these parents agreed that they needed help, but also because they (1) listened respectfully to my view of Kevin, which challenged their extremely negative perceptions of him; (2) showed commitment to each other despite strongly differing ideas about how to rear the children; and (3) allowed Kevin to be in the school's counseling program. With Kevin in the counseling program, we could monitor whether the family followed through on the agreed treatment plan.

When a Child Has Obvious Injuries

When a child has obvious injuries that leave little doubt in your mind as to their source, it is wise to have the nurse examine the child, but it is not necessary to take pictures. Do not require the child to remove his or her clothes, and always have another staff member present. These precautions are necessary because of the current climate regarding sexual abuse. The child should be interviewed by the designated reporter, who should be a person with expertise in talking with a child about sensitive matters, as shown in the following sample dialogue:

Teacher: *Those bruises look awful. They must hurt a lot.* (child may nod agreement) *What happened?*
Child: *I was in a fight.*
Teacher: *I think it was a grownup who was fighting with you.*
Child: (nods agreement or says) *It was.* or *How did you know?*
Teacher: (If the last question was asked) *Only a very large person could hurt you so badly.*
Teacher: *I think the grownup was mommy or daddy.* (Child may nod, look up or away, or say)
Child: *My mommy and daddy love me.*
Teacher: *Of course they do; but even though mommies and daddies love their children, they can get very upset or angry and hurt them without meaning to.*
Child: *If they find out I told, they'll hurt me more, and they won't love me.*

Teacher: *You didn't tell on your parents. I* guessed *that one of them hurt you. It isn't right for a grownup to hurt a child, no matter what the child has done. Your mommy (daddy) needs help to learn how to teach you to be good without hurting you.* (Say this earlier if the child insists that the beating was deserved because of acting bad.)

By telling the child what you think caused the injuries, without bad-mouthing the parents, the child will usually verify or correct your statements. Accurate information can thus be elicited without the child's feeling that he has betrayed his parents. The interview should be concluded by telling the child that you must inform the authorities (briefly describe Protective Services) so the parent can be helped.

Seeking Advice from Protective Services

School personnel have frequently been urged to report suspected abuse without being told which criteria to use in concluding that a child was probably being abused. As a result, many innocent families have had to endure the invasion of their privacy and the embarrassment of an official investigation.

When there is a nagging doubt in your mind about whether to report, discuss your concerns with the social worker or psychologist assigned to your school, or with the child-abuse consultant for your district, if you have one. If this does not satisfy you, call Protective Services and discuss the situation with one of their social workers without giving the family's name. The social worker should be able to advise you about whether a report should be made. If more people would use Protective Services as a resource, false reporting could be kept to a minimum.

STANDARDIZED PROCEDURE FOR REPORTING: YOUR RESPONSIBILITY

Impulsively reporting a family with little substantive basis for doing so should be guarded against, but it is also important to guard against the strong tendency to deny facts and ignore evidence of abuse. You have a moral duty to protect children, as well as a legal responsibility to report. Reporting is the best way to assure that abuse will be stopped. You cannot be held liable for reporting an unfounded case when you report in good faith. On the other hand, you can be sued for failing to report if a child is subsequently seriously injured and it can be shown that you had sufficient knowledge of probable abuse to have reported.

Experience suggests that reporting will be done most expeditiously and with the most satisfying results if there is a standardized procedure for reporting, and one person on the staff is the designated reporter for the school.[12] The person appointed is often the principal, but perhaps the school counselor/social worker or nurse are more appropriate choices. As the teacher is the one most likely to discover the abuse, he or she must make sure that a report is filed, although when there is a designated reporter, that is the person who carries out the actual procedure. Close collaboration between the teacher and the designated reporter is essential.

The steps to be followed in making a report, and the name of the agency to which the report is made, are not the same in each state, but your designated reporter will know how to proceed. Having one person trained to report eliminates the necessity for every staff member to have this expertise. It allows the teacher, who is the main contact person with the family, to maintain rapport with the family, and it allows the reporter to make and maintain a good working relationship with Protective Services.

Typically, the reporter will call a central abuse hot line, give the name, address, and phone number of the parents, the name and birthdate of the child and siblings, and the information that forms the basis for the report. Some states also require that a written report be filed within a specified time after the verbal report is phoned in.

Although the person reporting abuse is allowed anonymity, social workers who have had a lot of experience reporting physical abuse (but not sexual abuse) suggest that it is wise to call the parents and tell them, once a report is made. The parents may become angry, but they will most likely be less angry than if they receive a call from Protective Services without knowing that a report was filed. Tell them that there is a law that requires you to report; that you hope this action will bring some help to the family.

No matter how angry a parent becomes, try to remember that the parent is probably relieved to be "found out." You should always assume (until it is proven otherwise) that even though parents try to hide their abuse out of shame and fear, deep down most of them really want help. As in all matters requiring sensitivity and judgment, you may decide to discuss the situation with the parent before reporting, or you may think it is wiser not to tell the family that the report came from the school. Informing parents that you have reported them to Protective Services is not a general rule to be applied in all forms of abuse. For example, it is important to maintain anonymity in reporting family sexual abuse.

When a Child's Injuries Are Severe

If a child's injuries are severe, the police should be called and the child taken to the nearest hospital emergency room. Either the police or the physician can take protective custody, which usually involves admitting the child to the hospital. You should clarify with the police what further responsibilities you have, for example, who will inform the parents and so on. If the police have been called, this constitutes an official report, and it is expected that they will work directly with Protective Services. However, it is appropriate for you to ask exactly what will happen, and what further, if anything, you are to do.

Following Up and Collaborating with Others

Once a report has been made to Protective Services, you must hold them accountable for doing the job they are legally mandated to do:

1. Perform a thorough investigation of the child's total situation, including examining historical data.
2. Provide protection for the child.
3. Implement a comprehensive treatment plan for the family.

You should expect the assigned caseworker to consult with you to gain information about the child's school functioning and any insights you can offer. Legally, you cannot withhold information on the grounds of confidentiality; you must allow Protective Services or law enforcement officials to examine school records at their request. This is one instance where parental permission is not necessary.

There are two kinds of follow-up to consider, the first of which is most important. First, you will want to be sure that appropriate action is being taken. If you have not been contacted by a caseworker within two days after making a report, call the local office of Protective Services and ask to speak with the supervisor. If you learn that an investigation is not yet under way, demand that action be initiated immediately. You can tell them you will call the police or central registry unless you can be assured that they will act at once. Later follow-up involves inquiring about the outcome of the investigation (was the abuse substantiated or not?), learning about the treatment plan, and sharing information about what is happening at school.

Figures 2-5 and 2-6 illustrate the responsibilities and duties of the Protective Service workers and school personnel. These charts show how everyone involved collaborates to help the child and parents.

THE POWERS OF PROTECTIVE SERVICE WORKERS

LEGAL ACTION

- They can take or retain temporary custody of a child without the parents' consent if they believe the child is in immediate danger.
- They can use the threat of custody to obtain the parents' cooperation with the investigation.
- They can petition the court for continued custody when returning the child to the family is deemed not in the child's best interest.
- They can obtain court action to assure compliance with a proposed treatment plan

SERVICES

- Pay for regular or therapeutic day care, if required.
- Provide a homemaker service.
- Arrange for a lay therapist.
- Use a variety of counseling specialists to help a family reduce a particular source of stress, such as financial problems, a sexual dysfunction, marital conflict, and so on.

TREATMENT PLAN

- Coordinate and oversee the treatment plan.
- Provide continuity, support, and guidance.
- Encourage abusing parents to join a Parents Anonymous group.
- Act as liaisons with the school and other agencies.
- Offer direct counseling when possible.

Figure 2-5

SCHOOL PERSONNEL'S RESPONSIBILITIES AND ACTIONS

ADMINISTRATOR

- Provide support to staff to collaborate with Protective Services and community agencies in treatment plan.
- Offer outreach consultation and assessment services to nursery schools and day care centers where abused children are enrolled.

TEACHER

- Gain an abused child's trust by responding in a predictable way; by providing a lot of structure through consistent daily routines; and by consistently enforcing rules in a firm, calm, nonpunitive manner.
- Protect the abused child from being victimized by others.
- Don't emphasize a child's failures and negative behaviors to parents; rather, challenge the parent's negative view of the child by reporting positive behaviors (no matter how small) and emphasizing improvements.
- Don't expect the parent to help the child at home, as this creates more pressure on an already stressed family and increases the likelihood of more abuse.
- Recruit volunteers to provide maximum individual academic help to the school-aged child, or much needed loving attention to the preschooler; consider using successful older students, as well as adults from the community (especially retirees).
- Refer children with developmental delays or learning problems for Child Study Evaluation.
- Consider keeping the child in your class for two years if he or she has become attached to you and is just beginning to make progress at the end of the year.

COUNSELOR/SOCIAL WORKER

- Because there are few community resources for the treatment of abused children, you will play a major role in their psychological rehabilitation. Fostering attachment and permitting dependency are as essential as building esteem and teaching about feelings and interpersonal relating. Self-destructive behaviors will require confrontation, and aggression will need to be limited and rechanneled.

- Assume the major role in collaborating with other agencies. You may need to inform the directors of community agencies that you are the contact personal for your school, as agency workers are often inexperienced in working with school personnel.

- Use groups as well as an individual approach. These children need to have their self-worth validated through establishing an emotional bond with you, but they also need to develop social skills with peers via group process.

- Act in a nurturant way toward parent as well as child. Encourage parents to participate in all school activities and to volunteer in classrooms. Remind them to use the parental stress hot line, and encourage them to join a Parents Anonymous group if they are not already members.

PSYCHOLOGIST

- If your role is limited to assessment, work with the administration to write a job description that allows a broader role function.

- Use projective techniques in assessment; use any or all reputable ones you feel comfortable with.

- Be a co-leader with a social worker in a discussion group for parents who are having difficulty handling their children; these parents may be potential abusers, if they are not already identified as such.

- Teach a course in night school on child development for parents and prospective parents.

- Encourage the School Board to inaugurate an educational program for parents of infants to teach them to be effective parents; be willing to oversee and participate in such a program.

Figure 2-6

CHILD ABUSE TREATMENT AND PREVENTION PROGRAMS

Treatment programs, as crucial as they are, are only short-term, partial answers to the problem of child abuse. They interrupt the pattern in the present generation, attempt to ameliorate the damage already done, and in so doing may have some impact on the generational transmission.

Prevention programs take the long-range view. They attempt to lessen the chance that abuse will occur in the first place. Their goal is to assure children of a healthy and humane upbringing by preparing adults for parenthood and providing needed support services to families throughout the life cycle.

Although each form of abuse requires specific kinds of treatment approaches, the principles and premises of successful programs are the same, regardless of the type of abuse. They are: promulgation of a national policy, public awareness, adequate funding, use of volunteers, training of professionals, cooperation among agencies, and assuring that programs will be community centered. Let's examine each of these, and see where we stand.

National Policy

The Child Abuse Prevention and Treatment Act (PL 93-247) was signed into law January 31, 1974. This act is the closest we have to a statement of national policy, that as a nation we are committed to take actions necessary to stem the tide of child abuse. There are those who believe that a stronger and more definitive national policy is needed, one that spells out and mandates the kind of programs required to support families at all stages of the life cycle. However, PL 93-247 is a start. The act established the National Center on Child Abuse and Neglect (NCCAN), the purpose of which is to conduct and compile research, provide an information clearinghouse, compile and publish training materials, provide technical assistance, investigate national incidence, and fund demonstration projects related to prevention, identification, and treatment of child abuse and neglect. The National Center is a part of the U.S. Children's Bureau, and ten regional offices function as extensions of the NCCAN.

Public Awareness

The National Committee for the Prevention of Child Abuse, a privately funded organization established in 1972, has directed its efforts toward increasing public awareness, encouraging public involvement in prevention and treatment, and facilitating communication and cooperation among those involved in research and service programs. Activities of the Committee have included a national media campaign, publications, conferences, research, and establishing state chapters of the committee. Their efforts have resulted in the designation of April as Child Abuse Prevention Month.

Adequate Funding

How much is enough? Will there ever be enough? Do we have to wait for the federal government to allocate billions of dollars (that they don't have) to the cause, as some suggest is necessary? Is lack of money just one more excuse to deny the problem and do nothing?

The fight against child abuse is pulling together the people of many communities, and organizing to raise needed monies is part of that effort. We are a very resourceful people; perhaps adequate funding for programs will be generated if we can keep the problem in the public's awareness. Child abuse is a human problem with which most can identify, once denial of the problem is overcome.

Use of Volunteers

Volunteers are being trained and used as lay therapists, as lay health visitors, as telephone counselors on help lines, to present child abuse educational programs in schools, as helpers in Family Resource Centers, to help in shelters and crisis centers, and as associate leaders in self-help groups; in fact, in every aspect of child abuse prevention and treatment. In many instances, the volunteers are themselves trained professionals in psychology, social work, psychiatry, medicine, law, education, and the ministry. As discussed earlier, using volunteers in schools to give one-to-one help and nurturance to needy youngsters is another important aspect of treatment and prevention.

The use of volunteers requires that professionals share their expertise with others, accept the idea that less-educated people can be educators and therapists (although in a different way), and show respect and gratitude to them for their help.

Training of Professionals

Professionals must acknowledge that they have not had the kind of training that equips them to deal with the issues presented by child abuse. We must look for sources of training and avail ourselves of them. The National Center for the Prevention of Child Abuse and Neglect in

Denver, Colorado has been a leader in providing up-to-date education, research and clinical training materials to professionals. The Center was founded in 1972 and is funded by private foundations, the state of Colorado, and by HEW. It also serves as a regional center of NCCAN. The other nine regional centers, mostly located in or associated with universities, also provide resource materials and personnel for in-service training and consultation.

Cooperation Among Agencies

As we have seen, child abuse is a multifaceted problem involving all the major disciplines. If we are to be effective, we must not undermine each other's efforts. Despite our different orientations to the problem, it is vital that we understand and respect the purposes, goals, and realities of one another. Feelings about "turf" and "doing it better" must be confronted and resolved to assure cooperation rather than competitiveness.

Community-Based Programs

> Child abuse, both cause and cure, is rooted in the community—its attitudes, values and resources—and an effective prevention approach must tap all levels of community life.... All major community forces need to be utilized in this process, including service clubs, business and civic leaders, church groups, health professionals, trade unions, educators, child welfare professionals, and parent groups.... In addition, the resources of corporations and businesses must be tapped.[13]

At the Sixth National Conference on Child Abuse and Neglect, held in 1983 in Baltimore, Maryland, through a *Marketplace of Community Programs,* people from forty states shared what they do, how they do it, and what they know about treating and preventing child abuse. For each of 170 programs, objectives, key features, and what had been accomplished were stated; who sponsored the program, who was served and the source of funding were also indicated, and printed program descriptions were later made available through NCAAN to anyone interested. Through this dissemination of information and ideas, it became clear how the programs reflected the needs, and utilized the resources, of individual communities.

Hospital Programs. It is generally agreed that strengthening and supporting the family is a primary goal of treatment and prevention. Hospital-based programs offer the possibility of intervening at the earliest point in the life cycle. Programs that facilitate bonding between a mother and her infant (participatory birth experience, rooming-in and providing caring persons to give support and nurturance to the new mother); and those that identify "at-risk" mothers and follow up with home visits (that provide support for mother, educate about what the baby can and cannot do, and teach skills in how to care for and comfort the baby) are examples of hospital-based prevention approaches. Emergency room services, social work services, psychiatry clinics, and pediatric/neurology clinics that diagnose learning problems are hospital services important in the identification and treatment of children who have been physically abused.

School Programs. Through special education services, schools do a great deal to ameliorate the physical damage of learning processes and psychological damage resulting from child abuse. In this sense, educators provide an important component of the direct treatment of abused children.

In regard to prevention, programs that build self-esteem, teach social skills, life management skills, and how to care for young children prepare young people to become adults who are better equipped to deal with parenthood. For children who have missed out on these skills in the past, Ray Helfer proposes that schools offer "A Crash Course in Childhood for Adults."[14] Helping parents know how to enjoy, communicate, and support healthy development of their children through parenting groups, courses in child development, and so on, is also an important preventive approach that is most logically based in the schools.

Community Programs. Crisis nurseries, shelters for abused women and children, therapeutic day care, and Childrens Anonymous groups (self-help group therapy for children) are examples of needed treatment services for children that are usually organized on a community basis.

Parental stress hotlines, crisis intervention services, Parents Anonymous self-help groups (with a professional co-leader, usually a volunteer) and Comprehensive Treatment Centers (that offer group therapy, supervised mother-infant play, feedback about parenting via watching video recordings of their interactions with their infants, and child development classes), as well as the full range of more traditional therapeutic interventions, are services needed by parents to overcome their abusive behavior.

Family Resource Centers and centers for unwed teen mothers are the most promising approaches to prevention (along with the hospital- and school-based programs). The family center offers opportunities for both parents and children to socialize with peers; for parents to develop a support network and to have time off from parenting. Separate areas are provided where infants will be taken care of by others, and children can enjoy supervised play while their parents are nearby participating in adult relationships. Teen centers may provide classes for completion of high school; child care for children so the mothers can attend regular high school, or work; parenting and homemaking classes, as well as leisure and recreational opportunities with peers who are also parents. Counselors at both kinds of centers are usually available to refer parents to needed medical, legal, welfare, or social services.

Endnotes

1. Christine Comstock Herbruck, *Breaking the Cycle of Child Abuse* (Minneapolis, MN: Winston Press, 1979), p. 17.
2. C. Henry Kempe and Ray Helfer (eds), *The Battered Child*, 3rd ed., (Chicago: The University of Chicago Press, 1980), p. 67.
3. Harold P. Martin, "The Neuro-psycho-developmental Aspects of Child Abuse and Neglect," in *Child Abuse and Neglect, A Medical Reference,* ed. Norman S. Ellerstein, (New York: John Wiley & Sons, 1981), p. 96.
4. Ibid, p. 116.
5. Ibid, p. 105.
6. Ibid, p. 102.
7. Harold P. Martin, "Neurological Status of Abused Children" in *The Abused Child, A Multidisciplinary Approach to Developmental Issues and Treatment,* ed. Harold P. Martin, (Cambridge, MA: Ballinger, 1976), pp. 79-80.
8. Ibid, p. 81.
9. Ibid, p. 100.
10. Harold P. Martin, "Neuro-psycho-developmental Aspects of Child Abuse and Neglect," p. 98.
11. Study Findings, National Study of the Incidence and Severity of Child Abuse and Neglect, U.S. Department of Health and Human Services (DHHS Publication No. OHDS 81-30325), 1981, p. 43.
12. Kay Drew, "The Child and His School" in *Helping the Battered Child and His Family,* eds. C. Henry Kempe and Ray Helfer, (Philadelphia: J.B. Lippincott, 1972), p. 116.
13. Peter Coolsen and Joseph Wechsler, "Community Involvement in the Prevention of Child Abuse and Neglect" in *Perspectives on Child Maltreatment in the Mid '80s* (Washington, D.C.:U.S. Government Printing Office, 1984) DHHS Publication No. OHDS 84-30338, available from Superintendent of Documents.
14. Ray Helfer, *Childhood Comes First: A Crash Course in Childhood for Adults,* 2nd ed., (East Lansing, MI.: Ray Helfer, Box 1781, 1984). The book is both text for the student and curriculum guide for the teacher.

Chapter 3

Neglect: A Passive Form of Abuse

Parents who fail to feed and care for their children properly are guilty of neglect. Neglect also encompasses failure to provide needed medical attention, failure to provide the emotional nurturing necessary for normal growth and development, failure to send children to school, failure to provide the supervision required to keep children safe, and failure to provide protection from hazards that exist in the home or neighborhood. Exposing children to criminal or immoral influences is also generally considered to be neglect. *Parents who neglect their children are failing to meet their child rearing responsibilities.*

Child neglect has not been a popular subject for researchers; in fact there is a dearth of research data on the topic. The work of Norman Polansky and his colleagues offers much of the understanding we have of the problem. They proposed the following definition of neglect to guide their research efforts: "Child neglect may be defined as a condition in which a caretaker responsible for the child either deliberately or by extraordinary inattentiveness permits the child to experience *avoidable* present suffering and/or fails to provide one or more of the ingredients generally deemed essential for developing a person's physical, intellectual, and emotional capacities."[1] Unique among definitions, the emphasis placed here on *avoidable suffering* would seem to implicate the community as well as the parents; we must all assume some responsibility for allowing this suffering to exist.

Polansky found that there is strong agreement across social classes about quality of life matters that determine whether or not a child is receiving adequate care. That is, whether rich or poor, well educated or poorly educated, Americans generally agree about what constitutes *inadequate* child care. He and his co-workers devised a Childhood Level of Living Scale for rating adequacy of care in families reported for neglect. Polansky found that neglectful mothers know what the standards of child care are for their social group, but they do not practice them. During the research data collection, interviewers noted that neglectful mothers often *reported* doing for their children the proper things they knew should be done. Objective evidence was to the contrary.[2]

COMPARING NEGLECT AND PHYSICAL ABUSE

Since 1978, neglect has been classified, legally, as a form of abuse, and included in reporting laws. Yet we commonly speak of "abuse and neglect" as if neglect were something different. The way they differ is that abuse is an *act of commission* and neglect comprises *acts of omission*. They are really two sides of the same coin, the active side and the passive side, and there is considerable overlap between them. Neglectful parents also abuse their children, and many children who are physically abused are also neglected. As we shall see, the overlap extends well beyond this, particularly in terms of consequences. Both abusing and neglectful parents are dependent, have low esteem, and lack knowledge about children's needs and development, but the personality deficits in the mothers who neglect are more extreme and serious, and the consequences of their parenting are more profound.

There are no accurate statistics, but it is generally estimated that there are twice as many neglecting families as physically abusing families, which means four or five times as many neglected children. The most severe neglect occurs in lower class families.[3] While it is common for only one child in a family to be the target of physical abuse, in neglecting families all children will most probably be affected. The exception to this is when physical or psychological abuse is the primary problem, and only the child who is the object of that is neglected. Even though neglect and physical abuse often occur together, usually a mother who is basically neglectful does not have the energy nor notice the children sufficiently for abusive episodes to occur very often. A neglectful mother may abuse when she feels blamed for her children's developmental delays, or feels angry at caseworkers who are trying to get her to do something she doesn't want to do. The abuse will most likely *not* be of the same intensity as that described in the previous chapter, simply because neglectful mothers typically have very little energy, their feelings are deeply repressed, and they rarely show much of any kind of an emotional reaction.

Damaged Lives

Like physical abuse, serious neglect causes damage to a child's growth and development, but to even a more severe degree. Some define neglect in terms of the consequences for the child; for example, neglect is "a caretaker's indifference toward a child's basic growth needs, which results in physical, intellectual, or emotional damage to a youngster."[4] Whether focus is put on the parent's failure to provide what the child needs, or on the failure of the child to grow up normally, the sad fact is that the pattern of neglect will repeat itself in the next generation, even more certainly than physical abuse does.

Not only does the pattern of neglect repeat itself with the certainty of night following day, but the number of families involved in it multiplies with each generation. The cost to society has already become enormous, not only in monetary terms, but in magnitude of tragedies well beyond the sphere of the neglecting and neglected population. The link between abuse/neglect and crime/violent crime can no longer be ignored. The fact that violence has proliferated in this country to the point where innocent people can no longer feel or be safe in vast areas of our cities is proof that the consequences of abuse/neglect are not being contained.

Retrospective studies of delinquents, hardened criminals, and murderers reveal a high correlation between an abused/neglected upbringing and criminal behavior in adolescence and adulthood. Of the two, abuse and neglect, Polansky believes that it is the severely neglected group who commit the most brutal and coldblooded murders. He hypothesizes that severely neglected children, in order to tolerate their suffering, completely repress their feelings to the point where they are not aware of what it feels like to hurt. Because of this they cannot empathize with the hurt and suffering of others. This allows them to inflict suffering on other people with a coldness and calculation beyond the capacity of normal persons.[5]

Emotional Neglect

In general, when there is physical neglect there is also emotional neglect. However, as emotional neglect also happens to many children who are otherwise receiving fairly adequate care, and is prominent in middle and upper class families, it will be given specific emphasis in Chapter 5 as a subcategory of psychological abuse.

Emotional neglect is synonymous with such commonly used terms as emotional deprivation, emotional starvation, and conditional love. In emotional neglect, there is passive indifference to the child, what someone has called a "quiet nonrelationship." Nothing harmful is said or done to the child; the child is simply ignored, treated as if he or she didn't exist, or treated as little more than an inanimate object. Where there is emotional neglect, the mother does not form an emotional attachment to her child; she is too deprived herself to do so.

Poverty and Neglect

In contrast to physical abuse, which is spread across all social classes, neglect is *predominantly* a phenomenon of the lower classes. Because poverty and neglect are so often thought of in a cause-and-effect relationship, there has been a tendency to ignore the problem of neglect, explaining it away as an unavoidable consequence of poverty. However, when Polansky compared low income mothers who neglect with equally low income mothers who *do not neglect,* he found the critical difference between the two groups to be *character,* not how much money was available. This does not mean that we can ignore poverty as an important social issue, but rather, that simply erasing poverty will not solve the problem of neglect. What we have done about poverty so far is invaluable, instituting such vital programs as Head Start, Medicaid, school lunches, and food stamps to supplement the more general welfare benefits available to poor people. These programs have largely prevented *unintentional* neglect, but families who neglect do not necessarily make use of these programs; they must often be required to do so.

DEGREES OF NEGLECT

Neglect occurs on a continuum from mild to severe. Every parent is mildly neglecting of one or another of her children from time to time. As mild neglect is such a common occurrence, it is not a reportable offense. Latchkey children are an example of mild neglect (see Chapter 1). Children from wealthy homes who are supervised by non-English speaking maids are another example. Children of alcoholic parents are seriously emotionally neglected (see Chapter 5) but may sustain only a mild degree of physical neglect if their socioeconomic situation is generally adequate.

It is probably only appropriate to speak of a home situation as neglectful if the neglect is continuous and of long duration. Neglect following death or divorce may seem to meet this criteria, but it is more likely that the more protracted periods of neglect will be interspersed with some moments of joyful interaction and periods of sustained attention to needs. In these instances, neglect is logically related to a major life crisis and the children will have probably developed some character strengths with which to cope. This is not the kind of neglect that is a form of abuse.

Mild Neglect

In situations of mild neglect, there is a structured routine in the household, one or both parents work, and an effort is made to live in accord with community standards. Children have food, even if they must fix it for themselves; cleanliness is expected even if children must be responsible for cleaning the house and washing the dishes; and children are expected to participate in school and community activities even in the absence of much parental interest or involvement. Children suffering from mild neglect may be dependent and demanding of attention in school, but they will not necessarily stand out from the other children. On the other hand, children who are moderately or severely neglected will present visible evidence of their neglect. They will look dirty or unkempt, wear ragged, unclean or ill-fitting clothes, and smell offensive; they may cling to you, or grab food; they may look pale, have infected sores, or fall asleep in class. At the very least, they will stand out from the other children because of their apathy, and inability to enjoy themselves. Preschool children may exhibit excessive self-stimulation in the form of rocking, scratching, sucking hair, banging the head, and so on, as well as the same symptoms of neglect that school-age children show.

In moderate and severely neglecting families, there is chaos and disorganization, and parents cannot function to a greater or lesser degree. About half of these are single-parent welfare homes, who are in need of long-term help.[6] Most of the children will be attending city, inner city, or rural schools.

Moderate Neglect

A way to differentiate between moderate and severe neglect is to assess the degree to which chaos and disorganization are present in the home, and the degree to which the parents are dysfunctional. Moderately neglecting families function normally in at least *one major area*. For example, one or both parents may be employed, relationships with extended family may be unimpaired, or some semblance of routine can be discerned. Disorder and confusion will be evident, and probably the house dirty and dishes unwashed, but the children will be fed cooked food on some kind of regular basis, will be prompted to wash themselves, and will be provided with clean clothes some of the time. Most important, an effort will be made to send the children to school each day.[7]

Severe Neglect

Severely neglecting families, on the other hand, are disorganized and dysfunctioning in *every area of life*. The parents are unemployed, live in substandard housing, and make no attempt at housekeeping; what little food there is available is uncooked and not nutritious, and little or no effort is made to send the children to school. A high percentage of mental retardation, mental and physical illness, alcoholism, and drug addition are present in these families. "Children eat as they can, sleep when they must, and wander like lost souls in a world without order, without warmth, and without meaning."[8]

CHARACTERISTICS OF NEGLECTFUL MOTHERS

Several sources provide us with information about the characteristics of neglectful mothers: clinical observations, clinical research emerging from treatment projects, and direct research study. The literature tells us many things about neglectful mothers. The traits to be described are most pronounced in the mothers whose neglect is severe, possibly somewhat less marked in mothers whose neglect is of moderate degree. Mothers are singled out not only because they are the only parent in half the neglect situations, but also because they are the major force in the rearing patterns of low income families. When fathers *are* present, they function poorly, have similar problems as the mothers, and accept the way the mother is rearing the children.

Infantile Personalities

Caseworkers invariably find that neglectful mothers are like small children: they are extremely dependent, distrustful or strangers, impulse-ridden, are unable to express feelings in words, and don't seem to have much common sense.

Some feel that "infantile personality" better describes neglectful mothers because these women are not merely immature; their psychological development has been arrested at a very early stage of ego differentiation, leaving them character disordered. Polansky believes that these women sustained severe deprivation from infancy on, which limited their capacity for normal emotional and mental development.[9]

Because their most basic needs were never met, they cannot love or feel for their children. Mothers who neglect have experienced much deeper and more pervasive deprivation than abusing mothers. They re-create homes like those they grew up in, repeating a pattern of failure and futility that includes neglect of themselves, their homes, and their children. Thus, like other forms of abuse, neglect is a pattern passed on from generation to generation.

The implication seems to be clear: if neglect breeds infantile personalities, we will never break the cycle of neglect unless we find a way to rescue the children early in their lives, provide them with the nurturance they need, and give them a different role model. This does not mean foster home placement, which is often little better than their own homes, but rather it means adoption for the most severely neglected group and therapeutic day care for moderately neglected children.

Poorly Educated

Early deprivation causes severe language delay and pseudo retardation, which are never fully overcome. It is not surprising then, to find that neglectful mothers are poorly educated. One study showed that two-thirds did not go beyond the eighth grade in school,[10] and other studies have resulted in similar findings. Having entered school with serious lags in development, these mothers experienced continual academic failure until they were finally able to drop out at age sixteen. As adults they are functionally retarded, although they were probably born with the potential for normal intelligence. These women are without goals, consider themselves failures, and have no hope of bettering themselves. Most have never held a job, and as soon as they are sexually mature, they live with or marry the first or second man who shows an interest in them.[11]

Hostility and Lack of Trust

With deprivation beginning in infancy, neglecting mothers do not develop basic trust on which future normal development is dependent. As a result, they cannot master later developmental stages nor learn effective ways to cope with the fears that are part of normal growth. Without trust they remain deeply fearful and suspicious of everyone. This is the "stranger anxiety" of infancy that has never been conquered.

Viewing the world as a hostile place where no one can be trusted, neglectful mothers approach and react to others in hostile and aggressive ways. This serves as a defense against their deep-seated fears, and also against expected rejection, as they know they are outcasts from society. Because of the hostile barrier they create between themselves and others, it may be impossible to relate to these mothers unless a bond of trust can be developed.

Character Disorder

Neglectful mothers have distorted perceptions of themselves, of others, and of reality. Apathy and resignation to a life of hopelessness in which rejection is expected are features of their world view. These features are ingrained and impervious to change. It is important to recognize that we are dealing with a character disorder rather than immaturity in these women because treatment approaches must be adapted to this fact or be doomed to failure. We must relate to these individuals as a parent to a child, being nurturing and giving, as well as assuming an authoritative stance that includes setting limits.

There are two types of neglectful mothers: those who fit an "apathy-futility" syndrome, and those fitting an "impulse-ridden" character structure. Apathetic mothers are the ones who completely ignore their children, while the impulse-ridden ones react to their children but in totally unpredictable ways; when they want to escape, they simply abandon their children for a few days or longer.

With infantile personality development, neglectful mothers have only a primitive coping mechanism. When stressed, they develop psychosomatic illness or suffer a nervous breakdown. They may withdraw into themselves in a way that resembles depression, but it is more an emotional numbness[12]; or, they may run away all together. Periodic abandonment is one of the severest emotional traumas a child can experience. Escapism and denial of reality are pervasive ways of dealing with life for the neglecting population, and heavy use of drugs and alcohol, as well as withdrawal into the fantasies of television or romance novels, are common.

Lack of Knowledge, Judgment, Motivation

Often, neglectful parenting can be attributed to lack of knowledge, lack of judgment, and lack of motivation. Lack of knowledge about child care goes well beyond that of the physically abusing parent. While the physically abusing parent may have unrealistic expectations of a baby because of lack of understanding of development, the neglectful parent doesn't even realize that a baby needs to be fed every three or four hours, let alone be touched, talked to, stimulated, comforted, and diapered frequently. Out of ignorance and emotional detachment, the neglectful parent fails to form a basic attachment with an infant and fails to provide basic nurturance.

Lack of judgment on the part of neglectful parents renders them unable to realize when their children are sick, not developing normally, or in need of supervision. This is the kind of neglect that can prove lethal for a child.

Neglecting parents lack the motivation to change, largely because they do not perceive the way they live as harmful to their children. They have accepted the way they themselves grew up and the way they are now living and rearing their children.[13]

Still another worker in the field tells us, "Neglecting parents are so wrapped up in their own problems they seem to almost forget their children exist. They are capable of ignoring their children so completely that they virtually seem unable to see or hear them."[14]

All these insights show that compassionate understanding will allow us to find successful ways of helping and encourage us to persist in our efforts. Too often, using approaches that didn't work, professionals have tended to distance themselves from neglecting parents with an attitude of futility that mirrors the futility of the apathetic mother. Although caseworkers carry the biggest load in dealing with the problem of neglect, their burden will be lighter if we do our part in the school.

Mental Illness

In describing the deficits of neglectful mothers, we have skirted the edges of mental illness, but stopped short of placing them in this category. Many neglectful mothers are mentally ill, but the majority are not. Character disordered persons can become mentally ill, as can normal or neurotic individuals. It helps to think of mental states as a continuum, with normal/healthy adjustment at one end and mental illness at the other. Character disorders and neurotic conditions fall somewhere in between.

Two major classes of mental illness are the thought disorders (the schizophrenias) and the affective/mood disorders (unipolar depression and bipolar depression, formerly called manic-depressive illness). Although organic factors are implicit, these may be genetic in origin, produced by sustained emotional stress over a long period of time, or result from deprivation of physiological needs.

Mental illnesses can be distinguished from neurotic conditions, and personality and character disorders by the loss of contact with reality and lack of rational thought. Brain mechanisms that influence mood and thought do not function properly during an episode of a mental illness to the extent that the person is "not himself." Mood or thought are so drastically altered that almost anyone can recognize that the person is not behaving normally. However, psychiatric evaluation is necessary to make a diagnosis of mental illness.

A mentally ill person says and does things that make little sense to others; there is no way to predict what he will do or say. The mentally ill person may need to be placed in protective custody to keep him from harming himself or others, and to prevent destruction of property or "disturbance of the peace."

When a person lacks *rational* control of behavior, that person is psychotic. A person can become psychotic as a result of severe trauma or brain damage, during the late stages of alcoholism, as a result of prolonged sleep or sensory deprivation, by ingesting drugs or poisons, and from neuro-biochemical imbalance that is present in schizophrenia and manic depression. Persons suffering from mental illness become psychotic during an episode of the illness, but may be able to behave normally if the neuro-biochemical balance can be restored through medication. Treatment of mood disorders is much more successful with drug therapy than is treatment of the schizophrenias. Psychotherapy may be an important adjunct to drug therapy for many mentally ill persons.

IMPLICATIONS OF PARENTAL MENTAL ILLNESS ON CHILDREN

The tragedy of mental illness is that there is no good way to assure that medication and therapy will be continued once the patient is released from the hospital. Patients who are violent or have violent delusions may murder their children; those who withdraw totally into themselves will seriously neglect their children, and those who have irrational and sadistic ideas about how children should be reared will be severely psychologically abusive. In instances like these, parental rights should be terminated, either by court action or voluntarily, so children have a chance for adoption. I want to stress though, that children *can* grow up with a mentally ill parent and have few, if any, serious problems. This is particularly true of the mood disorders. When a parent is a depressive, periodic hospitalizations and suicide attempts cause separation anxiety and fear of abandonment for the children. Yet, the children can learn to cope, especially if the parent returns to love and care for them and they receive tender loving care from relatives or friends while the parent is hospitalized.

CONSEQUENCES OF NEGLECT

Most children survive being neglected, although statistics suggest that child deaths related to neglect are more numerous than those resulting from physical abuse. Neglected children who die do so as a result of unattended illnesses, accidents, or poisonings, or else by perishing in fires when they are left alone. Because of the unsanitary conditions in which they live, and the poor health care and nutrition they receive, chronic illness is prevalent. Growth failure and serious impairment of all aspects of development are the consequences of nutritional and emotional neglect.

Failure-to-Thrive Syndrome

This problem describes a child who, during the first three years of life, has suffered a marked retardation or cessation of physical growth. When this growth failure is not the result of organic illness, it is called nonorganic failure to thrive. In about ninety percent of cases, babies and young children who fail to thrive suffer from severe maternal deprivation and neglect, and show remarkable improvement when placed in a nurturing environment where they are fed properly and given tender loving care.

Babies with this syndrome are not given enough to eat, sometimes because the mothers are ignorant about how much to feed them, but more commonly because the mother is so detached she doesn't respond to her baby's hunger cries, and doesn't seem to perceive anything to be wrong when the baby is emaciated, even though it is obvious that the baby is acting hungry. The emotional detachment of the mother can also cause the infant to eat poorly even when food is offered. Some mothers offer food when the baby doesn't want it, not when the baby is clearly hungry. They have not learned to respond to the baby's cries.

Aside from the danger of starving to death, which can happen if there is no one around to tell the mother that something is wrong, severe and prolonged malnutrition during the first year of life can lead to brain damage and permanently diminished brain size.[15]

Lack of appropriate emotional nurturance in infancy not only results in failure to thrive, but also causes retarded or aberrant development of intelligence, speech and language, motor patterns, and emotional expressiveness. It has also been implicated as a causal factor in suicidal attempts by preschoolers[16] (see Chapter 12). Thus, neglected children present with the same spectrum of deficits as those described for physically abused children. However, unless there is brain damage from early malnutrition or some other organic cause, the developmental deficits of neglected children are potentially reversible.

Language Delay/Deficits

Infants and children need an attachment relationship to motivate them to develop language, and need a readily available human being responding to them to sustain their efforts at speaking. Children can learn to talk through imitation, and presumably television can provide a model. However, saying words does not guarantee comprehension or the ability to communicate and use language effectively. Hydrocephalic retarded youngsters are an example: these are loquacious children who can talk endlessly without conveying much that is meaningful. Although organic damage explains their communication difficulty, the point is that speech can develop while communication skills do not. In the case of neglected children, it is the lack of a two-way human relationship that impairs language development.

Neglected children, like those who were physically abused during their early years, should always be evaluated for learning disabilities if they are having trouble learning, aren't talking much, or often do not seem to understand. Remember that memory is linked to language comprehension: that which is not understood will not be remembered.

Language problems can be quite subtle, and may not unduly impair learning until third grade and beyond, when the comprehension of language and communication skills become major factors in academic learning. The degree of neglect, and whether or not a child has been in a compensatory program before entering school, will determine whether language problems are glaring. Language problems are seldom missed when neglect has been severe and prolonged, but may be overlooked when a child has experienced moderate neglect because the deficits will not be so obvious.

Pseudo-Retardation

Developmental delay has replaced the term retardation to describe the failure of young children to develop normally. The newer term seems to please everyone, parents and professionals alike, but I think it often creates false hopes when the child is organically damaged, along with excessive expectations that a child will catch up to his or her age peers in all ways when slow or abnormal development results from prematurity or neglect. I use the term *pseudo-retardation* because it is more descriptive of the degree of delay, connotes that the retardation is induced, and suggests that although the retardation is reversible, the child is not likely to attain full intellectual potential.

Child psychologists tend to believe that to fully reverse retardation resulting from early and severe emotional neglect requires substitute nurturance and stimulation within an attachment relationship that begins well before the age of three. Placing severely neglected infants in foster day care or a therapeutic nursery can provide the desired result, if surrogate care-givers are carefully chosen, trained, and given supportive guidance. Continuing assessment and special education services are also desirable for pseudo-retarded infants. Until recently, such services were not available and are now only found in a few states. However, many states are beginning to mandate special education services, including assessment and parental guidance, for the infant-to-three-years age group.

In the future, all new parents in Missouri will have access to an "infant educator" training program. This program should have a marked impact on the reduction of physical and psychological abuse (and hence, on enrollment figures of special education) because it teaches parents about child development, stimulation, language, discipline, and how to enjoy the child.

However, severely neglectful parents are themselves too damaged to benefit. In order to reverse pseudo-retardation of infants removed from severe neglect situations, infant education services may be needed by foster and adoptive parents.

REPORTING NEGLECT

There is disagreement among professionals about the merit and advisability of reporting cases of neglect to Protective Services. One of the reasons for this is that there is so much leeway in judging the degree of neglect. Another is that agencies such as the Salvation Army and child welfare societies, as well as churches, have frequently taken responsibility for helping neglectful families.

There is no doubt that neglectful families need many kinds of help and someone to coordinate and pay for a variety of services. Protective Services are legally empowered to do these things. Apparently, however, the law regarding reporting is often side-stepped in cases of neglect just as with other forms of abuse.

The largest group reporting neglect to the police or Protective Services consists of neighbors and relatives. This is understandable because they have the most direct knowledge of how the children are being reared. Frequently, the temporary abandonment of the children brings the situation to the attention of others. If the serious consequences of neglect are to be prevented or reversed, early reporting of severe neglect is essential.

By the time children enter school, many families will already be receiving help from special services. This may not be true for moderately neglectful families. The children in these families are not always identified early because their deficits are not extreme and those who know the family situation may feel that the parents are doing the best they can.

WHEN TO REPORT NEGLECT

When school-age children show symptoms of neglect, the first step is to determine if the family is receiving services through any community agency. If it is, contact the workers already involved with the family to discuss the problems observed at school and find out if the family is under the auspices of protective services. If a welfare worker or a public health nurse is involved with the family, they may not have seen the need to report the case to protective services. However, you may see the situation differently.

If the family needs help that can be paid for by Protective Services and no other source of funding for the service is available, this is a reason to report. Also, if the help being received is fragmentary and a person is needed to coordinate services, this is another reason to report. Other reasons include factors that specifically impair school progress and/or the child's physical or mental health, and apparent neglect in several areas of care.

In addition to physical neglect which is obvious to the observer, neglect falls into three categories:

1. medical neglect
2. educational neglect
3. emotional neglect

The discussions about them that follow will help you decide whether or not to report the case.

Medical Neglect

We all know that a certain level of physical health is needed for learning. If a family disregards your recommendations for medical evaluation of apparent sensory defects, or ignores malnutrition, infection, or follow-up care of chronic illness, then you should report medical neglect. However, report only as a last resort if medical neglect is the only issue. Before considering reporting, efforts should be made to help the family get the care needed by the child, through the services of a public health nurse or caseworker who already has a relationship with the family. Remember that neglecting mothers are frequently hostile and distrustful, so a worker who has an established rapport with the family is most likely to succeed in getting a specific task accomplished.

Educational Neglect

Chronic absence from school is another form of neglect that school personnel alone are in a position to document and report. Some neglectful parents do not register their children for school or make any effort to see that they attend. This kind of educational neglect clearly should be reported. Other parents do not require their children to attend school on any consistent basis. Even though registered, the children may be absent several days every week throughout the school year. Efforts should first be made to improve school attendance through voluntary compliance, using an authoritative approach: the law says the children must come to school. If this is not successful, careful attendance records should be kept, and a report made to protective services when absenteeism is obviously chronic.

Failure by the parents to cooperate with the school's request to assess a child's intellectual, academic, and social-emotional development for the purpose of determining an appropriate educational plan can also be considered educational neglect. Although there are other mechanisms within school law for solving this problem, they are time-consuming. If the situation is acute, reporting to protective services for neglect is an option to be considered.

John is a boy who could have been reported for neglect, although the school staff decided to use a more familiar tactic, that of requesting a hearing. In doing so, they were ignoring the fact that John's neglect was more pervasive than educational neglect.

John was failing third grade, but this was only one aspect of his problems. A psychological evaluation from his previous school showing he had a verbal IQ of 135 and a performance IQ of 85, qualified him for the learning disability program. However, his parents refused the special tutoring help offered. They said that they would provide tutoring outside of school. Efforts were made to help John make friends, but peers rejected him because of his many peculiarities, unusual statements, and irrelevant ideas. He openly masturbated, pulled his hair out, and ate dirt, crayons, and bits of tree bark. He hung around the school playground long after school hours and was often seen by neighbors sitting forlorn in his sandbox, unable to go in the house because no one was home and the doors were locked. He often came to school ill-clad and looking unkempt. He seemed tired much of the time and frequently brought no lunch. Although John gave evidence of being impaired in all aspects of development, his parents refused to consider psychological help for him, insisting his only problem was a learning disability. They would not allow the school to do a current child study evaluation and they continually failed to keep appointments with the principal and school social worker. When the parents were told that the school would take them to a hearing to force them to comply with an evaluation including psychiatric examination, the parents withdrew John from school and sent him to live with his grandmother in another suburb.

The value of reporting a case like this to Protective Services is that the family can be followed even if they move (or move the child) from one school district to another. Further, there was reason to suspect that John might be the object of sexual abuse because overt masturbation in a school-aged child is always reason to suspect sexual abuse.

Emotional Neglect

Confusion in reporting neglect occurs when emotional neglect seems to be the only kind of evidence. If emotional neglect is interpreted as psychological abuse, it may not be included as being reportable under the law. If it is reportable, Protective Services may interpret the law in such a way that they are not required to act. (See Chapter 5.)

Emotional neglect that cannot wait includes parental refusal to seek help when a child is suicidal or obviously quite emotionally disturbed. When families who do not take suicidal overtures seriously are investigated, it is often discovered that other kinds of abuse or neglect are present. This was true with Sue, an eleven-year-old girl who talked daily about wanting to kill herself, even describing the method she might use. While the staff was in a state of high anxiety for nearly two weeks as they tried to force the parents to seek help, Sue confided to a friend that her sixteen-year-old brother had raped her. The friend's mother then reported the family for sexual abuse. The school had not reported the family on the basis of their denial and resistance because they had always been cooperative, and at first said they would seek help. However, when it was learned that the "help" consisted of a conference for Sue with her minister, who gave her a book about the gift of life, and it became evident that her parents were denying the seriousness of Sue's threats and actually blamed the school counselor for putting ideas in her head, the school should have reported the family for neglect.

WORKING WITH NEGLECTFUL PARENTS

We cannot expect neglectful parents to help their children overcome academic problems, but we can hope to get them to cooperate with others who can help. The hostile barrier that these parents create between themselves and others is the first challenge to be met. As educators, we must build rapport with these people and try not to become too angry or frustrated ourselves.

The most severely neglectful mothers will probably remain hostile regardless of any efforts made to build trust and rapport. They will need the authority of the legal system to enforce compliance with recommendations that will safeguard a child's health and welfare. However, you may expect some success with moderately neglectful parents if you reach out to them in the ways shown in Figure 3-1.

HELPING NEGLECTED CHILDREN: BASIC STEPS FOR EDUCATORS

Helping neglected children obviously starts with seeing that they get to school, relieving their hunger, improving their health and hygiene, and making sure they have decent clothing. This can be done by:

1. Providing two meals a day at school
2. Using school showers and lavatories
3. Weighing and measuring the children regularly to be sure they are growing
4. Finding them clothes through P.T.A. clothing exchanges or the Salvation Army

Once basic needs have been provided for, acceptance by teachers and other children is possible. Then the task is to help children who have been unloved to become lovable.

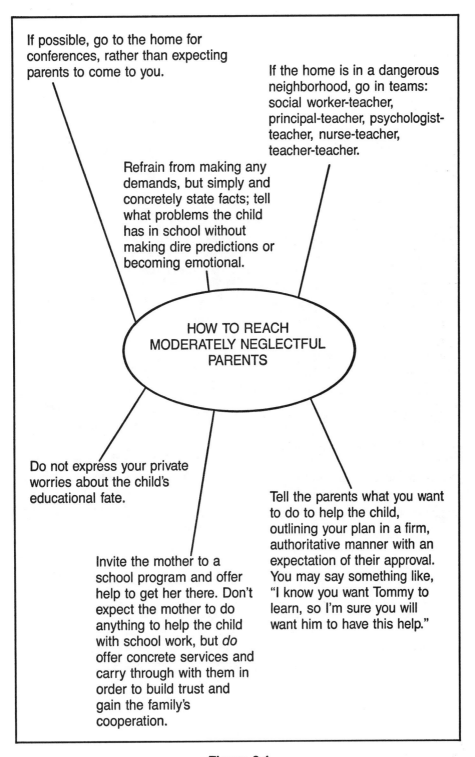

If possible, go to the home for conferences, rather than expecting parents to come to you.

If the home is in a dangerous neighborhood, go in teams: social worker-teacher, principal-teacher, psychologist-teacher, nurse-teacher, teacher-teacher.

Refrain from making any demands, but simply and concretely state facts; tell what problems the child has in school without making dire predictions or becoming emotional.

HOW TO REACH MODERATELY NEGLECTFUL PARENTS

Do not express your private worries about the child's educational fate.

Invite the mother to a school program and offer help to get her there. Don't expect the mother to do anything to help the child with school work, but *do* offer concrete services and carry through with them in order to build trust and gain the family's cooperation.

Tell the parents what you want to do to help the child, outlining your plan in a firm, authoritative manner with an expectation of their approval. You may say something like, "I know you want Tommy to learn, so I'm sure you will want him to have this help."

Figure 3-1

Unlovable Kids

Children who have been emotionally neglected for many years do not have much sparkle. They may be detached, remote and vacant, or superficially effusive and clingy. They are out of touch with their real feelings, having learned to repress them to avoid the inevitable pain of feeling unloved and bad. To win attention, they learn to use any device that has worked with anyone. Their neediness is like a bottomless pit, and they are indeed hard to love.

The following applies to physically and verbally abused children as well as neglected children, because in thinking and feeling themselves unlovable, they develop unlovable traits; yet all need to learn that they can be lovable. Caring adults must find their redeeming features and express a pleasurable response to them. Teaching these children that they are lovable is too big a job for just one person: many compassionate adults must become involved. At school, everyone from the custodian to the librarian has something to offer. Outside of school, Big Brothers and Sisters, scout leaders and church workers should be enlisted, and it is important to start as early in a child's life as possible. Nursery schools and day care centers, as well as the schools, need to recruit volunteers to help supply the emotional nourishment that these children need.

With unlovable kids, nothing is as valuable as your gift of self. You start by building trust, allowing the child to be dependent, and being there when he or she needs you. You find something unique about the child and let the child know that you have noticed it. You show that you are dependable and predictable in your actions and availability. When it comes to self-esteem, it is not a matter of reinforcing positive traits that are embryonic, but of *building* a positive self-image to replace the negative one already in existence. This is a process of reconstruction.

Helping a child like this construct a new, positive self-image will take years, and the teacher of each succeeding grade will build on what has been accomplished with the previous teacher. You must not be competitive in this endeavor. Each of you will recognize that the child has become attached as a result of the interest shown, and you will help the child ease the attachment to you in order to become attached to next year's teacher. This process can be rewarding when all the teachers cooperate and support each other.

You discover, then validate, a child's good qualities, as in the following dialogue:

(Judy thinks she is ugly; she has a reputation for being clumsy.)
Teacher: *How attractive your new glasses are. Did you pick them out?*

Judy: *Sort of; my mom helped.*
Teacher: *They certainly set off your beautiful eyes.*
Judy: *But I have a big nose.*
Teacher: *So who cares about noses? People really respond to beautiful eyes.*
(On another day you see her carry a pile of books to the shelf without
    dropping any.)
Teacher: *What a good job of carrying books. You didn't drop a single one.*
Judy (beaming): *I guess that is pretty good for a clumsy one like me.*
Teacher: *You're not as clumsy as you think.*

It is not easy to find things you can *honestly* give positive feedback
about (and your response to the child *must* be genuine), because the
unlovable aspects of abused children are hard to ignore. If you make a
conscious effort, you will find something good in every child. You will
need to become an expert observer.

Roy was a boy who believed he was dumb, and indeed, he
regularly got most of his work wrong. However, he was the only one in
his first grade class who knew the correct ending for an exclamatory
statement that the teacher dictated. Roy was vehemently told at home
how awful he was. Perhaps it was his experience with verbal intensity
that enabled him to recognize the emphatic statement that should end
in an exclamation point! At any rate, Roy's teacher capitalized on this
moment to help him challenge his view of himself as a dumb boy. "How
smart you are," she said. "Imagine, the only one in the class to get that
right. Congratulations!" Roy will remember this moment far into the
future. This event, along with other similar moments, will reinforce the
idea that he *is* smart.

TREATMENT AND PREVENTION OF NEGLECT

Even more so than other forms of abuse, the treatment and
prevention of neglect are inextricable. Improving neglectful mothers'
child rearing while supplementing their efforts with maximum emotional and cognitive input from caring adults in the community, we will
help the children now and reduce the evidence of neglectful parents in
the next generation.

We must be realists, however. Experience has shown that no
matter how much effort is put into trying to help severely neglectful
parents, change is not often possible. They simply do not make use of
the resources provided. The children in these families must be permanently removed, parental rights terminated, and an effort made to find
adoptive homes.[17]

The vast majority of neglecting families are in the moderate category, and much has been learned about how to help them change. Most of these mothers will show gradual but steady improvement in functioning if a long-term, sustained effort is made, utilizing a variety of resources simultaneously. However, even when physical neglect has disappeared, emotional neglect remains. These mothers cannot give their children the love and emotional support they need because they themselves have never received any. This must be provided by a substitute extended family consisting of day care workers, volunteer grannies, teachers, and counselors.

Neglecting families can benefit from the same kinds of services described in Chapter 2. However, neglecting mothers usually need a stable, "attachment-like" relationship with a caseworker who reaches out to them through home visits before they can avail themselves of such resources. Also, because of their neediness and verbal inaccessibility, they do not make as good use of self-help groups such as Parents Anonymous.

Comprehensive resource centers that provide a variety of services to both parents and children at one location seem to offer the best approach with neglecting families. Mothers are taught nutrition and health care, how to cook (particularly with the surplus food products they receive), sew, and do laundry. They learn how to engage in pleasurable activities with other adults, and how to enjoy their children. By assisting in the child care program, they learn effective ways of managing children's behavior, communicating with them, and knowing what can be expected of them. The staff become "good parents" to the deprived/neglectful mothers, and the center becomes an enriching home for the mothers and their children.

Homemaker Services

Similar goals can often be achieved through the use of homemakers. These people are mature, kindly, motherly women who are paid for by protective services to be in a home from a half-day to two days a week. They model home management and housekeeping skills, such as going shopping with and working along with the mother. They may also suggest alternative ways of dealing with the children if the mother seems receptive. They nurture the mother and children simultaneously, and withhold judgment. Unfortunately, current practice allows for only three to six months of this kind of service, while most neglectful mothers need it over a span of several years.

Day Care

Day care for the children is essential, both to meet the children's needs and to free the mother to learn housekeeping tasks and make progress with her own rehabilitation. This service is usually accepted by the mother if it is presented as something that will benefit her as well as the child. This principle holds for getting the mother to accept other services as well. If she sees them as something for herself as well as for the children, she is less likely to resist the offer. Emergency foster care and use of volunteer "Big Sisters" or grannies are services that are usually needed.

The kind of comprehensive resource center needed by impoverished families is not commonly available to more than a few. The question that continually comes to mind when thinking about the enormous rural and urban deprived population is "Why don't we transform the schools in these areas into just such a center?" Most of the mothers have serious educational as well as personal deficits that make them unemployable, and rehabilitation of neglectful mothers is primarily a matter of reeducation, so why not bring the mothers to school with their children? The school already has most of the resources needed for such a task, and is a logical choice because of the potential to instill positive attitudes toward education and staying in school even after the law no longer requires it.

Mothers with young children could learn how to play with them and teach them. Mothers of older children could have the option of "sitting in" on any class, helping in any class, or spending their time in a lounge playing games, working on crafts, reading, or socializing. They could learn to help in many aspects of school life. The sense of belonging and pride that would develop, the opportunity to identify with teachers, the improvement in self-esteem that they would achieve, and beginning to believe in their own potential would not only benefit them personally, but contribute, in an indirect way, to their children's educational growth. Parent and child would grow up together in such an environment.

Endnotes

1. Norman A. Polansky and others, *Damaged Parents: An Anatomy of Child Neglect* (Chicago: The University of Chicago Press, 1981), p. 15.

2. Ibid., p. 34.

3. Ibid., pp. 80-85.

4. Avis Brenner, *Helping Children Cope With Stress* (Lexington MA: D. C. Heath and Co., 1984), p. 115.

5. Polansky, *Damaged Parents*, p. 7.

6. Cynthia Mohr Trainor, *The Dilemma of Child Neglect: Identification and Treatment* (Denver, CO: The American Humane Association, 1983), p. 13.

7. Leontine Young, *Physical Child Neglect* (Chicago: National Committee for Prevention of Child Abuse, 1981), p. 4.

8. Ibid., p. 2.

9. Polansky, *Damaged Parents*, p. 43.

10. Robert M. Mulford and Morton I. Cohen, "Psychosocial Characteristics of Neglecting Parents" in *Neglecting Parents* (Denver, CO: The American Humane Association, 1967), pp. 6-8.

11. Polansky, *Damaged Parents*, p. 43.

12. Ibid., p. 39.

13. Hendricka A. Cantwell, "Child Neglect" in *The Battered Child*, 3rd ed., C. Henry Kempe and Ray E. Helfer, eds. (Chicago: University of Chicago Press, 1980), p. 184.

14. Christine Comstock Herbruck, *Breaking the Cycle of Child Abuse* (Minneapolis, MN: Winston Press, 1979), p. 33.

15. Ruth Kempe, Christy Cutler and Janet Dean, "The Infant with Failure to Thrive," in *The Battered Child*, 3rd ed., Kempe and Helfer, eds., p. 164.

16. Carol Austin Bridgewater, "Suicidal Preschoolers," *Psychology Today*, January 1985, pp. 17-18.

17. Young, *Physical Child Neglect*, p. 11.

Chapter 4

Sexual Abuse

Before 1975, what little was known about child sexual abuse was hidden, ignored, or denied. Everyone believed child molestation to be rare. Then women, abused as children, began telling their stories in the public arena. Psychotherapists gathered clinical data from women patients still haunted by the trauma of childhood sexual abuse; and research by an interested few provided new insights about the nature, enormity, and complexity of the problem. The literature on child sexual abuse is rapidly expanding; yet there remain unresolved differing points of view about some aspects of the problem, and also many unanswered questions. It is possible that ideas presented here may later need to be modified or changed, as knowledge evolves.

MAKING THE PUBLIC AWARE OF SEXUAL ABUSE

Women took the lead in creating public awareness regarding sexual abuse. Outraged by their sexual violation and exploitation, they developed rape crisis centers where abused women could obtain counseling and legal help. They founded shelters where women and their children could take refuge. As women talked more openly about their experiences, it became evident that many who suffered rape had also been sexually victimized during childhood. Prevention of child sexual abuse became an important goal, and to this end educational programs were developed. As these programs were presented to groups of parents, teachers, and children, public awareness increased. An immense media campaign followed.

The TV showing of *Something About Amelia* in early 1984 brought about a dramatic increase in reported sexual abuse, and in virtually every instance it was determined that children were telling the truth. Children were disclosing their abuse at school, to teachers and counselors, who found themselves cognitively and emotionally unprepared to handle the repercussions that followed disclosure.

One unfortunate outcome of the media attention to the problem was that some mothers began falsely accusing their estranged or divorced husbands in order to win custody battles, block the father's access to his children, or take revenge.[1] The incidence of children falsely accusing men other than fathers also increased.[2] These were disturbed children who had learned to manipulate their new knowledge about sexual abuse, and the public's reactivity to it.

Although we must not lose sight of the fact that most children do not lie about sexual abuse, it is also important to keep in mind that some occasionally do. The stigma of being falsely accused, and its economic and emotional repercussions are enormous. Anyone working with disturbed children and families, including all of us in schools, is a potential target for false accusation today. Whenever you have a question about a child's story, seek psychiatric examination of the child, preferably by a psychiatrist whom you trust and in whom you have confidence. It is also appropriate to ask that a child be given a lie detector test if the accusation is toward a respected professional.

HOW SEXUAL ABUSE DIFFERS
FROM OTHER FORMS OF ABUSE

We have seen that the best chance of helping physically abused and physically neglected children comes when we constrain our anger about their mistreatment and assume a nurturant, educative approach with mothers. By considering what damaged lives these mothers have experienced, we can generate empathy toward them.

Child sexual abuse is different; it produces intense emotional reactivity that allows no possibility of empathizing with the perpetrator. Upon disclosure, professionals, as well as the family and community, are shocked. Denial, anger, and retaliatory feelings churn within us and create conflict and confusion. We begin to wish we knew nothing and could forget the whole thing. Yet we know we must deal with the situation constructively if there is to be a positive outcome for the child. Too often, the child is betrayed in the aftermath of disclosure, and we professionals are left with guilt feelings and self-doubt about whether we did the right thing. It is reassuring to know that some of the experts in child sexual abuse admit to having made mistakes, and to having learned by trial and error. It is important not to be hard on ourselves if we find, after the fact, that there might have been a better way of handling a situation.

Child Sexual Abuse Is a Crime

A crucial difference between child sexual abuse and other forms of abuse is that it is a *criminal offense.* This makes it difficult to deal with, especially in the case of incest, because a young girl will feel threatened by the knowledge that telling on her father is tantamount to putting him in jail. Many of the educational programs and materials for adults and children do not make it clear that child sexual abuse is a crime. Children abused by a family member find out when they threaten to tell; parents use this fact to reinforce the need for secrecy.

Because it is a crime, child sexual abuse *must* be reported to the police; it is necessary for them to investigate such reports. If you report sexual abuse to Protective Services, they must inform the police. If the alleged perpetrator is not a caretaker or family member, protective services may not be required to investigate the report.

The most effective handling of the investigation of child sexual abuse reports requires the cooperation of law enforcement officials, medical personnel, Protective Service workers, and mental health professionals in school and community. To date, productive collaboration has not been achieved, except in a few communities. Instead, professionals have tended to work at cross purposes: the criminal justice system has been focused on proving guilt and punishing offenders, while mental health professionals' goals are to ameliorate the trauma and rehabilitate the family (when possible and advisable) to normal functioning. These are not really the contradictory goals they seem to be. Experience has shown that successful rehabilitation of the family is not possible unless the law is used to coerce the offender into treatment, set limits on his interactions with the family and child victim, and monitor his cooperation with the treatment plan.

Perpetrators Are Men

In the case of physical abuse and neglect, mothers are the abusers; in sexual abuse, perpetrators are nearly always men. Women and adolescent girls are occasionally guilty of molesting children, but they account for only five percent of the sexual abuse of girls and no more than twenty percent of the sexual abuse of boys.[3]

It is apparently difficult for many men to be objective about child sexual abuse because their own sex is incriminated by this offense. Male judges, defense attorneys, police officers, and social workers are prone to believe the rationalizations of offenders because they identify, either consciously or unconsciously, with them as members of their own sex. Offenders try to exonerate themselves by blaming their victims for having seduced them, and by claiming that the child consented to, or enjoyed the experience. They may excuse themselves by lying that the sexual activity happened only once (what's so bad about that?), or insist it only happened while they were intoxicated and thus didn't know what they were doing. Abuse of alcohol often correlates to family sexual abuse, but it is likely that the offender uses alcohol in order to get the nerve to engage in the sexual activity, rather than that he abuses *because* he is under the influence.[4]

DEFINITIONS

Before going further, let's consider some definitions of the terms commonly associated with sexual abuse in all its forms. Figure 4-1 briefly summarizes these definitions.

Child Sexual Abuse

Criminal codes vary from state to state, and it is important that you learn how your state defines and categorizes different kinds of sexual activity between an adult and child for the purpose of prosecution. However, the definition that follows is most pertinent for determining what should be reported.

Child sexual abuse is any sexual act *imposed* on a child by an adult or adolescent, whose age, size, and position of authority or dominance in relation to the child allows for coercion of the child into activities for the sexual stimulation or pleasure of the adult. The child's lack of emotional, maturational, and cognitive development disallows the relevance of "informed consent."

Incest: Family Sexual Abuse

Incest refers to sexual abuse by a close family member (father, mother, brother, uncle, aunt, grandparent, and so on) who may or may not be a blood relative. For our purposes, the term will also include anyone in a surrogate parent role (stepparent, foster parent, boyfriend, girlfriend or common-law spouse of a parent). Most of the sexual abuse that is reported is incest, and unless otherwise stated, the following discussion will pertain to incest. The terms *incestuous family* and *family sexual abuse* are used interchangeably, and most often the perpetrator will be assumed to be the father figure to a girl, although boys also can be victims. Brothers, uncles, grandfathers, and boyfriends often assume the father role when a woman with children is divorced or unmarried, so the perpetrator might be any of these.

DEFINITIONS RELATING TO
SEXUAL ABUSE

TERM	DEFINITION
child sexual abuse	any sexual act imposed on a child by an adult or adolescent
incest	sexual abuse by a close family member
pedophilia	sexual misuse and abuse of children
pedophile (child molestor)	an adult who is sexually aroused by children and gives in to impulses to act out sexually with them
fixated pedophile	an adult who has had primary or exclusive sexual attraction to children since early adolescence
regressed pedophile	an adult who has reached adulthood with a primary sexual orientation to age mates, but does not have well-developed personality strengths for coping with adult life, so may look towards children for sexual gratification
rapist	an adult who uses physical force or threat of harm in the sexual assault

Figure 4-1

Pedophilia

The sexual misuse and abuse of children constitutes *pedophilia*. Pedophilic offenders come from all classes and education levels, and are found in every profession. In the overwhelming majority of cases, pedophilic offenders are known and trusted members of the family, neighborhood, or community of a victimized child.

Pedophile (Child Molestor)

All child molestors are *pedophiles,* whether or not they have exclusively chosen children for sex partners or also have sexual experiences with adults. A pedophile is an adult who is sexually aroused by children and gives in to impulses to act out sexually with them. He is a person with deviant sexual interests; many pedophiles engage in deviant sexual activity other than child molestation. Researchers and therapists believe that a pedophile's sexual activity with a child serves a variety of psychological needs. However, this should not divert us from seeing their problem as sexual deviance. Pedophiles have developed an obsessive-compulsive drive to engage sexually with children, and each time they do so, their compulsion is reinforced. We do not know, and it may take many years of research to discover, why so many men develop a sexual attraction to children. (It has been suggested that four million American men are child molestors, but no one knows precisely how many there are.)[5]

Until recently, it was thought that men who molested their own children were not pedophiles; that it was only men who *exclusively* chose children for sex who were pedophiles. Many still believe this, but more and more it is being acknowledged that there is a *spectrum* of pedophiles, and incestuous fathers are one type. In more cases than we like to admit, incestuous fathers' sexual attraction to children antedated marriage; perhaps half of incestuous fathers abuse other people's children as well as their own.[6] It has been suggested that some men marry in order to produce children to satisfy their pedophilic appetites; others marry women who *have* children in order to have access to a child sex partner.

Nicholas Groth has differentiated three types of pedophiles: fixated child molestor, regressed child molestor, and pedophilic rapist. He divides the *class* of sexual offenders into two groups: child molestors and rapists (not all rapists are pedophiles). Pedophilic rapists differ from child molestors in that they are *sex-force* offenders. They use physical force or threat of harm to engage a child sexually, while child molestors use *pressure* techniques.

Fixated Pedophile

A *fixated pedophile* is one who has had primary or exclusive sexual attraction to children since early adolescence. As a teenager, he most likely avoided the usual pattern of socialization with age mates, such as dating and competitive sports, and as an adult he generally does not initiate or actively pursue mature sexual relationships.[7] His psychosocial and psychosexual development has not progressed through the normal stages, leaving him with a character/personality disorder. He has a strong tendency to prefer a male child, a child with a body like his own. Those fixated pedophiles who molest both boys and girls perceive the bodies of the children as primarily the same, simply discounting the genitalia. They are attracted to the size and looks of the child, the smoothness of the skin, the "little boy or little girl" smell, the lack of body hair, and so on.[8]

A fixated pedophile has a distorted perception of himself; he *experiences* himself as a child. This allows him to justify his sexual activity with a child partner as a peer relationship. He imagines that the child is enjoying the activity as much as he is, and he has no strong feelings of guilt, shame, or remorse. Cognitively, however, he does *know* that what he is doing is against the law and is considered wrong by others.[9]

Regressed Pedophile

Regressed pedophiles have reached adulthood with a primary sexual orientation to age mates. However, they do not have well-developed personality strengths for coping, and are prone to become over- whelmed by the responsibilities, demands, and stresses of adult life. They are usually married, or have been married, and their pedophilic interests seem to emerge when their sexual relationship with wife or girlfriend becomes conflictive or ungratifying. This kind of pedophile is most likely to prefer a female child as a sex partner, one whom he perceives as a pseudo-adult replacement for his impaired or lost sexual relationship with his wife or girlfriend. Because he has a distorted perception of the young female, as that of a miniature adult, he is able to rationalize his sexual relationship with her as being on a peer basis.[10]

Regressed pedophiles are more likely to have guilt or remorse about their behavior, yet there are many who do not. Sometimes they will say they are sorry and act remorseful to avoid the ramifications when they are caught; but subsequent attitudes and behavior will prove otherwise.

Rapists

Pedophiles who use physical force or threat of harm in their sexual assaults on children are called rapists. Although few in number compared to child molestors, the fact that they hurt children physically, either intentionally or unintentionally, makes them dangerous. These men have no emotional interest in the children they victimize; a child is used primarily to gratify the adult's sexual needs, but may also serve the purpose of discharging the rapist's hostility. Rapists are extremely angry men. For them, children are objects of prey to be stalked and hunted. This kind of offender may use a weapon to force compliance, or physically abuse the child to reinforce verbal threats. A small group of rapists are sadists who take pleasure in hurting their child victims; the physical harm they inflict is purposeful, often extensive and severe, and can result in murder. Those men who purposely seek out children to rape and murder are called lust murderers. Fortunately they are few in number.[11]

CHILD VICTIMS

There are no reliable statistics regarding the incidence of child sexual abuse, but we frequently hear that one out of four girls and one out of seven boys will be abused before age eighteen. These estimates are based on surveys of adult populations, which are fairly consistent in showing that girls are victimized two to three times more than boys.

There appears to be an approximately even distribution of fixated and regressed child molestors.[12] As fixated offenders tend to choose male children and regressed offenders choose females, we might expect boys to become victims as frequently as girls. Some believe that this will ultimately prove to be so. However, fixated pedophiles are not usually married, and they depend on "picking up" boys. They do not have as ready access to child sex partners as do regressed pedophiles who are married and have access to daughters and stepdaughters. This, and the generally recognized fact that boys are more reluctant to disclose their abuse than girls would explain why boys are less often reported to be victimized than girls.

Comparing Boy and Girl Victims

Figure 4-2 summarizes some facts regarding the differences between boy and girl victims.

Girls Who Are Vulnerable

Girls who are living with a stepfather are much more likely to become victimized than those living with their natural father. One study showed that a stepfather was five times more likely to abuse a stepdaughter than was a natural father, and stepdaughters are abused by their parents' friends, as well, possibly prior to remarriage while the mother is dating.[15]

COMPARING BOY AND GIRL VICTIMS

BOYS	GIRLS
• mostly victimized by men	• mostly victimized by men
• more likely to be victimized by someone outside the family	• more likely to be victimized by someone inside the family
• more likely to come from impoverished homes	• more likely to come from higher-income homes
• more likely to come from a single-parent family	• more likely to come from a two-parent family
• more likely to be a victim of physical abuse (by a parent)	• more likely to be a victim only of sexual abuse
• more likely to be reported to the police[13]	• more likely to be reported to a hospital or child protective agency
• mean ages of 9-12[14]	• mean ages of 8-11

Figure 4-2

The same study also confirmed the importance of mothers as protectors of daughters: when a natural mother is sometimes or always absent because of illness, death, or divorce, or is emotionally unavailable even when present, girls are at added risk to become victims. Mothers who are punitive in words and actions about sexual matters also contribute to their daughter's vulnerability, although the reason for this is not clear. When girls are bombarded with sexual prohibitions and punishments, they may have a difficult time learning to tell what constitutes danger; they may discard all warnings their mothers give about sex, including those about sexual victimization.[16]

INCESTUOUS FAMILIES

Incest does not happen in stable, harmonious families, but within the context of family dysfunction. (See Chapter 5 for a more detailed discussion of family dysfunction.) Two prominant patterns of husband-wife role relationship seem to be typical of incest-prone families: dominant husband/submissive wife, and passive-dependent husband/competent-mothering wife. Incest is more likely to occur in families where the rule of the father is absolute,[17] although it is apparent that there is more than one family pattern in which incest occurs.

Figure 4-3 provides a checklist of characteristics for incestuous fathers.

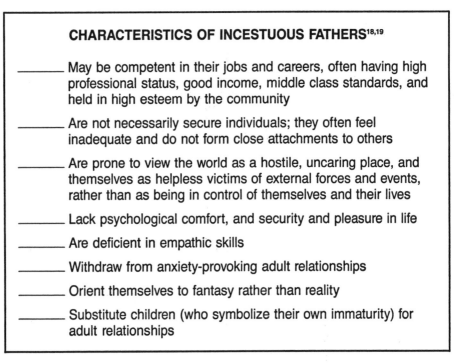

CHARACTERISTICS OF INCESTUOUS FATHERS[18,19]

_____ May be competent in their jobs and careers, often having high professional status, good income, middle class standards, and held in high esteem by the community

_____ Are not necessarily secure individuals; they often feel inadequate and do not form close attachments to others

_____ Are prone to view the world as a hostile, uncaring place, and themselves as helpless victims of external forces and events, rather than as being in control of themselves and their lives

_____ Lack psychological comfort, and security and pleasure in life

_____ Are deficient in empathic skills

_____ Withdraw from anxiety-provoking adult relationships

_____ Orient themselves to fantasy rather than reality

_____ Substitute children (who symbolize their own immaturity) for adult relationships

Figure 4-3

Dominant Husband/Submissive Wife Marital Pattern

In this marital pattern, reflecting the traditional patriarchal family structure, the husband assumes a dominant role, rules with an iron hand, and keeps his wife and children financially and emotionally dependent on him, as well as socially isolated from extra-family relationships. He reinforces any hint of insecurity or immaturity in his wife and children in order to maintain his position of power and control, and may even deliberately drive a wedge between the mother and children to prevent the mother from gaining strength through an alliance with the children.

In this kind of relationship, the wife is prone to become ill, either physically or emotionally, or both, and as a consequence is periodically unavailable to children and husband. When ill at home or in the hospital, she cannot be a protector to her daughter, and her unavailability to her husband causes him to turn to his daughters to fulfill his emotional and sexual needs. Since he feels that he owns his wife and daughters, he feels entitled to sexual favors from his daughters as well as his wife.

Passive-Dependent Husband/Strong Competent Wife Marital Pattern

In this marital pattern, the husband relates to his wife as if he were a dependent child. He looks to her to make major decisions, manage the household, bolster his ego, and take care of his emotional needs. Over time the wife begins to feel neglected and emotionally unsupported, and may turn elsewhere for emotional fulfillment and a peer social life. As she becomes increasingly self-sufficient, emotionally distant from her husband, and less attentive to his needs, he turns to his daughter as a surrogate companion-wife-mother. He requires his daughter to take care of him as he formerly expected his wife to do: she must get his meals, do his laundry, get him up for work, and spend her leisure time with him. Eventually, this emotional dependency and intimacy evolves into a sexual relationship.

PROGRESSION OF ADULT-CHILD SEXUAL RELATIONSHIPS

Sexual encounters between child molestors and children usually follow a predictable pattern. (See Figure 4-4.) The child is not forced into sex with the adult, but enticed or entrapped into complying. This is called the engagement phase. Following this are the sexual interaction phase, the secrecy phase, the disclosure phase, and the suppression phase.[20]

The Engagement Phase

The perpetrator is usually a person well-known to the child (when he is not the father), and someone who holds a position of trust that allows *access* to the boy or girl. The child molestor must also have the *opportunity* to be alone and in a private place with the child. Although the circumstances of access and opportunity may be accidental the first time a sexual overture is made, the child molestor will watch for, plan, and create opportunities for future private encounters. A daughter will be induced to participate by being told the activity is something special or fun. The power and authority of adulthood, and particularly of being the father, conveys to the child that the proposed behavior is acceptable and sanctioned. Sometimes a child will be offered rewards and bribes, but in most instances, the techniques used to engage a child will be subtle. The advantages of size, position of dominance, and mature intellect allow the pedophile to coerce the child into compliance without the need of threat or force.[21]

PHASES OF ADULT-CHILD SEXUAL RELATIONSHIPS

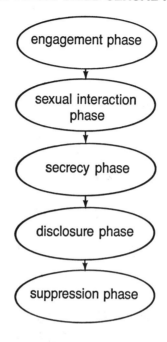

Figure 4-4

Sexual Interaction Phase

Pedophiles typically introduce a child into sexual activity slowly and gradually, becoming more overt and intimate with each encounter. The first encounter may go no further than disrobing and visually examining each other's bodies. Autostimulation or self-masturbation may come next, or the activity may progress directly to fondling. The perpetrator first fondles the child, starting by caressing the entire body, but ultimately focusing on the erotic body parts, then persuades the child to do the same to him. Fondling may be accompanied by kissing. Finally, the activity may progress to penetration of the child's body in one or more ways. Oral and anal penetration will probably precede vaginal penetration.[22]

The anal opening is very elastic and can be stretched to accommodate the adult penis without serious damage to the child. However this is not true of the vagina. A child molestor will typically "prepare" a little girl for intercourse over a period of time, using digital penetration of the vagina to increase its size. A medical examination will not be able to document anal penetration unless a venereal disease is disclosed, but the size of the vagina can be compared to what is normal for the girl's age as a way to validate vaginal penetration.

Secrecy Phase

In order for the activity to continue, and to protect himself from being accused of a crime, the offender must make certain that the child won't tell what is going on. His way to assure that no one will find out is to pledge the child to secrecy, and to keep reinforcing the idea that no one must know. He does this through persuasion ("If you love daddy, you won't tell"), through the offer of gifts and special privileges, and through verbal threats. The threat may be of separation ("Mommy will divorce me," "I'll be sent to jail," or "You'll be sent away"), or the child may be told that her mother will be angry, or someone will be hurt ("If you tell, I'll hurt your sister or you," or "I'll kill you").[23] The degree of threat will usually escalate in relation to a girl's threats or attempts to tell. If she does tell and mother confronts father, he will lie to protect himself, and mother will frequently believe him rather than her daughter.

Disclosure Phase

Many children *never* reveal the secret of their abuse; others do so only when they reach adulthood. However, with so much current attention to the problem, the secret is increasingly being disclosed while the sexual activity is ongoing. Accidental disclosure occurs when the activity is observed, when there has been physical injury to the child that brings her to the attention of the school nurse or a physician, when the child is found to have a venereal disease, when a girl becomes pregnant, or when a young child initiates precocious sexual activities with a peer or adult (such as mounting and humping, "French kissing" or other *adult* sexual acts). No one is prepared for accidental disclosure; it is always a shock, and it always precipitates a crisis.[24]

Purposeful disclosure also leads to a family crisis, but the crisis will be more or less traumatic depending on how it is handled. Girls who purposely disclose have reasons for doing so, and it is important to know what each particular girl's reasons are. Girls will probably need guidance following disclosure because they are usually unable to predict the intensity of the emotional reactions, and the disruptiveness of the family crisis that will ensue. Some reasons that older girls give for disclosing are: anger at father and a wish to punish him; fear of becoming pregnant; a wish to start dating (which father won't allow); and a desire for more involvement with peers (which he is restricting). Younger girls disclose for different reasons: it may take too much energy and effort to keep the secret; they may wish for a closer relationship with mother; or they may want relief from the hurt and discomfort of the sexual activity.

Suppression Phase

Family members have intense emotional reactions to the disclosure of sexual abuse, whether the perpetrator was a family member or someone outside the family circle. In the latter instance, the family is more likely to be protective and helpful to the child, yet they may deny that their son or daughter needs therapy, refuse to cooperate with the investigation, and be unwilling to bring charges against the perpetrator. For their own psychological comfort, they want to forget the matter, suppress publicity about it, and act as if the event has had little impact on their lives.

In the case of incest, repercussions in the family are great and the need for suppression strong. Everyone fears that father will go to jail, the family will break up, that they will be shamed by the community, and so on. Father can be expected to lie, act incensed at being "falsely accused," and do everything within his power to undermine the credibility of his daughter. This reinforces mother's normal tendency not to believe her daughter, and perhaps in one out of two cases she will join her husband in pressuring her daughter to recant. Father and mother will decide that their child is a pathological liar, mentally disturbed, or crazy. In the case of a young child, they may say that she dreamed what she said had happened, or created it out of her vivid imagination.

If the daughter is strong, and insists on sticking to her story, threats of the kind originally used to insure secrecy will be used, and possibly even physical abuse will accompany the threats.

Most family members will experience a conflict of loyalties, and hostility toward the one being blamed will be intense. Sometimes the child victim will be blamed, sometimes the mother, and only more rarely the father, the real culprit. Mother's dilemma is especially great, and the choices she must make are painful. If she chooses to believe and support her daughter, she automatically alienates her husband. She faces loss of economic and emotional support from him, and possibly even physical abuse.

HOW THE SCHOOLS CAN ASSIST
IN THE CRISIS OF DISCLOSURE

Educators *may* be able to help during the crisis of disclosure if the perpetrator was not a family member, if the disclosure did not occur at school, or if the mother has no doubts that the child's story is true. On the other hand, the school staff may be able to do little more than cooperate with the investigation. When the child is being actively pressured to change her story, the school staff must watch and wait because parents know they will be less successful if a counselor is involved. Parents may also suspect that someone at school made the report, even when this is not the case. The relationship between the school and the family may become strained, at least temporarily, if they believe this.

The needs of family members during the crisis of disclosure are outlined here so that if you are in a position to help, you will know what direction to follow. *The goals of intervention are to keep everyone functional and to reduce suppression as much as possible.*

Keep Family Members Functional

Following the disclosure of incest, everyone is at risk of emotional breakdown. Suicide attempts are common. People act as if the world had changed, as if they don't know how to perform ordinary daily tasks. Each person in the family needs someone to give him or her support and tell him or her exactly what to do.[25]

The first task is to get the father to leave the home. If he at first resists, the mother and children should be taken to a shelter until someone can convince the father to leave. If there is a Parents United or similar group in the vicinity, a formerly incestuous father who belongs to the group may be called upon to talk to the perpetrator. He will not only try to persuade the father to move out, but will advise him to admit his wrongdoing and to desist from pressuring his daughter to recant. The Parents United father is a source of support for the father, and his involvement can help to reduce suppression as well as to keep the father functional.

As soon as disclosure takes place, there will need to be medical evaluation of the child. The child will need support through this procedure, and also upon return to school. She and her siblings will be thinking "everyone knows" (even though they usually don't) and may be reluctant to return to school to face their friends and classmates. If they do come back immediately, they may be inclined to "tell everyone" to ease the anxiety they feel. They need help to make decisions about whom to tell, and to sort out their feelings about school and friends. Also, mothers need to be told that they must send the children to school. In this crisis, mothers may cling to their children and keep them home unless specifically told not to.[26]

General principles of crisis intervention should guide counseling with the mother. No matter how competent she is, her anxiety, guilt, and fear disorient and immobilize her and make her feel that she can't cope. The mother needs help to sort out and clarify her feelings, and to order her priorities: what must be done immediately, what can wait, what others can be asked to do. Deciding whether to file charges against her husband will be one of the most painful decisions she will be asked to make.

Shoring up the mother's confidence is also crucial, and in the case of the very dependent wife, learning new skills (such as driving a car, or managing a checking account) may need to be planned for. Mothers should be commended for the positive steps they have taken, and reassured that they *will* cope without falling apart or breaking down.

The mother may need to be told what to say to the daughter or son who has been abused, and how to talk to the other children about what is going on. She needs to tell her daughter (probably many times) that she believes her, that it was not her fault, that she's sorry it happened, and that she will do her best to protect and support her in the future. She also needs help to overcome her own self-blame, by being reassured that the responsibility for what happened is entirely that of the perpetrator.[27]

Reduce Suppression

If the father can be kept from pressuring his family to deny what has been disclosed; if the daughter can be strengthened in her determination to stick to her story; if the mother can be given enough support to overcome *her* denial, and if the investigation is well handled, the suppression phase, normally lasting two weeks, will have been constructively maneuvered. An important way that the school staff can help is to stand firm in their belief of the disclosure story. This is easier said than done. Experience shows that investigating professionals have a high potential to join the family's denial system, and to be strongly influenced by the contradictions in children's interview responses that reflect the pressure being brought on them to change their stories. Those who first heard the disclosure and then reported it, will also feel the pressure to join in the denial because disbelief will be expressed by colleagues at school and by the investigating team, as well as by the family. With one Protective Services worker mulling doubtfully over contradictory statements made by the child, a teacher or counselor can say, "But she has been brainwashed by her parents!"; or, in another case, "All five-year-olds make up stories, that is no reason not to believe this one"; or with still another case, in which the child suggested that maybe she had just dreamed what she said had happened, "But we mental health professionals *know* you didn't just dream it."

The suppression process will have less impact if the girl can be interviewed by an official investigator *before* the family learns of the disclosure. This is done more easily in the case of an older girl, by getting a police officer to come over immediately to interview her before she goes home, or by asking her to tell no one else until she *can* be interviewed. The older girl can understand the investigative process and the need for silence once she has disclosed the situation. If the reality of her family's predictable upset reaction is also discussed with her at the time of disclosure, she can be guided in how to handle and resist the family's pressures and threats.

When disclosure occurs at school, the teacher, principal, counselor, psychologist, or social worker should expect to remain with the child while she is interviewed, offering support and reassurance as needed. Some investigative interviewing is excellent, but in other instances the interviewer may be insensitive or insufficiently empathic. When disclosure does not take place at school, or immediate investigative interviewing is not possible, the school is still the most logical place for such interviewing to take place. There is so much emotional reactivity in the home, where the sexual abuse took place, that it is difficult for a child to freely communicate about her experience in that environment.[28] Be prepared to find a pleasant, quiet, private place for the police officer or Protective Services worker to hold the interview. Even when the school is not involved in the disclosure and reporting, it is appropriate to expect a school person to be present during the interview. The younger the child, the more important it is for her to have someone she knows with her.

REPORTING CHILD SEXUAL ABUSE

Extreme caution is advised in reporting sexual abuse unless you are relatively sure it can be validated. The stigma for all family members, the intense reactivity of the community as well as the family, and the potential for reports of this kind of abuse to backfire are reasons for conservatism. Educators filing a report (even when their identity is not revealed) may have their credibility questioned, be intimidated by lawyers, and become the object of hostility from colleagues as well as from the family. They may be left with enormous guilt and/or anger if the report is determined to be untrue.

Abuse Must Be Reported by Law

Sexual abuse *must* be reported if there is definite evidence. Explicit disclosure by the involved child, a close friend of hers, or the parent;

physical evidences such as blood-stained underwear or symptoms of venereal disease (and the mother won't take her for medical evaluation); or observation of the sexual activity are ways you *know* sexual abuse is occurring. If you don't report it, you are not only breaking the law, you are also colluding with the family in keeping the abuse a secret.

If, while actively involved in counseling the child or parents, you should learn that someone in the family is either a perpetrator or victim of sexual abuse, you must report even if you risk losing your rapport with the family. In this instance, it makes good sense to tell the child or parents that you must report the situation, and simultaneously anticipate and plan for the repercussions of reporting. Another instance in which you might want to openly discuss your need and intent to report the problem is when the perpetrator is *not* a family member, such as a babysitter.

In situations of incest, it is best to keep the identity of the reporter concealed. If others in school know who has reported, they are obligated to keep the fact confidential, and they will need to be told this. To protect themselves (if they feel a finger is being pointed at them as a possible reporter), some teachers may be tempted to reveal the identity of the person who reported. When the staff member who reports sexual abuse keeps facts confined to those few who need to know (probably only the principal, the child's teacher, the counselor, and the psychologist), problems of confidentiality are not likely to arise. As soon as possible after the report is made, the few who are to be informed should meet to share feelings, anticipate reactions of the family, and plan for dealing with problems that are expected to arise.

Powerful parents, with clever lawyers, may try to intimidate and scare those suspected of being the reporter. If this happens, seek support from administrators and ask for legal consultation with the district's counsel. You need to *know* you will be protected; the threat of a lawsuit can be quite disturbing.

SUSPECTING CHILD SEXUAL ABUSE

Short of purposeful and explicit disclosure, children often give clues about what is going on behind closed doors. Several ways in which we come to suspect that a girl or boy is being molested are: behavioral changes (symptoms), overt sexual behavior, casual comments containing suggestive hints, and drawings. Figure 4-5 summarizes these warning signs of sexual abuse.

WARNING SIGNALS OF CHILD SEXUAL ABUSE

A. Change in Behavior (check specific change)

_____ develops somatic complaints (headaches, stomach aches, etc.)

_____ begins to stutter, or scrambles ideas in expressing self

_____ becomes silent, uncommunicative or unresponsive

_____ becomes disruptive, antagonistic, or overly aggressive

_____ becomes sad, weepy; or has angry outbursts

_____ withdraws from social activities, alienates friends

_____ shows signs of being suicidal

B. Overt Sexual Behavior

_____ open display of precocious sexual knowledge or activity

_____ compulsive masturbation

_____ excessive interest in sex

_____ excessive interest in the opposite sex during ages 5-10

_____ persistent sex play with toys or peers

C. Decline in Academic Performance

_____ young child's failing work, although of apparent normal intelligence

_____ older child's sudden decline in academic performance

D. Development of New Fears

_____ fears not characteristic of normal children in this age group

_____ new fears that elude explanation

E. Symptoms Reported by Mothers

_____ loss of appetite

_____ threats to run away

_____ worry about keeping clean

_____ unexplainable new fears

_____ refusal to go to favorite places or stay with specific persons

_____ sleep disturbances

_____ bedwetting

F. Drawings

_____ drawings show genitalia or other sexual parts (not usually drawn by children)

Figure 4-5

When our radar picks up a cluster of these signals that includes B, E or F, what do we do next? Talk privately with the child? Discuss our observations and thoughts with the parents? Talk to the principal or the counselor? Recommend a child study evaluation? Get parental permission for counseling at school? Report on the basis of the "clues"? Depending on the circumstances, each one of these actions is appropriate, regardless of the warning to be cautious about reporting.

When a child has not *clearly* disclosed sexual abuse, what to do is a matter of judgment and individual conscience, which each professional must make. Teachers will usually want to share thoughts about possible abuse with the principal, counselor, or psychologist; the counselor or psychologist, when the clues emerge in an ongoing interview, will be faced with deciding whether to bypass the clues or pursue them. We know that children try very hard to keep their abuse secret. They are frightened about what will happen to them if they reveal it, and they usually feel guilty about betraying the secret when they do disclose the situation.

How then do we resolve the dilemma of whether or not to pursue the clues left by the child? Confidence in our knowledge about child sexual abuse will be one factor; confidence about our interviewing skills and rapport with the child will be another. We must be able to interview children in a nondirective and nonthreatening way, without probing, and we must be sensitive enough to discontinue pursuing the matter when the child, either verbally or nonverbally, indicates that he or she wants to stop. The interview must be held in a private place, and the child accorded all the considerations of an adult: everything possible must be done to make the boy or girl feel comfortable, the child's dignity and rights must be respected, and the child must not feel pressured to say things he or she doesn't want to say. By all means, ideas must not be put into the child's head.

Behavioral Symptoms

As with other forms of abuse, when children are distressed about the sexual abuse (not all children are), they are likely to develop symptoms. Some of these are common to all kinds of abuse and emotional trauma (see Figure 4-5, A.,C.,D.), but others are more specifically characteristic of sexual abuse. The marital patterns typical in incestuous families, and/or the presence of a stepfather should not by themselves cause us to suspect sexual abuse, but when either or both coexist with generalized symptoms in the child, together with symptoms specific for sexual abuse, the constellation of factors will be strongly suggestive.

Overt Expression of Sexuality

Children who are being sexually exploited may give no hint whatsoever of what is going on, or they may express their involvement in quite explicit ways. Of all the behavioral symptoms associated with sexual abuse, the most specific are overt expressions of sexuality. Although school-age children are curious about sex, they typically hide their sex talk and experimental play from adults, and *they do not know what adults know about sex.* Therefore, an open display of precocious sexual knowledge or activity, compulsive masturbation, excessive interest in sex (or in the opposite sex when this is not usual in ages five-ten) and persistent sex play with toys or peers are indications that a child is *probably* being sexually abused.

Decline in Academic Performance

Children who are being sexually abused do not always have trouble with learning. Sometimes they try to excel, to undo the bad feelings they have about themselves. However, failure in a young child of apparently normal intelligence, or a sudden decline in academic performance of an older child should always be investigated. A child study evaluation should be recommended.

> Frank was a kindergartener who showed an atypical interest in the opposite sex, couldn't concentrate on schoolwork, and was showing a poor level of learning despite apparently above-average intelligence. During the child study evaluation, he drew a person as requested by the psychologist, then said that it was his baby sitter, Richard. (Children invariably draw themselves; it is *very* unusual for a boy or girl to draw a baby sitter when asked to draw a human figure. A discussion about what he liked and didn't like about Richard led to the disclosure of sexual abuse. Frank was handling his fear of boys by choosing only girls to play with. This behavior was a puzzle to his mother and teacher, as was his learning problem, until we learned of his sexual molestation by the male teenage baby sitter.

New Fears

The development of *new fears* that are *not* characteristic of normal children this age and that elude explanation should alert you. Those particularly suggestive of sexual abuse include fear of the dark; fear of strangers or a particular family member, relative or friend; fear of being alone; fear of sleeping alone in the child's own room; fear of males. These fears may generate other symptoms such as sleep disturbances, nightmares, or bedwetting (when this had not been a problem before). These symptoms may continue even after the sexual molestation has ceased. One retrospective investigation of child victims, following apprehension of a child molestor, revealed a high incidence of bedwetting that had continued for years after the event of the molestation.

Symptoms Reported by Mothers

Symptoms seen only at home such as loss of appetite, threats to run away, worry about keeping clean, refusal to go to favorite places or stay with specific persons, as well as the abovementioned fears and sleep disturbances, will not come to your attention unless the child's mother is worried about them and discusses them with you. Although these are all behaviors associated with sexual abuse, do not jump to conclusions about their meanings, but *do* ask, "What could be going on to cause that to happen?" "What are your ideas about what that means?" After eliciting all of the mother's ideas, discuss them with her to see if she really believes any of her theories. If she does, advise her how to follow up to find out if her ideas are correct.

If the mother remains puzzled and perplexed following such a discussion, ask her if she has considered the possibility that the behaviors might reflect distress over sexual abuse. If this idea is rejected, simply state that these behaviors have been found to be associated with sexual abuse, but could be indicative of something else, and end the discussion. If she is receptive to the possibility, explore with her whom she suspects the perpetrator might be, then tell her how to talk to her son or daughter to elicit further information.

> NOTE: When you suspect possible sexual abuse, and neither of these approaches seems feasible, nor is an interview with the involved child a reasonable option, follow the guidelines given for physical abuse: keep notes of observations and interviews. They may help to substantiate sexual abuse if a report from another source is later being investigated.

Detecting Abuse from Drawings

In drawing pictures of the human figure, children do not normally draw genitalia or other sexual parts such as breasts or buttocks. When they do so, this is strong evidence that they are preoccupied with sexuality, but does not prove that they are being abused. Depending on the context in which the drawing is made, and your relationship with the child, you may wish to use the drawing to elicit information that would open the door for disclosure. Being careful not to probe, comment about the child's obvious interest in those parts of the body and ask, "What makes you interested?" If she responds freely and seems open to further discussion, go on to a series of questions in tiny steps, each increasing in intimacy, such as:

"Do you have names for these body parts?" (if not already verbalized)

"What do you call them?" (then use the child's names, perhaps adding that they are also called this correct name)

"What do you know about these parts?"

"Do you want to know more?"

"Are you worried about yours?"

"Do other people seem to be interested in yours?"

"Is it wrong to be interested?"

"In what way is it wrong?"

"Has anyone ever wanted you to do anything you think is wrong?"

"What happened?"

The interview can be stopped when the child is no longer willing to respond. If there is emotional blocking or the need to escape (that is, to get a drink of water or go to the bathroom), ask if he or she wants to continue or stop. Then respect the child's decision, offering support and reassurance if the child chooses to continue.

CONSEQUENCES OF CHILD SEXUAL ABUSE

Drawing conclusions from clinical populations, it has been suggested that many cases of homosexuality (or lesbianism), drug addiction, prostitution, or mental illness in adults may be the result of childhood sexual abuse. It is also thought that women who were victimized as children are vulnerable for becoming rape victims or battered wives in adulthood, and that the sexual victimization of boys contributes to their becoming pedophiles and rapists. However, the fact that large numbers of adults presenting with these problems have a history of childhood sexual exploitation does not necessarily prove that their sexual abuse was the *cause* of the adult problem. As yet, few of our beliefs about the consequences of childhood victimization have been subjected to scientific investigation. Until research can give us more definitive answers, we must be tentative about conclusions.

One researcher gives evidence that childhood sexual victimization contributes to sexual problems and sexual deviations in adulthood,[29] and this kind of relationship to later sexual functioning would seem logical. I think the impact of keeping secrets, impaired intrafamily relating, betrayed trust in adults, and restricted peer socialization, factors commonly associated with sexual abuse, need to be investigated before we can hope to have a clearer understanding of the damage done by this kind of abuse.

PROTECTING CHILDREN FROM SEXUAL ABUSE

As yet, it is not known how and why men come to be sexually attracted to children, so preventing men from developing into pedophiles is not a viable answer to protecting children from sexual abuse. Pedophilia is probably a chronic, uncurable disorder which, in a high percentage of cases, can be controlled through long-term treatment. However, sufficient treatment resources are not available; and we do not have adequate mechanisms for controlling and monitoring pedophiles at large in the community. Educating children to protect themselves from sexual abuse seems to be the only feasible approach to the problem.

Educational Programs

Educational programs have been presented and evaluated in many localities over the past several years, to children of preschool age through high school. We *know* that children can be given information about sexual abuse without unduly upsetting them; that they can learn the principles of self-protection; and that they will disclose their own sexual abuse more freely following open discussion about this kind of abuse. But whether or not they will retain and apply what they have learned, when confronted with a seductive situation, has not been determined.

Empowering Children to Protect Themselves

Teaching children to protect themselves involves empowering them. Empowering children to resist adults who are determined to get what they want may prove difficult, although the developers of the Child Assault Prevention Project (CAP) believe that it is possible. CAP stresses children's rights to be "Safe, Strong, and Free." To this end, the program emphasizes the importance of:

1. self-esteem
2. self-assertiveness

3. mutual support and help among children

4. independent thinking and problem solving

5. the ability to evaluate potentially dangerous situations

6. children's right to be respected by adults

Children are taught a special yell to be used *only* when they are in trouble (*never* during play), to respond to a friend's yell for help, and the basic elements of self-defense.[30] This very comprehensive program goes well beyond that of other programs, in which teaching the difference between good and bad touches and how to avoid situations where they could be entrapped are the major objectives. If we are to expect children to truly be able to protect themselves, this kind of total approach is necessary.

Empowering children requires that we reinforce their capacity for assertiveness, an idea that many adults are not ready to accept. Somehow, a child who stands up to an adult is viewed as insolent and "out of line," and punitive action toward the child usually follows. This inhibits assertiveness. The success of the CAP kind of program will depend on allowing children more leeway to stand their ground with adults. Adults who are ready to listen to children's feelings and viewpoints, who believe in encouraging children to think for them-selves and to become independent problem-solvers will not react punitively when confronted with a child's argument.

For more information about CAP, contact:

National Assault Prevention Center
P.O. Box 02005
Columbus, Ohio 43202
(614) 291-2540

Sexual Abuse Education at School

Parents seem to be in favor of sexual abuse education being provided in schools. A research survey showed that eighty-nine percent of parents support the idea[31] of giving students this information.

Before embarking on a program of sexual abuse education, seek the support of other school staff and parents, and consider the climate of the community in regard to the open discussion of sexuality. Then, move into this subject area slowly and gradually, starting with work-shops for teachers and parents that explore their feelings and reactions, and their ability to assimilate rather than deny the information given. "Officer Friendly" can be asked to expand his talks with children to include self-protection from sexual abuse. Groups in the local community that have developed programs can be invited to present them after school or in the evening, so that attendance can be voluntary. It may take several years before a total program modeled after CAP can be established, and in some communities parents may insist on maintaining control over this delicate area of their child's education, as they have done in regard to general sex education.

Parents as Educators

Research has shown that only twenty-nine percent of parents had talked to their children about sexual abuse, and that many of these were mothers who themselves had been sexually abused as children.[32] If parents are to carry out this educational task, they may well need the encouragement and help of the school, The school's role would be to provide instructional programs for parents and develop a library of materials that can be borrowed by the parents. Materials are available in many forms: books, videotapes, film strips, comic books and play scripts. Puppet show presentations and live theater are available in many communities and parents can attend these with their children, especially when this kind of program is given at school with the support of the administration.

SEXUAL ABUSE BY EDUCATORS

It is clear that children are not safe from sexual abuse at home, church, camp, day care or even school. A spate of alleged abuse by area educators (most of it verified) was reported by the *Chicago Tribune* in 1985; and in one case the teacher had had two previous convictions for child molestation. As a result, the Illinois legislature has made it mandatory for applicants for employment by schools, both certified and noncertified, to be fingerprinted and to undergo a criminal background investigation before they may be hired. The speed with which the Illinois General Assembly acted attests to the public's outrage, and similar laws will undoubtedly be enacted in other states.

A school administration should be informed when a child has accused a school employee of sexual molestation, but this does not always happen. On the other hand, the school administration should not be the only ones to be informed, because they might do their own investigation and take the employee's word against that of the child. Because of the stigma involved, and the chance that the child's accusation may be false, it is appropriate to keep the child's story out of the newspapers, but it should be properly investigated by the police.

HELPING A VICTIMIZED CHILD

The degree of trauma that a child suffers from sexual abuse will be greater or less depending on the stage to which the sexual activity has progressed, the duration of the abuse, the amount and kind of threat or force used, and the nature of the relationship with the perpetrator. Sexual engagement between a six-year-old and his sixteen-year-old babysitter, which has not progressed beyond the fondling stage and has occurred only a few times, has much less impact than father-daughter incest that has progressed to intercourse and has been ongoing for several years. Yet, both children need therapy.

The trauma is not limited to the sexual activity but encompasses:

1. betrayal of trust in a caregiving person
2. sense of doing wrong (and thus, being bad)
3. fear of revealing the secret (and guilt for doing so)
4. impaired relationship with the mother and (possibly) siblings
5. disturbed functioning (sleep, toileting and eating disorders)
6. impaired communicative ability
7. impaired school performance

It is believed that all children who have been sexually abused need at least short-term therapy. There are two problems about this: parental resistance to the child's being in therapy (particularly when the molestor was not a family member), and lack of treatment opportunities. Schools can potentially solve both problems if they are willing to risk intervening in the aftermath of disclosure. School professionals attending training workshops on sexual abuse have expressed a reluctance to engage in social work or mental health interventions.[33] However, the resources of the school offer therapeutic possibilities for victimized children, and parents may ultimately look to the school for the help they initially deny they need. The following goals for helping may be worked toward by school staff whether or not the parents permit counseling. If permission is given for counseling, and the counselor (social worker or psychologist) has attended a training workshop for treating sexually abused children,[34] more in-depth goals are possible.

Advocate for Court Appearance

To prevent further traumatization, a child who must appear in court needs a trained advocate to prepare her for the experience, accompany her to court, and guide and support her at each step of the legal proceedings. Advocacy groups exist in major large cities, and are proliferating. If you do not know of one, consult your telephone directory, inquire of your mental health association, protective service worker, or legal aid society; or call a sexual abuse hot line. *Finding an advocate* to be with the child during court proceedings is a major way you can help. Even if you only advise the parent and the parent locates an advocate, you are performing an important service.

Help the Child Regain a Sense of Normalcy

Girls who have sexual knowledge and experience beyond their age feel set apart from peers and somehow get the idea that they are not normal. They need reassurance and validation of their normalcy. Encourage them to dress and groom like their peers, and to participate in the usual group activities for their age. Discourage premature sexual interest in opposite sex peers by helping her see that she can be liked for her personal qualities.

Help the Child Make and Maintain Peer Relationships

Several factors conspire to alienate a sexually abused girl from her peers: shyness and verbal inhibition (resulting from a need to keep the secret), social restriction by her father, symptoms that make her seem less than normal to others, as well as to herself. Help in making friends, or encouragement and support in maintaining friendships are commonly needed. Anything that will boost her self-esteem will contribute to increased confidence, belief in normalcy, and an improved capacity for relating.

Help the Child Believe He or She Is Not to Blame

It will be difficult for a girl to fully absolve herself of self-blame unless her father tells her the responsibility for what happened was entirely his. It usually falls to the mother to give her daughter continuing reassurance that it was not her fault, but if she mentions it to you, be prepared to emphasize that she is not to blame.

Monitor the Child for Signs of Continuing Distress

When parents initially resist counseling for their son or daughter, evidence of continuing distress may prompt them to reconsider. At a later point they may agree to counseling on the basis of the symptoms the child presents, not linking them to the sexual experience, which they have perhaps totally repressed. It is not necessary for them to perceive or acknowledge the link. Your knowledge of the family must guide you in deciding whether to suggest a cause-and-effect relationship should they still be resistant to therapy. A wise course of action would be to start with school counseling on a limited goal basis and gently condition the parents to the need for more specific therapy around the issue of the abuse.

In incest situations where it is known that the family is receiving therapy, continuing symptoms should be reported to the protective service worker who may be able to persuade the mother to allow school counseling to be coordinated with other services.

Recommend Arts Therapy

Therapies through the arts—dance, music, drama, and art—can be very helpful to traumatized children, and are forms of therapy that parents can accept while rejecting verbal therapy. These kinds of therapy are also useful adjuncts to other more traditional forms of verbal therapy. Explore the possibilities for this kind of help in your community. If your arts staff is interested in the therapeutic use of their media, encourage them to get further training, and to experiment with techniques.

TREATMENT OF SEXUAL ABUSE

The treatment of family sexual abuse takes a minimum of two years. It is most successful if the father has admitted the abuse, the mother believes that the abuse occurred and gives support to her child, and the father apologizes to his child and accepts responsibility for the abuse. A wide range of treatment approaches is necessary, including:

1. crisis intervention
2. casework counseling
3. individual, group, and family therapy
4. marital therapy if the couple does not divorce

Treatment begins with individual sessions for the father, the mother, and the child, and progresses to participation by each in separate groups of peers. Rehabilitating the mother-daughter bond is an important initial goal, and the two are seen conjointly to achieve this. The father is brought into these sessions when he is ready to apologize to his daughter. Family therapy may begin after these beginning goals have been accomplished. Finally, marital therapy will be pursued if the couple wants to restore the marriage and keep the family intact.

PREVENTION OF SEXUAL ABUSE

Based on our limited, inadequate knowledge of why men molest, the following are the current major orientations toward prevention:

1. Protect children from being molested (so they won't become further victimized, or become victimizers in the next generation).
2. Identify and intensively treat young adolescent boys when they first begin to molest.
3. Change the way boys/men are socialized.

I have already emphasized the need to protect children, and the ways in which this can be accomplished. The treatment of young adolescent boys, when they first show pedophilic inclinations, depends on these factors, none of which is yet receiving adequate attention: having sufficient treatment resources; reporting and bringing charges against guilty youth (in order to mandate treatment), or voluntary acceptance by the youth and his family of the need for therapy; comprehensive and long-term treatment of the youth and his family; in-patient treatment facilities for repeat offenders or those who have used force with their victims.

The outcome of the Women's Movement may determine whether it is possible to change the ways in which boys are socialized for their adult role. The male's resistance to relinquishing his societal position of dominance (which may well have its roots in biology), and the fact that society condones violence and reinforces male aggression suggest that we will not see any radical changes in the psychology of men very soon.

Endnotes

1. "Uncovering a False Charge of Child Sex Abuse," *Pediatric News,* January 1985.
2. John Crewdson, "The Stigma: Being Wrongly Accused of Child Sex Abuse," *Chicago Tribune,* February 24, 1985.
3. David Finkelhor, *Child Sexual Abuse: New Theory and Research* (New York: The Free Press, 1984), p. 184.
4. Judith Lewis Herman, *Father-Daughter Incest* (Cambridge, MA: Harvard University Press, 1981), p. 76.
5. *Frontline,* PBS video broadcast, April 16, 1985.
6. Anne H. Rosenfeld, "Discovering and Dealing with Deviant Sex," *Psychology Today,* April 1985, pp. 8-10.
7. A. Nicholas Groth, "Patterns of Sexual Assault Against Children and Adolescents" in Ann Wolbert Burgess et al, *Sexual Assault of Children and Adolescents* (Lexington, MA: D. C. Heath and Co., 1978), p. 6.
8. *Frontline,* April 16, 1985.
9. A. Nicholas Groth, Ph.D., *Child Sexual Abuse: Victims and Offenders* (Investigation and Assessment), Training Workshop, Chicago, IL, May 9, 1985.
10. Groth, "Patterns of Sexual Assault Against Children and Adolescents," p. 9.
11. Ibid., pp. 13-14, and Groth's workshop, May 9, 1985.
12. Ibid., p. 22.
13. Finkelhor, *Child Sexual Abuse,* p. 166.
14. Ibid. p. 161.
15. Ibid., p. 25.
16. Ibid., pp. 26-27.
17. Herman, *Father-Daughter Incest*
18. Ibid., pp. 71-72.
19. A. Nicholas Groth, "The Incest Offender" in Suzanne M. Sgroi, M.D., *Handbook of Clinical Intervention in Child Sexual Abuse* (Lexington, MA: D. C. Heath and Co., 1982), pp. 229-230.
20. Suzanne M. Sgroi, Linda Canfield Blick and Frances Sarnacki Porter, "A Conceptual Framework for Child Sexual Abuse," in Sgroi, *Handbook of Clinical Intervention in Child Sexual Abuse,* p. 12.
21. Ibid., p. 13.
22. Ibid., pp. 14-15.
23. Ibid., p. 16.
24. Ibid., pp. 17-18.
25. Debra Chase, "Dealing with the Sexually Abused Child: Theory and Practice of Working With These Children in a School Setting and a Family Setting," workshop section of Helping Children and Their Families in the 80's Conference, Glencoe, IL, March 15, 1985.

26. Suzanne M. Sgroi, M.D., *Child Sexual Abuse: Victims and Offenders* (Investigation and Assessment), Training Workshop, Chicago, IL, May 9, 1985.

27. Lois Loontjens, *Talking to Children/Talking to Parents About Sexual Assault* (Santa Cruz, CA: Network Publications, 1984), p. 60.

28. Sgroi, workshop, May 9, 1985.

29. Finkelhor, *Child Sexual Abuse,* pp. 192-196.

30. Sally Cooper, Yvonne Lutter and Cathy Phelps, *Strategies for Free Children: A Leader's Guild to Child Assault Prevention* (Columbus, OH: Child Assault Prevention Project of Women Against Rape, 1983).

31. Finkelhor, *Child Sexual Abuse,* p. 103.

32. Ibid., pp. 136 and 141.

33. Ibid., p. 208.

34. Training workshops can be arranged through Forensic Mental Health Associates, 3 Ireland Road, Newton Center, MA 02159 (617-322-0228).

Chapter 5

Psychological Abuse

Psychological abuse is the most prevalent form of abuse; it always accompanies physical abuse, physical neglect, and sexual abuse, but also occurs in the absence of other forms of abuse. It is not hard to identify psychological abuse, but it is hard in a legal sense to prove the cause-and-effect relationship between what a parent does or fails to do, and the psychological impact on the child. Thus, even though the child abuse statutes of at least thirty-six states include psychological abuse (sometimes called mental injury) as a reportable offense, it is common for reports to go uninvestigated by child protection agencies unless they are associated with physical or sexual abuse or neglect.

PSYCHOLOGICAL ABUSE IMPAIRS DEVELOPMENT

Educators must be concerned about psychological abuse because this kind of mistreatment impairs a child's ability to develop a sense of competence and self-worth, without which normal social and emotional development do not occur. Psychological abuse is probably at the root of most motivational problems and also accounts for most of the placements in behavior disorder classes and alternative school programs. It is a new way of conceptualizing and understanding children's social-emotional problems.

DEFINING PSYCHOLOGICAL ABUSE

Although it is common to use the terms *psychological abuse* and *emotional abuse* interchangeably, our understanding is increased by differentiating three categories of psychological abuse: emotional neglect, emotional abuse, and verbal abuse. However, these three forms usually do not occur in isolation. Psychologically abused children will probably be suffering from some combination of the three, with one form possibly more obvious than the others.

Emotional Neglect

Emotional neglect is the failure to provide a child with the emotional nurturance needed for adequate development. It encompasses failure to promote and facilitate emotional attachment between parent and child; failure to give a child support as he or she encounters obstacles or defeat in attempting to master developmental tasks; failure to encourage socialization; and failure to show an interest in a child's schoolwork and other achievements. We are all guilty of a modest degree of emotional neglect because the stresses and strains of life prevent us from always responding optimally to our children's emotional needs. However, it is the impact on development that determines whether neglect is significant. As we have seen, when emotional neglect begins in infancy, it will have the most profound effect on development.

The Impact of Emotional Neglect. Children whose parents don't respond to them emotionally grow up seeing themselves as nonentities; they have no trust in themselves nor their abilities and their feelings. They lack a sense of self, and feel an emptiness inside. They are the children who, when asked to draw a person, draw only a face, a robot, or an imaginary figure. Depending on the age of onset and the degree and pervasiveness of emotional neglect, a child may be extremely shy or isolated, may not know how to make friends, may be a clingy, whiny child who is indiscriminate about seeking attention from strangers, a mean child who is callous and uncaring about others, or one who is quite disturbed.

Neglected children have not felt loved, and therefore do not believe themselves to be lovable. They need substitute nurturance, and need to develop an identity through attaching to and identifying with a caring adult. However, their neglect has made them so unappealing that they have little with which to attract the healthy attention of others. This makes them easy prey for child molesters.

Emotional neglect can begin at any age, and all developmental stages that follow its onset will be affected. Chapter 3 discussed the consequences of emotional neglect that begins in infancy. We will pick up here with emotional neglect that occurs in the absence of general neglect and has its onset at a later stage of development. This problem often accompanies other types of psychological abuse.

Emotional Neglect in the School-Age Child. The kind of emotional attention needed by a child changes as he or she moves through developmental stages. Some mothers do a good job of meeting the needs of infants and young children, but then become cold and distant when the children are independent enough to go to school. Validation of the child's worth and lovability, a central aspect of emotional nurturance, may not be continued once the child shows a mind of his or her own. More often, though, emotional neglect that starts with the school-age child reflects a chronic family problem such as alcoholism, mental or physical illness, or a major crisis such as death or divorce.

Because parental alcoholism is a major traumatizing event in and of itself, and is also the prime factor in many abusive situations, the alcoholic family will be used to illustrate the effects of emotional neglect on the school-age child. Children in alcoholic families suffer all forms of abuse, but they feel most keenly the emotional deprivation, alienation from their parents, and their own social isolation. Even when they are not otherwise abused, they pay the heavy price of being emotionally neglected.

Alcoholism and emotional neglect. It is estimated that twelve to fifteen million American children live in alcoholic families.[1] This means that perhaps four to six children in your class have to cope with an alcoholic parent.[2] There are just as many alcoholic mothers as alcoholic fathers, and in many families both parents are alcoholic. Alcohol and drug abuse often exist together, and are present in nearly twenty percent of the families who are reported for child abuse and neglect.[3] However, the majority of abusive alcoholic families do not get reported. The National Council on Alcoholism estimates that sixty percent of alcoholic families in treatment have experienced domestic violence.[4] Children are traumatized by the violence even when they escape physical attack. When alcoholism precipitates physical abuse, the initial treatment approach must be to get the alcohol abuse under control.

What children experience in an alcoholic family. The following are children's statements, quotes taken from a report of a rare study of children from alcoholic homes:[5]

- I don't go places with my friends and their parents because I can't ever take my friends places.

- Everybody at our house is angry all the time.

- I worry all afternoon at school about how things will be when I get home.

- The kids at school all talk about the fun they have with their families. It makes me feel sort of left out.
- I can take it when one of them drinks, but I really get scared when they both start.
- Mom doesn't look after us. I have to be the Mom myself.
- Why did they have us at all if they weren't going to take care of us?

In Cork's study of children in alcoholic families, reasonably adequate physical care of the children was evident, but emotional needs were largely unmet. She found that sensitivity to the children's needs was lacking, and communication between the parents and between parent and child was hostile and negative. The children had no sense of security, received no encouragement in the face of obstacles, and neither parents nor children had productive relationships outside the family. The children viewed the parents as less mature than themselves and were ashamed of them. The older ones tried to parent the younger siblings. They protected themselves from shame and embarrassment by not inviting friends to their homes. Most of the children succeeded in getting passing grades in school, but could not achieve in keeping with their abilities. They cited the fighting, chaos, and instability at home as making it impossible for them to study and concentrate on homework. At school they also had trouble concentrating because of their preoccupation and anger about the family problems. Concentration difficulties increased in the afternoon, and especially toward the end of the school day when they began to anticipate with dread having to go home.[6]

What educators need to know about alcoholism. As a society, we are no longer kidding ourselves about the significance and magnitude of the problem, but individually some of us get entrapped in the family's denial system and fail to recognize that the *basis* of the family problems is alcoholism. Like the spouse, we fall into the habit of "understanding" and "excusing" the drinking because we agree with the spouse that the person is not alcoholic, and believe the spouse's explanations for drinking. The spouse, for example, may justify drinking as a reaction to job loss, illness, disability, or a child's problems. When a child's problems are accepted as the excuse for drinking, he or she becomes the family scapegoat.

Solid research evidence has established that alcoholism *is an illness*. Alcoholics are people who cannot control their drinking "because of a chemical imbalance, usually genetically transmitted, coupled with cultural permission to test it....The pathology seen in active alcoholics is not the cause of the illness, but rather the result of the illness. There is no pre-alcoholic personality: All kinds of personality types develop the illness...following initial recovery, only about 10 percent of alcoholics need psychotherapy, apart from on-going attendance at Alcoholics Anonymous meetings."[7]

A generally accepted definition of alcoholism is that it is the *loss of control* over how much one drinks and when or where one drinks it. The loss of control precipitates a deterioration in one or more major areas of a person's life—family, work, health, social.[8] Thus, if a person's drinking results in abuse of family members, trouble with the law, absenteeism from work or job loss, poor health, social isolation, or marital problems, a "curbstone diagnosis" of alcoholism can be made. It is not necessary to know how much or how often alcohol is consumed to know that a person is an alcoholic. Patterns of alcohol consumption vary. It is the consequences of drinking that distinguish a heavy social drinker from an alcoholic.

When you recognize that a child's parent is an alcoholic, family problems, as well as those of individual family members, should be recognized as resulting from alcoholism. The alcoholism must be acknowledged as central, and if the alcoholic is unwilling to be treated, the spouse and children must be helped to understand how to live with and deal with the alcoholic to avoid becoming co-alcoholics and destroying themselves in the process. When family members stop protecting and excusing the alcoholic, and refuse to tolerate physical and verbal abuse, while simultaneously confronting the alcoholic about the need for treatment, a crisis is usually precipitated. This crisis provides an opportunity to get the alcoholic into treatment. Experts tell us that alcoholics need not *want* help in order to benefit from it. In fact, alcoholics rarely want help, but don't want to lose their families or their jobs, so they seek treatment. Those alcoholics who will not begin and continue attending AA, and those who are at the stage of experiencing blackouts, need to be in the controlled environment of an in-patient facility in order for treatment to be effective. Counselors and "significant others" should confront the alcoholic strongly at the point of crisis to get him or her to accept in-patient treatment.

Teaching children about alcoholism. Clearly, alcoholism is not only a social problem, but also a health problem; information about it belongs in the school's health curriculum. Children of alcoholics are at high risk to become alcoholics because of the genetic transmission of the biochemical imbalance mechanism. Interestingly, preliminary research data suggests that there is a genetic link between alcoholism and the forms of major psychological depressions. Perhaps some day there will be a test to determine whether one has a genetic predisposition to alcoholism or depression. Meanwhile, children who have an alcoholic parent may be able to resist drinking if they know they are at risk of becoming alcoholic.

Drug awareness programs are now commonly presented to students, starting in fifth grade and up through high school. The best programs are those stressing self-esteem and the satisfactions of a constructive lifestyle as reasons to stay away from drugs and alcohol, while also involving the parents as important allies for the program's success. These programs teach about the destructive aspects of drug use (alcohol is a drug) and inform the children that anyone can be pulled into this kind of lifestyle, even though it is avoidable.

The subject of alcoholism and drugs can also be successfully introduced to children as early as Kindergarten, if it is done with the proper sensitivity and restraint, and an emphasis on the facts is maintained. If a quarter of all children are living in alcoholic homes (the current estimate), then the concrete realities of their lives provides these children with a kind of knowledge base about alcoholism. Very young children can still learn to differentiate between good and bad kinds of drugs, to recognize alcoholic behavior, and to understand blackouts, and given this information and knowledge, actively avoid falling into the same trap.

An important warning is needed here: drugs and alcohol are sensitive curriculum topics. Because of the Hatch Amendment (discussed later in this chapter), these topics must be treated like other academic material: information and facts are to be given, and the discussion limited to *thoughts* and *ideas*. Children must not be encouraged to divulge information about their families, be expected to make judgments, express feelings, or discuss decision making about drinking or drugs during class. If they spontaneously divulge anything that can be considered "private family business," you must be careful not to probe. However, if you feel the child is endangered by the situation, you may want to consult the school psychologist or social worker. You are on safe ground provided you did not elicit the information directly from the student.

Discussing alcohol use and its consequences on health and behavior with children is a way to protect them, and parents must understand that this is the reason the subject is in the health curriculum. Having alcoholism as a curriculum topic for young children may help us learn which children are having to cope with an alcoholic parent, and this knowledge can make us more effective in helping them. However, this is not the main reason for making it a part of the educational program. Children rarely talk openly about their parent's drinking because they understand that it is a family secret; the alert teacher will most likely discover the secret when he or she asks the class "What do you know about alcoholism?" Answers from the children will range from stereotyped ideas they have gained from movies or cartoons, to factual data about drinking and driving gained from television public service announcements, but will also include what an alcoholic says and does to a spouse and children. According to Claudia Black, the child who vividly describes what alcoholic behavior does to a family most likely comes from an alcoholic home.[9]

Responding to alcoholism. It does not help a family to agree with the nonalcoholic spouse's denial of the alcoholism. The following is a typical case of spouse denial that we must be bold to challenge:

> Steven B., a second grader, was receiving L.D. help and counseling, and the staff involved were closely monitoring his progress with monthly parent check-in conferences. When Mr. B. failed to come to one of the meetings, carefully arranged on his day off from work, his wife was asked for an explanation. She said that Mr. B. had been drinking all afternoon and was in no condition to come. Further inquiry revealed that when Mr. B. drank, he did not usually stop until he passed out. In addition, he often physically abused Steven when he was drunk, but he did not remember doing so, nor did he remember other things he did or said when drunk.

Mrs. B. had just described an alcoholic: a person who could not control his drinking, who abused when drunk, and who had blackouts (amnesia for events that occurred when he had been drinking). Mrs. B. had also done what most alcoholic spouses do: she denied he was alcoholic, and excused his abusive behavior on the basis that he *didn't know what he was doing.*

Steps to take in helping the alcoholic family. Alcoholics need to be confronted about their drinking, and required to take responsibility for their behavior. We in the school can help by taking a firm position with the co-alcoholic spouse (one who helps to perpetuate the problem by denying it, caring for and covering up for the alcoholic):

1. The school social worker should tell Mrs. B. that her husband is an alcoholic and that she is making matters worse for herself, Steven and the other children by her acceptance of the situation.
2. The long-range goal would be to get Mr. B. into an alcoholic treatment facility; meanwhile, Mrs. B. and Steven should be given support and education about alcoholism.

3. As an initial step, Mrs. B. should be urged to join Al-Anon and told how to stop being a co-alcoholic.

4. Steven could be taught practical ways to avoid being abused when his father is drinking.

5. With the alcoholism out in the open, the social worker could create structured play scenarios and rehearse Steven, through role-playing, in what he should do and say when his father approaches him while in a drunken state.

In this case, Steven's emotional problems became acute: he began to hurt himself and talked of killing himself. This crisis scared his mother sufficiently into making an appointment with the community mental health center. Another event also reinforced her willingness to seek help: She attended a lecture on the relationship between alcoholism and manic-depressive illness, now called bipolar depression. Mr. B.'s sister was a manic-depressive, a fact that had not been reported to the social worker when the family history was taken. Steven's mother now became worried that Steven would grow up to be either an alcoholic or a manic-depressive.

Neither Steven's abuse nor his father's alcoholism were revealed to the school until his parents accepted voluntary referral to the mental health clinic. Reporting the case to protective services was not necessary because the parents were intelligent, insightful, and cooperative about seeking help. Steven was abused physically only when the father was drunk, so alcoholism, not abuse, was the primary problem.

Verbal Abuse

Verbal abuse is the use of words as weapons in expressing anger and disappointment toward a child. It is an assault on the child's whole sense of integrity. This form of abuse comprises a verbal barrage of negative and deprecating labels that destroy self-esteem and make the child feel rejected, unlovable, and bad. The negative labels run the gamut from "lazy good-for-nothing," "dumb idiot," and "jerk" to "whore" and "bastard." Belittling nicknames, often assigned in a spirit of jest, can also hurt. When a child is subjected to verbal abuse on a regular basis, his or her sense of self-worth is so undermined that he or she feels incompetent and unable to win friends. If a child has little hope for success either in school or socially, and feels totally inadequate, his or her motivation will be nil. The verbally abused child is usually failing in school, shy and isolated, may act out, have psycho-somatic problems, or habit disorders.

Verbal Abuse at Home and School. Verbal abuse that is hurtful to children occurs in all kinds of settings and can be inflicted by teachers, nurses, coaches, and substitute caretakers as well as parents. The demeaning and derogatory labels that the adult puts on the child become a part of the child's self-image. This negative self-image expresses itself in a wide range of negative, self-defeating, and destructive behaviors. The negative behaviors in turn reinforce the negative self-image because they are reacted to negatively by others, and both are perpetuated in a vicious cycle.

Verbal abuse, like physical abuse, is an intense expression of strong emotion. Something the child says or does (sometimes only a look on the child's face) evokes the negative emotion, which may be fury, disgust, revulsion, and so on. The adult may experience the impulse to physically abuse the child and perceives the *verbal* attack as a more acceptable way of expressing the intense feeling aroused. Indeed, teachers and others officially in charge of children usually get away with verbal abuse, while they lose their jobs if they physically abuse their students.

Adults who are verbally rather than physically abusive delude themselves that they are not hurting the child. Rather than feeling guilty, they may congratulate themselves that they controlled their impulses to physically attack. However, adults who have been both physically and verbally abused as children report that it is the verbal abuse that has the most lasting effects. Physical wounds heal and can be forgotten, but negative labels are incorporated into the developing personality and last forever unless they are extricated through enduring positive relationships. This is what a therapeutic relationship is all about: helping a child find that he is lovable and good, after years of believing that he is a horrible person.

Verbal abuse in the classroom. At one time or another, every school has at least one teacher who verbally abuses children to such an unacceptable degree that he or she should not be allowed in a classroom. Whether it is one child or several who are the target of the teacher's verbal attack, all the children will suffer to some extent because each one is afraid he or she will be the next one attacked. The teacher's verbal outburst is sometimes accompanied by ripping up a child's paper or otherwise destroying what the child has produced; or, the teacher may throw the papers at the child. To the child, the teacher's action is symbolically experienced as a direct physical attack, and he or she is threatened by it. In essence, in destroying a student's papers, the teacher also destroys a bit of the child.

Pediatricians are sometimes the ones who first become aware of an abusive teacher because children develop physical symptoms, such as nausea, and a reluctance to go to school, which the parents bring to the attention of the doctor. Krugman and Krugman (pediatricians) report an instance of seventeen third and fourth graders from one class who showed noticeable behavior and personality changes within two weeks after a school term began. (See Figure 5-1.)

Some of the children were transferred to other classes at the request of the parents, and their symptoms ceased shortly thereafter. The principal refused to make further changes but the parents persisted, insisting that the teacher be replaced. When the teacher was finally replaced, the majority of the children's symptoms resolved themselves. The two children who required psychiatric help were undoubtedly quite vulnerable to traumatization. Ten children in the class of twenty-seven had been able to withstand the teacher's abuse without developing symptoms.[10] Even though about a third of the class was not visibly hurt, my guess is that these children were quite frightened and would remember that school year into adulthood. This is the kind of teacher who should be suspended pending further evaluation of the inappropriate behavior.

I experienced the phenomenon reported by the Krugmans, first as a mother, then later as a school psychologist. Years ago, when parents had less power, it was more difficult to get an abusing teacher replaced. Even now, many children must suffer through an entire school year with an abusing teacher, and often fall behind in their academic skills as a result.

Sometimes teacher abuse is not so pervasive and threatening as that described by the Krugmans, and children's symptoms are milder. Parents discover from other parents whose children have passed through that grade that their children bounced back the next year, and that they can help their children tolerate the situation. This may be an acceptable reality adaptation for bright and healthy children from stable homes, but these children are now a minority group (the ten asymptomatic children from the Krugmans' report were in the minority). The additional insults to health and emotional development sustained by today's vulnerable children is a heavy price to pay. Administrators must persist in helping verbally abusive teachers to change their behavior or else place them in jobs other than classroom teaching.

```
Symptoms of Children with an Abusing Teacher
        as Reported by Krugman and Krugman

Problem                                    Number of Children Affected

excessive worry about performance _____ 15

change in self-image _____ 13

change in perception of school _____ 13

verbalized fear that the teacher
would hurt them _____ 7

excessive crying about school _____ 6

headaches _____ 6

stomach aches _____ 5

decreased functioning in social
situations outside school _____ 5

nightmares _____ 4

school avoidance _____ 4

withdrawal _____ 3
```

Figure 5-1

Dynamics of Verbal Abuse. The reasons that teachers verbally abuse children are the same ones that explain parental abuse: the teacher (and parent) may be under severe stress, suffering from physical or mental illness, or be self-hating.

Physical and Mental Illness. As in all professions, there are educators who have depressive or paranoid conditions, resulting from biochemical imbalance, generally classified as mental illnesses. In many cases, these illnesses can be treated successfully with medication that restores normal mental functioning. These are chronic illnesses in the same sense that diabetes is; as such, stress, failure to take medication, or some other reason will cause periodic exacerbation of the symptoms of the illness. Because it is the nature of mood/attitude illnesses to cause behavior change, verbal or emotional abuse that comes on only periodically probably correlates with physiological changes of the illness. In these instances, the teacher will be asked to take sick leave until the illness is under good control.

It is also a reality that some teachers are alcoholics, have epilepsy, cancer, or other illnesses that cause behavior or personality change, either because of the illness itself, or as a side effect of medication. One teacher I knew had a rather sudden change in personality that expressed itself in verbal abuse, physical outbursts, and extremely erratic behavior. Although we did not know until later, these behavior changes signaled the presence of a brain tumor, which was subsequently removed.

Typically, children who fail to live up to a teacher's or parent's expectations, who are needy and vulnerable, or who dare to criticize or find fault with the adult, become the butt of verbal abuse. These may be bright children who are doing a reasonably good job of learning and completing assignments, but the teacher or parent wants them to be outstanding. They may be slower learners who make the teacher feel inadequate and the parent disappointed. Painful feelings evoked in the adult by the child's neediness or vulnerability can result in a negative outburst.

Emotional Abuse

Emotional abuse is more subtle and usually less visible than the other forms of psychological abuse. The parents are likely to impress us as wonderful people, and their pathogenic attitudes toward their children and unhealthy modes of relating within the home are not usually apparent in social/superficial encounters.

Emotional abuse has many variations, among which are the following:

1. exploitation (using a child to serve the needs of the parent)
2. scapegoating (making the child the object of blame for everything that goes wrong in a family)
3. an overly punitive attitude (excessive punishments, far out of proportion to a child's naughty or wrongful act)
4. bizarre punishments (that humiliate and publicly shame a child)
5. excessive restricting of a child (so he or she misses normal and needed social experiences)
6. obsessive, unfounded concern over a child's physical or mental adequacy (causing a child to believe there is something seriously wrong with him- or herself)
7. inconsistent and unpredictable reactions to the child (that cause the child to be uncertain about how he or she is to behave and what is expected of him or her)

In essence, emotional abuse stifles a child's normal progress toward autonomy, independence, and social involvement with peers and adults outside the family. The paradox of emotional abuse is that parents and teachers who are guilty of it usually are unaware that their attitudes and treatment are harming the child.

Emotional Abuse at Home and School. The process of emotional neglect and verbal abuse takes place between one adult and one child, is easily observable, and the harm done to the child is readily recognizable. This is not the case with emotional abuse, which is the outcome of a systemic process involving numerous interlocking relationships, rules governing the system's functioning, communication patterns within the system, and pressures from both inside and outside the system. The psychological process involved in emotional abuse is not readily apparent; it must be tracked down by psychological detective work if it is to be discovered as the basis for the symptoms that make it manifest. As numerous explanations for the symptoms are possible, one cannot immediately conclude that it is emotional abuse that is the root cause. If emotional abuse *is* the basis of the symptoms, is it occurring only within the family, only within the school, or does it result from a combination of the two?

I think most of us ignore or deny psychological abuse that occurs in school, so I want to make it clear that the same mechanisms that produce emotional abuse in families also operate in school systems, in the same manner, and for the same reasons. School staff should always be ready to ask themselves, "How might I, because of inner conflicts produced by school policies I do not agree with, or because of pressures I am subjected to, or the stress I am under because of personal or family problems, be contributing to the symptoms I am observing in a child?"

Dynamics of emotional abuse. Whether we are talking about emotional abuse that occurs in families or that which occurs in classrooms, the mechanisms are the same:

1. People react to pressures and harassment.
2. There are difficulties communicating effectively.
3. Misinterpretations of each other's verbal and nonverbal messages occur.
4. People get into double binds.
5. There is a lack of problem-solving and conflict-resolution expertise.
6. People either protect each other too much or fail to offer each other support.
7. There are boundary problems.

8. There are misguided goals.

9. People have too rigid or too loose a set of rules governing them.

10. Families and schools experience problems with the control and appropriate expression of anger.

Essentially, emotional abuse is the use of intimidation, manipulation, blame, and punishments within a power relationship to accomplish an adult's goals for a child. Although the adults' purposes are usually self-serving, they delude themselves that their words and actions are to serve some legitimate goal such as to teach the child a lesson or help the child overcome a problem.

The end result of emotional abuse is that the child suffers variously one or more of the following:

1. burdensome guilt

2. shame and humiliation

3. extreme embarrassment

4. overwhelming anxiety

5. crippling fear

These emotional reactions become manifest in symptoms that impair one or more areas of the child's functioning and stifle social-emotional growth. The symptoms are a child's distress signals, a cry for help, and if they go unheeded, they will multiply to become more serious and further affect the child's life.

Status striving. Emotional abuse may occur in a school system that is trying to achieve or maintain a particular image, such as being the highest achieving school in the state, or having the best football team in the county. The pressures and harassment that teachers are exposed to, the conflicts of values and conscience, and the frustrations resulting from unsuccessfully trying to meet the demands of the system create an unhealthy emotional climate that affects everyone, children as well as teachers. On the other hand, when striving to achieve the image of a compassionate school, a healthy emotional climate will emerge, one that enhances the growth and development of teachers and children.

Families also try to maintain an image, one that will bolster family esteem. They want to be seen as the ideal or perfect family, or at least a family without problems. However, this is not the main reason the dysfunctional patterns that produce emotional abuse (and other forms of abuse) develop. It is the "emotional baggage," a set of unresolved conflicts, misguided beliefs, distorted perceptions, and unfulfilled aspirations, left over from growing up in an imperfect family (everyone's is) that each person brings to marriage and parenting, that forms the basis of family dysfunctioning. This is an extremely common problem.

One of the reasons that failure to learn has become such a common symptom of family dysfunctioning is that as a society we place too high a value on competition and striving, on social and status images. Too many families do not allow normal childishness and the assertion of natural inclinations in their quest for perfect, high-achieving offspring. It is as though, at just the point in history when we know what children need for healthy growth and development, we stop allowing them the freedom to be the children they are.

In the following case, Jamie's failure at school had his teacher baffled because the family's dysfunction and their emotional abuse of Jamie were hidden:

> Jamie was a bright fifth grader who had always been a poor student. The school staff had vacillated over the years from thinking he had a learning disability to being equally sure he didn't. His mother, a former teacher, engaged in a power struggle with the staff over the diagnosis. When the school thought he had a learning disability, the boy's mother was convinced of a psychological causation, and vice versa. Meanwhile, Jamie became an expert at failing in a variety of patterns that kept everyone off balance. Aside from his below grade-level performance, Jamie was a delightful person, socially at ease, and popular with the brightest kids. This pleased his mother. He went out for all kinds of sports and took lessons to increase his athletic skills. This pleased his father. However, every time he tried to please himself and followed his own inclinations toward normal exploring and experimenting, he was berated, punished, or bribed into doing what pleased his parents. It seemed that the only way he could assert his autonomy and have any sense of being in control was to fail in school. In the process he was also punishing his parents, who wanted him to be best in everything *they chose for him,* and that included school work. Theirs was a complicated family process and very subtle mechanisms involved in the emotional abuse made Jamie appear to be incompetent in school. He later showed that he was not the failure he seemed to be; he had actually acquired all the skills necessary for academic success, but had just refused to use them.

Dysfunctioning families. Families that produce healthy, goal-oriented children who are able to enjoy life and cope with stress have been studied, and the family processes that contribute to healthy development of the children have been identified. This gives us a standard against which to compare the processes that characterize dysfunctional families, those that produce varying degrees of pathology in their members. Even when a child is the symptom bearer of a dysfunctional family, other family members may have more serious problems than that child.

Symptoms of dysfunctioning families include the following:

1. Mutual respect, emotional support, and empathy for one another are often lacking.

2. The children are continually punished for normal expression of curiosity, for initiative in trying to solve problems on their own, or for not acting in accord with adult social standards when they are learning to socialize.

3. Someone is commonly scapegoated to protect others from feeling guilty or getting depressed.

Nearly always, when learning disability is not the cause, a child's immaturity, acting out, inability to relate successfully, or failure to achieve reflects a dysfunctional family system. One six-year-old's behavior looked like immaturity but instead was the expression of a family problem:

> Tim was a likable first-grader who had done well in Kindergarten but was now disruptive, unable to settle down to work, and usually out of his seat. He sometimes talked baby talk; and he did strange things like tying himself to his chair with his sweater and walking around with the chair on his back. Although the teacher considered him immature, the psychologist found him to be a bright, clever, mature boy who wanted to learn, but also one who was anxious about his family. He wanted to be at home rather than in school. He was sure that his mother could teach him because she was very smart. The projective material from the psychological evaluation suggested that the mother might be alcoholic (this was later confirmed) and that the parents might be on the verge of divorce. Tim was an only child who wanted to keep his mother functional and his family intact. He was anxious at school because he could not monitor his mother's drinking. He had discovered that he could keep her from drinking if he kept her involved with him. If she could be his teacher, he reasoned, that would keep her from drinking. Tim's role had become one of meeting his mother's emotional needs in order to keep her from drinking. In this family, the alcohol problem would need to be addressed before the family dysfunction could be dealt with.

If you, as an educator, assume that there is a family problem when a child is showing symptoms in school, approach parents as an information gatherer rather than as an advice giver. By doing this, you will avoid appearing to have an explanation for the child's behavior, and will be able to report specific task and social behaviors without injecting your opinion about what they mean. Begin by asking parents for advice in order to find out what works and what doesn't work at home. You will thus discover much about the family dynamics by asking questions and showing an interest in the family's struggles, and this will help you give better advice when it does become essential to do so. Teachers who are expert information gatherers are invaluable to social workers and psychologists who are trying to piece together a diagnostic impression in order to develop strategies for helping a child.

THE HATCH AMENDMENT AND PSYCHOLOGICAL ABUSE IN THE CLASSROOM

Child Abuse in the Classroom is the title of a book published in 1985 that is catching the attention of parents and should be read by all school professionals."[11] This book has the potential to create parental hysteria and irrational condemnation of valid school programs. Edited by Phyllis Schlafly, the book contains excerpts of testimony given by parents, teachers, and interested citizens at hearings held in March, 1984 by the U.S. Department of Education at seven sites across the country. The hearings were held in regard to proposed regulations to implement the Protection of Pupil Rights Amendment (also known as The Hatch Amendment), Section 439 of the General Education Provisions Act. Part A of the Amendment was passed in 1974, and Part B in 1978. It is your responsibility to know the regulations pertaining to the Amendment and what constitutes a violation.

The testimonials in Ms. Schlafly's book document violations of The Hatch Amendment, and I have to agree that what is reported clearly *is* psychological abuse. However, we cannot be sure how widespread this kind of classroom abuse is because testimony about the programs and practices was limited to a *relatively limited number of school systems.*

It is unfortunate that the abuses described in the book occurred in the name of implementing programs of affective sex, death, parenting, and drug education. If we want to be successful in our efforts to teach children about death, sex, and drugs, how to take care of their health and protect themselves, as well as how to relate to others and cope with stress, we must seek the involvement and support of parents, and we must be sure that *teachers and counselors know what they are doing*. The educational programs used should be those that have been tested and proven effective, and which meet with parental approval.

Parental evaluation of materials and methods should be sought, and they should be welcome visitors in the classroom when programs are presented. Parents should be helped to understand that emotional reactivity can impair intellectual functioning: anxious and depressed children have difficulty concentrating, understanding, and remembering. The most effective use of the intellect, that which makes achieving academic goals possible, will result if appropriate and sensitive attention is given to affective issues. This does not mean that the teacher should play psychologist; it does mean that we cannot ignore the feelings and stresses of children.

REPORTING PSYCHOLOGICAL ABUSE
IN ALL ITS FORMS

Obviously you cannot consider reporting psychological abuse (including emotional abuse and neglect) unless your state's laws include it as a reportable form of abuse; but even so, protective services may ignore reports of this kind of abuse. Thus, even when your primary concern is psychological abuse, always try to find substantive evidence of neglect or physical or sexual abuse that can be used as the basis for reporting. Remember that psychological abuse that is extreme enough for you to want to report it is often linked with other forms of abuse. If a child's emotional problems are serious and glaring and the parents refuse to seek help, you should consider this neglect and report it as such.

Unless a child is threatening suicide, psychological abuse is not an emergency, and there is time to collect data that will document this kind of abuse. I can't stress enough the importance of having a dated, written, anecdotal record of incidents that constitute psychological abuse. Protective Services workers can get no help through the courts unless they have *evidence* of abuse.

HOW TO REPORT PSYCHOLOGICAL ABUSE

I suggest two approaches to reporting this form of abuse in those states where it is included in the law:

1. Keep reporting when *you* think it is warranted, even if you get no action. When voluntary approaches with the family have failed and all available resources for helping the child within the school have not gotten results, there is nothing to lose by reporting.

2. Ask a protective service worker to meet with your staff and discuss what kinds of situations the Department of Children's Services consider serious enough to investigate.

WAYS TO HELP PSYCHOLOGICALLY
ABUSED STUDENTS AT SCHOOL

Discussed below is how each particular staff member can help a psychologically abused student at school.

What the Administrator Should Do

Be certain that psychological abuse does not occur in your school, and that parents are not using the school to carry out their abusive methods.

If a parent sends a child to school wearing a sign that reads *I wet my bed, I am a jerk, I am a liar,* or something similar, do not allow the child to wear the sign in school. The same goes for other humiliations that the parent wishes to be carried out in school. Let the child know that you are in charge at school and that you will not allow it. Also inform the parents of your authority and let them know that they cannot use the school in this manner.

To prevent psychological abuse in school, apprise your staff of The Hatch Amendment and all the regulations relating to it; then carefully supervise their implementation of any controversial programs, offering advice as needed and disapproving methods that constitute violation of the Pupil Rights Amendment. Listen to students and parents who complain, and investigate all complaints. Prohibit practices that humiliate, confuse, or upset students.

Be sure that there is some kind of teacher support system. (See Chapter 11.)

Steps the Teacher Can Take

Become an information gatherer when dealing with parents, and also *ask questions and listen* to what the child has to say. You can make educated guesses about a child's behavioral messages, but only he or she really knows what that behavior expresses. Ask such questions as:

- Are you trying to let me know you are (hurt, angry, frustrated, hungry, worried)?
- Do you need a private space for working?
- Could it be that you want me to pay more attention to you?
- Do you want help?
- Does it bother you to have Eddie watch you draw?

In dealing with problem behaviors, it may be wise to try a different approach if efforts to *correct* the behavior through limit setting or disciplinary actions are not working. Think of the behavior as a symptom or distress signal and schedule a private interview with the child where you can sit together in a relaxed environment.

1. Tell the child that you want to help him or her change the specific thing he or she is doing or not doing because it impairs the ability to achieve, make friends, or feel good about him- or herself.

2. Tell the child that you believe he or she is the only one who really knows what would help him or her change.

3. Encourage the child to express his or her ideas about why it happens and what would help.

4. If the child can't give ideas, suggest some of your own, but always add, "What do you think about that? Do you think it might work? Are you willing to give it a try?"

5. Make a bargain about what each of you will do.

6. Agree on a private signal you can give to let the child know when he or she is living up to his or her part of the bargain, and another to let the child know when he or she is not.

7. Try what is agreed upon, then evaluate how it is working when you have a follow-up private conference a week later.

If direct approaches with the child don't work, either because the child is too young, not aware, or verbally inaccessible, get ideas from the parents about what works and what doesn't work at home. If they insist that nothing works, suggest ideas you'd like to try and ask for their approval, but don't involve them. (Don't make demands of the parents, but ask them to *stop* doing what they have found to be *unsuccessful.*) Whenever parents report that conflict ensues when they try to help the child with schoolwork, *always* ask them to *stop helping*.

In dysfunctional families, those where psychological abuse occurs, it always exacerbates a child's learning problems when parents insist on trying to help a child academically. This is a paradoxical phenomenon, where the more they try to do something about the problem, the worse it gets. If they ignore the problem, you will have more success working directly on the problem with the child. It is usually not easy to get parents to stop helping, but you should persist in recommending that they stop, even if it means that the child might fail. Until a child is fully in charge of whether he will succeed or fail, he has the capacity to frustrate all your efforts, just as Jamie did.

The Role of the Counselor/Social Worker/Psychologist

Although you can do much to ameliorate mild forms of emotional abuse through counseling, learning resource help, diagnostic study, and direct guidance to teachers and parents, many families need to be referred for psychotherapy outside of school. No matter how imperative you feel it is for the family to seek outside help *now*, do not use tactics involving threats or dire predictions to get them to call a counseling service. Express your deep concern, but maintain rapport with the family, which you cannot do if you intimidate them. Be patient but persistent in recommending help, and always be on the alert for any crisis that can be used to get them into therapy.

In getting parents to move toward therapy for the child or the family, it helps to be personally acquainted with therapists in community agencies and the private sector who are reasonable referral sources. Consider having a Therapist Invitational soon after school starts each fall. Invite therapists whom you have not met to an open house. At the meeting ask each one to speak about background and training, kind of cases preferred, theoretical orientation to therapy and so on. When inviting them, ask them to bring copies of their résumés to distribute to the staff. Share information with the therapists about school programs, and discuss boundary issues and ways of collaborating. You will need to involve your administrators in planning and implementing an event of this kind, but both the school staff and the community therapists will benefit from it.

TREATMENT AND PREVENTION
OF PSYCHOLOGICAL ABUSE

The most seriously psychologically abused children and youth will need special class placement, "alternative education," or residential schooling. Some children may require psychiatric hospitalization where they will receive multiple forms of therapy as well as educational services.

The treatment of choice for mild and moderate psychological abuse is family therapy. This is a mode of therapy that sees the family's ways of thinking, perceiving, reacting, and interacting as the elements that need to be changed, rather than just the behavior of an individual child who is having symptoms. When parents are not willing to acknowledge that a child's symptoms stem from a family problem, they may be able to accept individual counseling for the child at school or elsewhere. Later on, they may be more open to accepting family treatment, particularly if a crisis occurs, or another family member develops symptoms. A child's improvement from individual therapy will cause changes to occur in the way other family members act and react. Sometimes these are positive changes, but more often the family dysfunction just shifts around a bit, bringing out symptoms in other family members. It is often found that the symptomatic child becomes competent and strong, as in the examples of Tim and Jamie, and the more serious problem resides in the parent or the marital relationship. However, emotional abuse that is not treated at an early stage will eventually cause greater impairment of a child's development, so that by adolescence, individual as well as family therapy may be necessary.

Prevention of psychological abuse is closely linked with the prevention of other forms of abuse. It is a chicken-and-egg question: Which comes first? As psychological abuse is always an aspect of other forms of abuse, treatment/prevention that is effective with physical abuse, neglect, or sexual abuse will also have an impact on lessening psychological abuse.

Psychological abuse arises out of attitudes, expectations, and esteem issues, all of which are embedded in societal values. Faced with the high rate of drug and alcohol abuse, suicide, divorce, violence, and crime, we are being forced to reexamine those values and confront our humanity in new ways. An important cultural change that must take place is people's attitudes toward "being helped." People with psychological problems and families that are dysfunctional need help, whether this comes in the form of self-help groups or through professional counseling. We must remove the stigma and implied sense of failure that is currently attached to the idea of obtaining help for our human problems.

Endnotes

1. Claudia Black, *It Will Never Happen to Me: Children of Alcoholics* (Denver, CO: M.A.C. Printing and Publications Division, 1982), p. 26.
2. Avis Brenner, *Helping Children Cope with Stress* (Lexington, MA: D. C. Heath and Co., 1984), p. 151.
3. Jeanne Sullivan, *Catapulting Abusive Alcoholics to Successful Recovery* (Chicago: National Committee for Prevention of Child Abuse, 1981), p. 1.
4. Black, *Children of Alcoholics*, p. 136.
5. R. Margaret Cork, *The Forgotten Children* (Toronto: Paperjacks, Ltd., 1969), pp. 22-31.
6. Ibid., p. 44.
7. Sullivan, *Catapulting Abusive Alcoholics to Successful Recovery*, p. 3.
8. Ibid., p. 2.
9. Black, *It Will Never Happen to Me: Children of Alcoholics*, p. 171.
10. R. D. Krugman and M. K. Krugman, "Emotional Abuse in the Classroom: The Pediatrician's Role in Diagnosis and Treatment," *American Journal of Diseases of Children*, 138: 284-286, 1984.
11. Phyllis Schlafly, ed., *Child Abuse in the Classroom* (Westchester, IL: Crossway Books, 1985).

PART III

CHILDREN TRAUMATIZED BY SEPARATION AND DIVORCE

No one doubts that parental divorce is a terrific blow to a child, even when it frees him or her from an abusive situation. However, most of us do not appreciate the enormity and complexity of the emotional dilemmas that a child confronts, nor that the trauma of the divorce crisis reverberates for years to come.

Children who are separated from a parent for any reason suffer a sense of loss, and become insecure for varying lengths of time. The chapters in Part III will consider the psychological tasks of children of divorce, the impact of being separated from parents either on a temporary or permanent basis, and what schools must do to accommodate single-parent families.

Chapter 6

Helping Children Cope
with Separation from
a Parent
and Placement Outside
the Home

The impact of separation trauma has been recognized for some time. Separation trauma explains why children have so much more difficulty dealing with parental divorce than single parenthood per se, because the separation from the parent who moves out is a deeply felt loss.

This chapter considers the emotional and behavioral reactions of children who are separated from parents for reasons other than divorce or death. Separation experiences are more or less traumatic depending on the age and coping capacity of the child, the reason for the separation, and whether or not the child is cared for at home, by familiar adults, during parental absence. Those children who remain in their own homes or in those of relatives with familiar persons and possessions, do not have the same reactions as children who are placed elsewhere; yet they may exhibit troublesome separation reactions at school. Understanding these for what they are allows us to respond in ways that do not aggravate a child's emotional pain. Even when separations are only temporary, children will suffer some degree of anxiety, and will be dealing with fear of abandonment or fear that the absent parent will meet some terrible misfortune and never come back. Let us briefly consider some attachment/separation phenomena.

ATTACHMENT

In order to appreciate children's reactions to separation, we must understand the meaning of attachment (also called bonding). Attachment encompasses both biological and psychological phenomena, the purposes of which are to assure survival and foster normal development. It is the observable emotional connection between a mother and her infant. In healthy attachment there is an interplay of touching, cuddling, smiling, talking, and singing, by the mother that either elicits, or is a response to smiling, cooing, gurgling, reaching, touching, and laughing in the baby. Normal attachment develops as the mother consistently and lovingly responds to her baby's signals of distress, discomfort, or hunger, and recognizes the infant's need for physical contact, social interchange, and stimuli.

Crying and Clinging

Crying and clinging are attachment behaviors manifested by normal human infants at the ages of six months and older, that serve the purpose of keeping the mother close. Crying and clinging are instinctive modes for assuring that the mother (or a mother surrogate) will be there to protect and nurture the child. As a child develops beyond age two, he or she learns other behaviors that elicit mother's presence, but crying and clinging will always be used to signal acute distress. Remember that children of all ages (as well as adults) cry and cling when frightened or seriously upset, and in situations of loss or threatened loss. These behaviors are very basic, biologically determined indicators of distress and should always be responded to sensitively.

Disturbances in Attachment

The importance of bonding for healthy development is underscored when we look at the consequences of *anxious attachment* (produced by mild to moderate degrees of abuse and neglect); *disturbed attachment or bonding failure* (severe degrees of neglect, physical, and psychological abuse); and *disrupted attachment* (separation due to divorce, death, or placement). Mental health practitioners are increasingly acknowledging that disturbances and disruptions of attachment may be the root cause of most personality disorders and emotional disturbance. A significant number of case histories of young suicide victims reveal bonding failure. Dr. Mary Giffin believes that bonding failure during infancy may ingrain a suicidal impulse that is later activated by any kind of problem a youngster must face, particularly if he or she senses a lack of support.[1]

Causes of Disturbed Attachment

Disturbances in attachment may result from:

1. separation of mother and infant during the earliest weeks and months of life (as occurs with premature babies who must remain hospitalized; or serious mental or physical illness of the mother following birth that requires *her* to remain hospitalized)

2. prolonged separation after attachment has occurred (that is, because of illness of the child or mother)

3. loss of the attachment figure through death, divorce, or placement in foster care

4. many changes of caregivers during infancy (a working mother who cannot provide for consistent care from the same babysitter)

5. a neglecting, unresponsive mother

6. a mother who persistently miscues in response to her infant out of ignorance or her own emotional disturbance

SEPARATION

Anxiously attached children have had frightening experiences, traumas, or prolonged separations during their early years that have not been followed by an opportunity to recover a sense of security and reestablish a close bond with attachment figures. These are children who feel anxious about whether someone will be there for them when they need someone. They are the least prepared to cope with future separations and loss, and most vulnerable to having acute or chronic separation reactions. Unhappy or unresolved separations are cumulative in their impact: the more that have been experienced, the greater the sense of threat produced by subsequent, even insignificant separations.

Separation Anxiety

There are children who are experiencing mixed up or upsetting feelings related to attachment/separation in every classroom, at every grade level. In younger children separation difficulty is frequently obvious and readily recognized:

1. A child protests going to school, and/or cries and clings to the mother when it is time for school.
2. A child breaks into tears in the middle of the day and says he or she wants mother.
3. A child has frequent headaches or stomach aches and asks to go home.
4. A child frequently asks for permission to call mother.

Failure to learn, or learning that depends on making an attachment to the teacher and keeping her close through constant requests for help, are less readily recognized manifestations of a separation problem.

Older children have learned to suppress tears and to deny their desire for emotional and physical closeness with their teacher. Their reactions to separation operate at an unconscious level and can be completely inexplicable to us unless we know that a separation has taken place or is imminent, or that a particular child is vulnerable to having irrational separation reactions. One danger of not recognizing separation reactions for what they are, is that we may conclude the behavior is manipulative, and thereby become involved in an unproductive power struggle with the child.

Reasons for Separations

Reasons for separations from a parent range from the benign experience of parental vacations, business trips, or military duty, include the stigmatizing experiences of parental incarceration and hospitalization for mental illness, and encompass separations posing a serious threat of loss, such as foster care placement and parental hospitalization because of a serious accident or life-threatening illness. A child's own hospitalization is a special kind of separation, alleviated to a great extent by modern policies of having the mother stay with the child, providing instruction about and preparation for special procedures and surgery, having a child-life program available in the hospital, and so on. However, the child will still be separated from friends, school, and normal activities, and will feel apprehensive about what will happen in the hospital, as well as why he or she is there.

Recognizing Separation Reactions

Reactions to separation shown by children include changes in behavior, symbolic clinging, and excessive shyness or withdrawal from others.

Sudden Changes in Behavior. Nine-year-old Jack, an excellent student whose behavior was usually beyond reproach, brought a toy pellet gun to school (which he knew was against the rules) and spent recess shooting pellets at other children on the playground. Eight-year-old Barry, usually good natured and cooperative, began to have temper outbursts at school. Seven-year-old Rhonda became weepy, whiny, and demanding in constrast to her usual age-appropriate behavior.

Jack, Barry, and Rhonda were all reacting to impending parental vacations. Separation reactions to parental vacations without the child typically precede the trip. Consciously or unconsciously, children hope that their parents will change their minds and cancel the trip, or at least decide to take them along. We can't know that behavior changes reflect a separation dilemma unless we are told that a separation is anticipated or ongoing. Always ask the parents about sudden behavior changes.

Symbolic Clinging Behavior. Children whose parents are seriously ill are often admonished to be brave, to show how well they can take care of themselves, and so on. Instead of crying and clinging, they may express their threat of loss by "holding on to others" symbolically, through helplessness and excessive social contact with others. Tina's mother had been hospitalized several times for cancer surgery and treatments. At home, Tina acted maturely; physical clinging would have made her seem immature, so she clung to others symbolically: at school she talked constantly and continually sought social interaction with her teacher and her peers.

Excessive Shyness or Withdrawal from Others. Paula's mother had been hospitalized twice for manic-depressive illness, but Paula had not been told why. Word that Paula's mother was crazy began to circulate through the neighborhood. Paula withdrew into a shell, cut herself off from her friends, and stopped talking to anyone at school.

Carol's mother was in jail. Carol was ashamed and afraid that others would find out and tease or reject her. She played alone at recess and did not talk to the teacher or to other children. After school, she always went directly home to her grandmother's house. Verbal inhibition and social withdrawal were ways in which Paula and Carol protected themselves from being humiliated, and also served to conceal their fears related to their mother's absence. Cutting themselves off from others justified staying home where they felt safe.

Chronic Separation Reactions

Children's chronic separation reactions include "up and down" learning patterns, negative attitude toward the parent, or teacher, and not being able to adjust to more than one teacher.

Learning Patterns. Children who are anxiously attached may have difficulty forming new relationships and also *relinquishing* attachments. They may have difficulty adapting to new routines or substitute teachers, and in meeting the increased demands of higher grade levels, such as working independently, getting along with more than one teacher, or working on a long-term assignment. These children typically have trouble adjusting and learning at the beginning of each new year. They may do well most of the year, but show a sharp decline near the end of the year when separation from school and their teacher, to whom they have become attached, is imminent. If the learning pattern is plotted, it may be discovered that learning also falls off before and after vacation periods, and that Fridays are often "bad days" when little learning takes place. These children have a greater than usual need for an attachment relationship with the teacher; their learning depends on it.[2]

Negative Attitude Toward and Deprecation of the Teacher or Foster Parent. Children continue to seek closeness and love from their parents and do not want to be separated from them, even though they may have experienced rejection, neglect, or physical or emotional abuse. They wish for closeness and love, but if they have not received it at home they can't accept receiving it elsewhere. The most deeply hurt children, those who cannot endure the pain and possibility of further rejection, protect themselves from becoming emotionally connected to others through a variety of negative behaviors. These may be displayed toward anyone (teacher, principal, counselor, coach, foster parent) who is making an effort to establish a relationship with the youngster.

One form that this defensive posture assumes is deprecation of the adult who is showing the caring, or by accusing the adult of unfairness. The negative behaviors in essence carry the message, "I'll reject you before you have a chance to reject me."[3]

Difficulty Adjusting to More than One Teacher. Children who have attachment/separation problems and depend on establishing a relationship with their teacher in order to learn may not do well with more than one teacher. These are children who can handle only one attachment. They have not reached the stage of emotional development where they are able to handle attachments to several people simultaneously.[4] Special education classes, multigrade classes in which the student can remain with the same teacher for several years, or other arrangements that allow the student to have the same teacher for every class may need to be considered for these youngsters.

PREPARING CHILDREN FOR SEPARATIONS

Separations from two major influences—parent and teacher—can affect a child. Let's take a closer look.

Separation from Parents

Whether an anticipated separation from a parent is considered benign or is laden with threat, children will be able to cope in more constructive ways if they are prepared for what is to take place and given sufficient support for the anxieties that will be aroused. Preparation involves giving children the real reason for the parent's absence, permitting them to ask questions, even if they ask the same ones several times; responding to the questions patiently, so the children receive accurate information (emotional reactivity may cause them to distort the information being given); and allowing the children to express fears, anger, and worries they may be feeling. They should also be told that it is okay to cry, be angry, and feel lonesome in the parent's absence, and that if they misbehave they will still be loved. They should also be allowed to use "crutches" such as thumb sucking to help them tolerate the situation.

Need for emotional crutches. The kind of crutches a child needs while a parent is absent are those that offer comfort and reassurance, and those that reinforce the image of the parent and the child's knowledge of the parent's love.

A child may handle the separation more satisfactorily if he or she:

1. has a picture of the absent parent at bedside or to carry in a purse or paste on a notebook
2. is allowed to use a night light
3. is not criticized for returning to thumb sucking
4. is allowed to bring a doll, teddy bear, or other favorite object to school or the hospital
5. receives something special from the departing parent or is lent something that belongs to the parent before going away
6. receives an empathic note of encouragement from the teacher

Of course, these are what mothers usually do to reassure and comfort very young children. The point is that older children may also need these sources of comfort and emotional connection, at home or at school, when separated from a parent for any reason. Children who do not need to use crutches of this kind will feel comforted by knowing they *could* use them if they wanted.

Meeting the substitute caretaker. If at all possible, children should have a chance to:

1. meet the sitter who will care for them before parental departure
2. tour the hospital, meet the nurses on the pediatric ward before hospitalization
3. visit the foster family in their home before placement
4. meet or be told who the substitute will be (if he or she is known to the children) when a teacher is to be away

In addition to the chance for brief acquaintance with the stranger who will be taking over intimate care, children might be told anecdotes that illustrate how the substitute caretaker will take care of them.

Child's fears or concerns about the upcoming parental absence. If children are giving indications at school that they have concerns or need information about an imminent separation and are afraid to talk to their parents about it, it is wise to arrange a conference with parents at which the child is present, and encourage a dialogue between them and the child.

1. Get the child started by asking her to tell her parents what she has been afraid to talk about, and give the child any prompts and support that may be needed.
2. In turn, offer the parents support and help in responding to the child's fears or questions, being sure to remain neutral if the dialogue precipitates a negative interaction between parents and child.
3. With a child who is too shy to talk, be her "voice" and convey to the parents what she wants them to know.

Separation from the Teacher

All children form some degree of attachment to their teacher and feel uneasy in her absence. Children with healthy family relationships, those who have coped well with normal separations, do not become excessively anxious when their teacher is sick, or away for some other reason. However, the accumulation of mild anxieties within twenty or thirty individual children creates a climate in which they can easily lose their self-control. There may also be a few students within the class who are vulnerable to chronic, irrational separation anxiety, and they may express their anxiety in disruptive or unruly behavior. The out-of-control behavior of a class with a substitute teacher is well known, but it is seldom attributed to separation anxiety. When a teacher is to have a planned absence, preparing the children in keeping with the principles given for parental absence, as well as incorporating some of the following ideas may reduce the children's reactivity. Separation rituals before vacation periods and on Fridays help vulnerable youngsters handle separation at these times. The ritual may consist of:

1. reading a special story at the end of the day
2. shaking each child's hand as he or she leaves for the weekend
3. giving a treat or special card to each child before holidays
4. asking the children to write a letter or keep a journal to be shared later
5. sending pictures during long vacation periods

Unplanned Teacher Absence. When a teacher's absence is unplanned, class unruliness may be minimized by following these suggestions: The principal comes to introduce the substitute; explains the reasons and expected duration of the absence (if known); allows the children to ask questions and express worries; then asks them to suggest ways in which the class can be helpful to the substitute. The children should be told that the substitute will probably not run the class exactly the way their regular teacher does, but that they should cooperate with her and follow her methods. It is sometimes too much to expect a substitute teacher to have to refer to a seating chart to find out a child's name in a particularly difficult class. In some cases, it may be helpful to establish a school policy that requires children to wear name tags when their teacher is absent, just as grownups do at large meetings where people don't know each other.

By modeling sensitivity and concern for both the substitute teacher and the children, and letting the children know they must have different expectations of her than they have of their regular teacher, we set the tone for mutual respect and cooperation. The emotionally stronger children will be helpful to those vulnerable students who are prone to exhibit troublesome behavior. Another benefit is that you will have taught some basic coping strategies that many children will be able to generalize and apply when future unexpected happenings make them anxious.

CHILDREN IN PLACEMENT

As previously discussed, placement of abused and neglected children is no longer the rule, yet it is still the only viable solution for a great many children. In about fifteen percent of confirmed reports of abuse or neglect, the children must be placed in some form of foster care. It is a paradox that the children who are least able to handle separation because of serious attachment disturbances are the ones who must be placed in foster care. It is to be expected that the placement, aimed at giving the children the protection and nurturance they need, will be fraught with hazards.

Difficulties Adjusting to Foster Care

Children in placement are doubly traumatized: first from their severe abuse or neglect; then from the added experience of separation trauma. Despite the hostile, neglectful, punishing, and ungiving home environment from which they come, children yearn for their parents (and mourn their loss); they may run away in an effort to return to them. They can have trouble adapting to a nurturant environment because they will bring to it the patterns of adapting to an unfavorable one.

Most children enter foster care with emotional problems, and often also manifest bizarre behavior that reflects adaptation to a chaotic, confusing, rejecting family. They come with learning deficits and medical problems. Is it any wonder that they have difficulty at both home and at school?

Children have trouble attaching to their foster parents because they fear further rejection and the pain of another separation when they must return home, but also because of identity issues. The parent is internalized as part of the self, and any criticisms they hear about the parent will be felt as a criticism of themselves. They continue to carry their birth family name and have a sense of loyalty to their family of origin. Their identities are linked to siblings as well as to parents, and once apart from the family they tend to idealize their families and remember their past lives as a fantasy construct; that is, how they wished to have been treated rather than how they were actually treated.

Parents also have a strong sense of ownership of their children, and often want more contact with them than placement caseworkers consider advisable. Placement caseworkers know that contact with the parents is important, not only because of the strong likelihood that the children will be returned to the parents, but also as a way for children to maintain a *reality* rather than a fantasy of the way their parents actually are. However, meetings with the parents are often extremely difficult for everyone to handle emotionally, and the fragile stability that a child may have gained in the foster home can be lost and not be easily reestablished after the child meets with his or her birth parents. Birth parents can also complicate matters at school by hanging around the playground, seeking conferences with the teacher or principal, and causing the child to become disruptive because their presence arouses conflicts in the child.[5]

Children who are resilient may adjust well and form a positive relationship with their foster parents, given time and continuing acceptance, regardless of initial adjustment difficulties. They are not in great need of contact with their parents, and may even ask to be relieved of the stress of parental contact. As these children become more deeply attached to their foster parents and develop fantasies of being adopted by them, they may wish to be called by the foster family name rather than their birth family name. Placement workers consider this a healthy sign, and recommend that teachers respect the child's wish, by not only accepting the child's use of the name, but also by addressing the child and introducing her by that name, even though the legal birth name must be on the official records.[6] This seems a reasonable concession to the child's needs, and should not create conflict for the teacher.

Embarrassment at School

The placed child tends to feel self-conscious about his or her status as a foster child. On top of this dilemma, the child enters a new school knowing no one, and is most surely going to be out of sync with the curriculum. If the child has been so severely abused or neglected as to warrant placement, he or she is also going to have language and academic deficits that will be hard to reverse. As a result, this child is going to stand out from others not only because of academic problems, but also because he or she is often treated differently from other children in ways that may be viewed as demeaning, or at least embarrassing. For example, I have been told by placement caseworkers that foster children are humiliated by having to stand in a separate line for hot lunch because their meals are free. Those few who ultimately get adopted are thrilled because they can now bring a bag lunch from home, and do not have to stand in that line anymore. They are also sensitive if their free bus pass is different from those of the other kids; they feel hurt because they can't afford to buy their school pictures;

and they are embarrassed when the teacher puts their names on the board because they haven't brought money for a field trip.

Some teachers and administrators are seemingly insensitive to foster children because they resent the problems they bring with them. Caseworkers have found that all too often teachers give up on foster children; they do not have expectations that the child can learn, and therefore do not offer them the academic assistance they require.[7]

It is true that children don't do much learning when they are in the throes of a major adjustment such as placement; but this should not become the basis for having no academic expectations. Assignments should be given to placed children even if they do poorly in completing them. It *is* possible to make a child feel good when his or her work improves, even if the quality is below that of the rest of the class.

It is not necessary to emphasize the difference in children's circumstances. Practices such as making the children stand in separate lines, or giving them odd-looking lunch or bus passes that "mark" them only add to the children's problems in adjusting to difficult personal circumstances. These practices should be ended immediately by all humane, compassionate educators.

RETURN TO BIRTH FAMILY/ REPEATED PLACEMENTS

Most children who require out-placement probably should not be returned to their parents, but the judicial system has not yet evolved to the point of terminating parental rights on nearly the scale that is needed. The sad fact is that far too many children are returned to their hurtful, abusing birth families, usually over the objections and recommendations of social service caseworkers. After repeated placements, children tend to become more and more seriously disturbed, and show even more severe learning deficits. It is crucial that schools help in every way possible by gathering evidence (in the manner described in Chapter 5) that documents the severity of parental abuse and neglect for use in proving that parental rights need to be terminated; and by obtaining as extensive a diagnostic study as is possible, through special services staff or a local mental health clinic, of a foster child's abilities, skills, and personality strengths.

HOW TO HELP FOSTER CHILDREN IN SCHOOL

The best foster families are those who are motivated by an altruistic spirit and have a high intuitive capacity for responding to children in an empathic and genuinely accepting way, regardless of the problems they present. The mother typically grew up in a large family where she was the oldest child who "mothered" many younger children, became used to having many children around, and also learned to enjoy the company of a flock of children.

Most frequently these foster families, who think of their work as a "calling," are found in rural areas. Unfortunately, rural schools usually have few if any specially trained psychological staff to help with the complex kinds of problems foster children present. In recognition of this fact, the following suggestions are directed to the principal, although any staff member could begin implementing them.

Develop an Appreciation for Foster Families

Make a special effort to know foster parents well, and find some way to show appreciation for the nobility of their work, either privately or publicly. Perhaps they could receive an award for having the largest number of children in school, and honoring them could include a display of photographs of the many foster children (along with their own children) the family has parented. If the school has a career day, invite foster parents to tell about having a career as surrogate parents: what motivates them, what the rewards are, and how they work with social services. Have them tell about other types of foster parents such as those called "house parents" who work in group homes. The same kind of information can be given in the context of studying about different family structures, such as in family living classes or home economics courses. The foster mother could be asked to visit the class as a resource person during discussion of the topic.

Appoint a School Advocate for Each Foster Child

Foster parents attempt to "act for" their foster children when problems or misunderstandings arise, but they often do not have enough clout or are not given the respect needed to get a child's side of the issue heard. For this reason, each foster child should have a school advocate, a specially concerned person, other than the foster parent or caseworker, to intervene on his or her behalf when difficulties occur in the school setting. Depending on circumstances and the availability of psychologically trained staff, the advocate could be the principal, nurse, school psychologist, counselor, special education teacher within a school, or a volunteer from the community who has been trained by the local mental health unit. The school advocate would have intimate knowledge of a child's needs and problems, a positive relationship with the child and the foster parents, and the authority to negotiate with others on the child's behalf. The school advocate would also be expected to interpret a child's needs to his teacher, intervene when the teacher's efforts or attitude are misguided, and encourage the teacher to look to his or her professional peers for support and advice.

Establish a Staff Support System

For example, the teacher assistance team described in Chapter 11 could be established. Teachers will be less inclined to resent having children with problems in their classes if they have a source of help for dealing with the children's difficulties.

Arrange for Diagnostic Study

Request a child study evaluation through your special education services for every foster child who has a background of abuse and neglect. Do not accept the rationalization that the child would not be learning well because of his bad background. In all likelihood, the child will qualify for some type of special education service.

Implement the Suggestions Contained in the Abuse Chapters

In addition, be sure to incorporate in your family life curricula discussion of family change and differing family structures, as outlined in Chapter 7. Foster children are less likely to feel different and set apart if other children understand what foster families are all about. Establish policies that eliminate the demeaning differentiation of these children, as discussed earlier in this chapter.

Be Sure You Are Well Informed

The child's placement caseworker should let you know about changes in the child's situation or legal status that are being considered.

Endnotes

1. Mary Giffin and Carol Felsenthal, *A Cry for Help* (Garden City, NY: Doubleday and Co., 1983), pp. 187 and 215.
2. Ner Littner, *Five More* (New York: Child Welfare League of America, Inc., 1980), pp. 40 and 42.
3. Ibid., p. 43.
4. Ibid., p. 42.
5. Interview with State of Michigan Social Service Department (Northern Division) placement staff: Roger Quinn, Barbara Varley, Beverly McGurk and Juanita Pickett, November 12, 1985, Traverse City, MI.
6. Ibid.
7. Ibid.

Chapter 7

The Impact of and Coping with Divorce and Remarriage

Divorce, for children, is a crisis second only to the crisis of death. Children feel that they are being abandoned by the parent who leaves, and worry that the other parent will also abandon them. They worry about running out of money, and being "out in the cold." They blame themselves for the difficulties between their parents, and try, in whatever way they know, to reconcile them. Their fantasy that parents will reconcile lasts a very long time; a women I know still had not let go of this fantasy at the age of fifty.

It is difficult to remain neutral and unbiased about divorce. School professionals who have experienced divorce may have continuing unresolved conflicts and ambivalent feelings, as well as insights, that affect their attitudes and reactions. Those who have stayed married against the odds perhaps believe that others could do the same if they were more committed and made more of an effort. Still others are opposed to divorce on moral and religious grounds, although they make exceptions for situations in which violence endangers the wife and children, or where pathology in a spouse hinders healthy development of the children.

Whatever our feelings or individual biases (and it is important to be aware that we all have them), we all know that divorce is a fact of life and the trend toward more and more families becoming dissolved is not likely to reverse itself soon.

DIVORCE DOES NOT ALWAYS MAKE THINGS BETTER

There is no doubt that some children are better off following parental separation. The earliest studies of children of divorce, done in the 1960s, indicated that children improved in their overall functioning once they were no longer living in a family where the parents were unhappy and conflictive. Perhaps at that time divorces were primarily between parents who were putting an end to a very destructive marriage, and the outcome proved beneficial for everyone. However, that is no longer true for the majority of divorces.

Divorce has become an epidemic. Parents are parting for personal reasons that often do not make sense to the children. It would appear that divorce is a solution for adults to which children must adapt. Research now tells us that children hardly ever want their families to break up; only a small percent (less than 10 percent in one study) feel relief. The aftermath of divorce is wrenching, frightening, and devastating for most children, and the fact that there is a high rate of divorce in a community does not mitigate the distress. Divorce represents the collapse of a structure that provided support and protection to a child; it leaves a child feeling insecure, alone, and adrift in a world of unknowns and imagined terrors.[1]

THE IMPACT OF DIVORCE IS LONG-LASTING

Teachers usually observe changes in children's learning and behavior at the time a marriage is coming apart, even if they don't know the reasons for the changes until later. In their study of 131 children of divorce, Wallerstein and Kelly found that only one-third of the children *did not* present observable symptoms of distress in school. Many of these children were showing vigorous emotional reactivity at home, however.[2]

After their parents separate, children typically have serious concentration problems that affect their ability to do schoolwork. Although a majority of children are back on track at the end of a year, two out of five may not be.[3] Considering the enormous number of children affected by divorce, a significant group will need psychological help.

Divorce is not a self-contained crisis. Children who rally within the first year after the family breakup may present problems later, as new crises and disruptions are encountered, and as new developmental tasks must be mastered. The aftermath of divorce is a continuing cycle of crises and readjustments for the parents, and children do better or worse depending on how well their parents deal with them. What the children know and feel about the changes, and how well they can disengage from parental distress are also factors in how well they cope.

THE POST-DIVORCE ADJUSTMENT PROCESS

Although the number of fathers who have custody is increasing, the most recent census figures indicate that in nearly ninety percent of divorces, it is still the mother who becomes the custodial parent.[4] Fathers experience emotional pain at being separated from their children, and have their own set of adjustments to make, but here I will discuss the new nuclear family, made up of a mother and her children.

The post-divorce period is a difficult time for a woman, even when she is the one who wanted out of the marriage, and/or planned carefully for the divorce. There is no real way she can prepare herself for the wrenching caused by the division of property; the psychic pain of developing a new identity as a "single parent" (that often involves cutting off old associations and creating a new network of friends); the sense of loss at having no one to share her worries with or to help her make decisions. Working out the legal aspects of a divorce is emotionally draining; the need to work outside the home is both exhausting and time consuming. A mother in this situation has no one to take over the children when she needs a little time for herself.

Becoming a single-parent family has its burdens for both a mother and her children. Many new realities must be dealt with while also experiencing feelings of loss, despair, anger, confusion, and a sense of chaos. Schedules and household routines must be revamped, priorities set, and roles and rules must undergo restructuring. A major restructuring in the children's status and their responsibilities will occur in a majority of families.

New Responsibilities for Children

Out of necessity, children will be drafted to help with a multitude of household tasks that are normal to daily living. Mother can't do it all the way she did before. Older children will learn to cook, clean, and care for the younger ones. The younger children will be expected to do more for themselves, become independent at an earlier age than usual, and find ways to comfort themselves rather than looking to others when needing support.

Children Elevated to Adult Status

As part of negotiating a fair deal with the children who must assume responsibilities beyond the norm for age, their mothers will elevate them in status to nearly that of a peer.[5] In this elevation of status, the child gains the right to negotiate not only his needs, but also the way he wants to live. This is a heady experience for children aged nine and up; but in time the determination and manipulative skill they use in getting what they want is likely to lead to conflict with the mother, difficulty in adjusting when in their father's home, and resistance to authority at school and in other situations.

Being granted adult status in the home is a mixed blessing for most children. As part of their new role, they may be used as confidante-therapist by the parent; may be allowed too much decision-making power that confuses and upsets them; and may not be shielded from a host of adult concerns which become a burden to know about because the child has no way of helping. Worries about money and how bills will get paid and concern over parental depression on the part of children are common.

Decline in Economic Status

Divorce means a reduction in the amount of money available and a limitation on material possessions, and always results in a change in economic status. The most wealthy may still be comfortably well off, but private schools and lessons, designer clothes, and expensive cars will usually be replaced by public school attendance, modestly priced clothes and small, inexpensive cars. The family home may be maintained for a while, but a move to a smaller, less expensive one will usually be made within a year. We may not be inclined to feel sorry for families who are economically reduced by only this much, but the loss of status for mother and children is keenly felt, and it is experienced as a blow to self-esteem. When self-image is constructed around status symbols, their loss requires identity restructuring.

For families of more ordinary means, the decline in economic status may create an extreme degree of insecurity. If the mother should lose her job, if there is a reduction or stoppage in the father's support check, or if unexpected expenses arise, a new crisis will face the family. "How are we going to survive?" becomes the issue; obviously this is a more pervasive anxiety than just doing with less.

The presence or absence of a support check from the father may make the difference between staying off or going on welfare. For mothers and children, the frequent necessity to use welfare, at least for a time, damages self-esteem and doesn't solve the family's poverty problem.

Visits with the Children's Father

Most studies indicate that when children have regular contact with their father, their adjustment is eased. Financial support from the father and the interest he shows about their welfare is very meaningful to children. If efforts are made, in the weeks and months following separation, to sustain the father's involvement, he is less likely to drift away and stop sending support checks. The school can help in this process by sending the father reports, inviting him to conferences, and reinforcing with the mother that there are positive benefits for the child in having his or her father involved (see Chapter 8).

When the father's instability or violent nature poses a threat to the child's safety, or when the father has deserted the family, the child must come to understand the reason (or reality) that he or she cannot see the father. However, we must remember that men are sometimes not as unstable or as vicious as their ex-wives claim. If our perception of the father is different from that held by the mother, we should let her know how we see him, and explore whether it wouldn't be wise to allow children to visit with the father in a safe place like school or church.

The increased appreciation of the father's importance to his children is resulting in more custody disputes being resolved in his favor, and wider experimentation with joint custody and joint physical custody. There are many emergent patterns of living at Mom's house and living at Dad's house, some of which are not necessarily beneficial to the children. However these are matters that need to be ironed out by the parents with input from the children. It does seem to help both the father and child to have a more normal and satisfying parent-child relationship when the father can experience the full range of parenting duties and have his children live with him for several days or longer at a time. Children are better oriented and feel a greater sense of belonging when they have a "place" of their own and an accumulation of possessions at their father's house that allows them to come and go without the need for extensive packing and remembering what is needed for each change of household. With this arrangement, Dad and Mom don't become split into the good and the bad parent; the parent who brings goodies and fun versus the parent who must set limits and provide discipline.[6]

PARENTAL REMARRIAGE: A NEW CRISIS

Remarriage of either parent is often more difficult for children to handle emotionally than the original separation or divorce. It stirs up feelings and conflicts previously put to rest, and again requires major readjustments in family structure, rules, routines, and so on. The new spouse usually requires a shift back to the traditional family structure in which the adults are authoritarian and the children are expected to obey. This is a difficult adjustment for children who have grown used to negotiating on a peer basis with a parent.

In remarrying, a parent gains a close and intimate relationship with another adult, a position formerly filled by the child. Although this is a healthy change, it makes the child feel displaced and excluded. Thus, while a parent feels happy about the remarriage, a child may feel quite sad. In addition to feeling displaced, the children of a remarrying parent face numerous emotional dilemmas: jealousy, resentment, or fear of loving the new stepparent; competition with new siblings; conflicts of loyalty; renewed feelings of rejection; worry about the natural parent who is not yet remarried. No matter how the marriage is anticipated by the adults, there are bound to be problems, and the more thought given to the potential difficulties before the marriage, the better prepared the family will be to handle them.

The task of family reorganization is full of hazards; as many as half of second marriages fail. Counseling for the remarried family is advisable just to assure its success; it is imperative if problems occur. However, counseling can be unsucessful if the therapist does not appreciate the uniqueness of the issues involved, nor have a plan for intervention that is appropriate for step-relationships. In referring these families for counseling, special consideration should be given to the maturity of the therapist and his or her previous experience working with step-families.

DIVORCE AND DEVELOPMENTAL PROGRESS

The critical question regarding the impact of divorce is whether it impairs a child's developmental progress. Developmental arrest occurs when a child remains fixated or "stuck" at the level he or she had reached when the divorce trauma was experienced. That is, the child does not regain developmental momentum following the emotional setback the divorce creates. The "arrest" may encompass social, emotional, and cognitive development and be manifested by either social or learning problems or both. Learning failure over a prolonged period always interferes with development, and may be a good indicator of developmental arrest. Poor achievement may be the only persistent symptom, so monitor this carefully following divorce.

POST-DIVORCE PSYCHOLOGICAL TASKS*

Based on a ten-year follow-up of children from divorced families, six psychological tasks must be mastered by children over a period of years if their development is to proceed unimpaired. It is important to recognize that these divorce-related tasks impose an *extra burden,* because there are still the normal developmental tasks to be dealt with as well. The challenge of the added tasks overtaxes the coping capacities of many children. An understanding of these tasks provides a framework for constructing both preventive and treatment strategies with these children.

Beginning Tasks

The most immediate tasks children face are:

1. Acknowledging the reality of the marital rupture
2. Disengaging from parental conflict and distress/resuming customary pursuits

Most children master these tasks within twelve to eighteen months after parental divorce.

Children ages seven and younger have great difficulty dealing with the reality of the divorce. Even when parents have carefully explained the reasons for the divorce and the changes taking place, children this age usually can't understand what is happening. They have a poor grasp of the concepts of marriage, separation, and divorce, as well as limited comprehension of the concepts of time, calendar, space, and distance. Their difficulties in separating fantasy and reality also make them particularly vulnerable to being upset by frightening fantasies. Preschool children usually respond by crying, clinging, seeking comfort, and staying close to their mothers. Even children ages

---

*This section was adapted from an article by Judith S. Wallerstein, Ph.D., "Children of Divorce: The Psychological Tasks of the Child," *American Journal of Orthopsychiatry,* Vol. 53, No. 2, pp.230-43, ©American Orthopsychiatric Association, Inc. Used by permission.

six to eight are prone to develop school phobias, based in separation anxiety. Their learning blocks may be severe.

Older children and adolescents have little difficulty acknowledging the reality of the divorce (which is different from accepting the permanence of it), but they have considerable difficulty staying out of the parents' problems and returning to their customary activities of school and play, with their usual capacity for learning and enjoyment. In order to disengage from parental problems and return to normal activities, older children and adolescents must establish a degree of psychological distance from their parents, and emotionally separate themselves from the parental distress and conflict. This is hard to do because the older children realistically worry about a parent's capacity to cope, and perceive that one or both parents look to them for nurturance and support. A lot of support and guidance from outside the family is needed if this task is to be accomplished by older youngsters.

While most children withdraw from their usual activities during the divorce process, and we must respect their need to do this, we must also be ready to offer support when we feel that they are ready to become reinvolved. As we notice their anxiety and depression diminishing, we can start encouraging them to resume their usual activities. Individual and group counseling, and opportunities for closeness with a favorite teacher will usually provide the gentle prodding needed.

Ongoing Tasks

The remaining tasks are ongoing. These are:

3. Resolution of loss
4. Resolving anger and self-blame
5. Accepting the permanence of the divorce
6. Achieving realistic hope regarding relationships

These ongoing tasks cast a shadow over childhood and often are never totally mastered.

Resolution of loss. Resolution of loss demands that a child overcome the sense of rejection and unlovability that the departure of a parent brings out. There are multiple other losses to mourn as well: home, school, and neighborhood; status and a sense of security; familiar routines, family togetherness and holiday rituals; and so on.

Resolution of Anger and Self-Blame. Children and adolescents do not believe in no-fault divorce. They may blame one or both parents, or they may blame themselves. Younger children think their badness caused the divorce; older ones blame themselves for not being able to reunite the parents. Older children and adolescents have enormous anger with which they must come to terms. Mastering this task requires that children forgive themselves as well as their parents. If they can forgive themselves, they may well be able to forgive their parents.

Accepting the Permanence of the Divorce. Children cling tenaciously to the fantasy of family reunification; and if old enough and clever enough, try very hard to get the parents back together. One of the reasons remarriage is so threatening to children is that they must confront the death of their wish for parents to "undivorce" themselves and reform the original family. When either parent also yearns for restoration of the marriage, the adult's fantasies reinforce those of the children, and make it even harder for children to accept that the divorce is going to be permanent.

Achieving Realistic Hope Regarding Relationships. This task is one the children face when they reach adolescence. To some extent, children feel betrayed by parents who divorce. They lose faith in their own capacity to love and be loved because they have seen that their parents' love did not endure. They are frightened that they too will fail at love and marriage. To master this task, adolescents must risk getting involved in a loving relationship, recognizing that it may fail, but having realistic hope that they will ultimately find a relationship that will endure. If they have mastered the previous tasks they will probably do well with this one also. However, some residue of anxiety regarding relationships may haunt an individual into the adult years.

HOW THE SCHOOL CAN HELP

School personnel can do much to help children ease the stress of and cope with divorce.

Administrator: Establish New Programs

A large number of latchkey children are children of divorce. Thus, the suggestions for before- and after-school child care, activity programs and survival skill training discussed in Chapter 1 apply here as well. Older elementary-age children and junior high students can sublimate their anger and psychic pain through intense involvement in extracurricular activities, and may particularly benefit from creative art and creative writing clubs. Peer tutoring is another after-school activity that will help reduce the number of youngsters falling behind academically.

Review the family life curriculum materials to see if they encompass the idea of family change and alternative family structures. If not, consider adding a program on family change like the one described in the next section. Implementing the suggestions in the following chapter will benefit both the children and their parents.

Counselor/Social Worker/Psychologist:
Crisis Intervention and Use of Groups

Children can benefit from brief, focused individual crisis counseling during the weeks immediately following the parental decision to divorce.[7] If parents request this, and you are able to offer it, follow these guidelines:

For children aged 6-8

1. Plan for two to four sessions to be closely integrated with the parents (two sessions with the child, two with the parent).

2. Children of this age are often very sad, close to tears, and unable to talk very much about what is happening. Explain why you are seeing them, that you want to make them feel less sad and upset.

3. Ask them to draw pictures about what is happening in their family and to draw how they are feeling.

4. Talk about the pictures and empathize, clarify, and reassure as the need presents itself.

5. Offer facts about divorce and what other children their age usually feel like and worry about, either in a monologue fashion, or by reading passages from a book such as *Divorce Is a Grown-Up Problem* (second half).[8] After each feeling is presented, ask, "Do you feel like that?" Also watch for nonverbal reactions.

6. Use the insights gathered to work out a plan with the parents for helping the child cope.

For children over age 8

1. Older children readily recognize their conflicts and have many reality issues they are eager to discuss with someone besides their parents. Often, these children are trying to solve their parents' problems and need to be told that these issues are not the province of children, no matter how mature.

2. Reinforce the children's ego and role boundaries.

3. Ascertain the strength of their support system, and make them aware of where and to whom they can turn for help.

4. If the support system is weak, work towards finding additional sources of support within the school.

5. They may not be able to utilize peer support from friends until later, after the initial crisis has past, but if you help them consolidate sibling bonds, brothers and sisters can offer each other support.

Groups to help children cope with divorce have been utilized successfully in schools, and appropriate techniques have been described in professional journals and books. There are pros and cons about divorce counseling groups, and each school system must decide whether offering such groups is something they want to do. A program called *Rainbows,* using specially trained lay leaders, is offered in many Catholic schools, and has the potential of being adapted for public schools. Although the use of lay leaders is necessary in private schools that do not have mental health professionals on staff, public schools should not have to use paraprofessionals. A social worker, counselor, or psychologist on the school staff should be selected to plan and conduct the groups. The training and experience of each professional should determine the choice, not a job description.

The following are guidelines for those who want to set up groups for children of divorce:

1. Groups should be for children in grades three and above. Younger children (even some third graders) have difficulty talking about the divorce, and the pressure to do so may impair their ability to cope. Younger children's psychological defenses are tenuous, and care must be taken not to put further stress on them.

2. Decide on a fixed number of sessions (five to eight) and schedule meetings of the group outside regular class time: during recess, noon hour, or before or after school.

3. Involve parents in the planning and give them individual feedback at the end of the series of sessions.

4. Have a narrow age range for each group and limit size to five to eight children.

5. Participation must be voluntary; gain parental permission first, then ask children to make their own decisions about signing up.

6. Be clear about goals; don't try to diagnose or treat emotional problems through the group. However, reactions of children in group sessions may help to identify those in need of therapy.

7. Don't use questionnaires that probe feelings to gain information about the youngsters' personal situations.

8. Develop a structure for each session and write a proposal of the plan that includes goals and methods to be used; present this to an administrator and the parents for prior approval.

9. Use activities, stories, or filmstrips to stimulate discussion and to develop understanding. Consider using games such as Ungame, Family Happenings, Conversations, and The Changing Family Game,[9] as well as games of your own construction.

When working with groups of children, you should keep in mind certain goals. These are given in Figure 7-1.

There will be some communities in which parents do not believe that divorce groups are appropriate in the school. However, these parents may be open to the idea of a program that focuses on family change. Such a program has been designed and it has been successfully implemented in schools. The previously mentioned group guidelines were generally followed, but the group was open to *any* child in the eight- to twelve-year age-range, and met for five consecutive one-hour sessions.[10] The objectives of these sessions are given in Figure 7-2.

The desirability of this approach is that it is basically educational, does not point a finger at a single group of youngsters, and gives children a broader perspective of family change, from incorporating a new member (new baby, grandmother, or a foster child) to losing a member (older sibling leaving home, death of a family member, and so on).

CHECKLIST OF CHILDREN'S DIVORCE GROUP GOALS

_____ Clarify the child's feelings about the divorce.

_____ Help the child understand that others are experiencing similar feelings.

_____ Help the child gain a realistic picture of the divorce situation.

_____ Assist the child in learning new ways of coping with the feelings associated with divorce.

Figure 7-1

Ideas taken from G. S. Wilkenson and R. T. Bleck, "Children's Divorce Groups," Elementary School Guidance and Counseling, *February 1977, 11:205-213.*

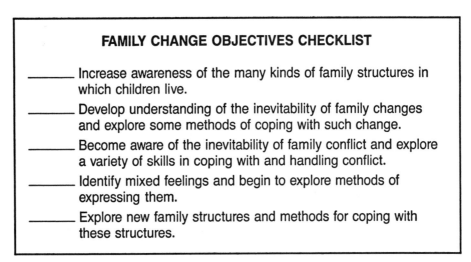

Figure 7-2

Ideas taken from S. Holdahl and P. Casperson, "Children of Family Change: Who's Helping Them Now?" The Family Coordinator, October 1977, 472-477.

Resources for Parents. Consider typing a list of community resources and books helpful to divorced parents (see also Chapter 8). Include addresses and telephone numbers, making sure that local bookstores carry the books or that they are available in the library. Have copies of the resource list available in the school library and with each teacher, as well as in your office. Develop a small library of books to lend to parents to use in talking with their children.

Teachers: Classroom Strategies

If the child's learning was satisfactory before the divorce, he or she probably does not have a learning disability. Learning blocks, regressions in thought and speech patterns, math problems that center on subtraction and division (because of the symbolic meaning of these processes) may worry you, but it is important to maintain confidence in the child's learning capacity. The following suggestions relate to the difficulties that children have with memory, organization, concentration, inner tension, conflict, chaos at home, and so on:

1. Maintain a definite structure and predictable routine in the classroom.
2. Teach memory reinforcers: making lists, writing notes to self, using colored yarn or stickers as "prompts," placing notes on lunch bag or jacket.

3. Help with organization: compartmentalize desk with boxes for different objects; cover books in different colored paper for each subject and have bookmarks of the same color that can also be used to write down and date assignments; at the end of the day check to see that proper books and bookmarks are taken home.

4. Ask the child where he or she does homework and from whom he or she seeks help. If the child likes to have homework when he or she visits the father, coordinate assignments accordingly. If the father's home is a place where the child *can't* do homework, try to give homework during weekdays rather than over the weekend. If possible, see that the child gets all work done at school if he or she is persistently failing to turn in homework. Perhaps the home environment or added responsibility prevents the child from doing the work.

5. Use attention-aiding devices to bring the child out of reveries. Also, have children work in teams. This will increase interaction and interest while reducing the tendency to daydream.

6. For children who can't think of anything to write when confronted with a creative writing assignment, suggest that they first draw a picture, then write a story to go with the picture; or offer several pictures for them to choose from to serve as stimuli for a story.

7. Read stories and/or play music at the *end* of the day, as well as at other times, to reduce tension.

8. Offer personal conference time: set aside one recess period or part of the lunch period for children to use if they want to sign up for a private talk with you. Availability at other times can be more casual and spontaneous.

9. Use bibliotherapy wisely: suggest books for children to read that will help them cope with the divorce.

10. Hold a classroom discussion about divorce based on a story or book that you read to the class.

Endnotes

1. Judith S. Wallerstein and Joan Berlin Kelly, *Surviving the Break-Up: How Children and Parents Cope with Divorce* (New York: Basic Books, 1980), p. 35.
2. Ibid., p. 270.
3. Ibid., p. 279.
4. "Playing Both Father and Mother," *Newsweek* Magazine, July 15, 1985.
5. Robert S. Weiss, "Growing Up a Little Faster: Children in Single Parent Households," *Children Today*, May-June 1981.
6. Isolina Ricci, *Mom's House, Dad's House: Making Shared Custody Work* (New York: Collier Books, a division of Macmillan, 1980), pp. 122-123.
7. Judith S. Wallerstein and Joan B. Kelly, "Brief Interventions with Children in Divorcing Families," *American Journal of Orthopsychiatry,* 47 (1): 23-29, 1977.
8. Janet Sinberg, *Divorce is a Grown-Up Problem* (New York: Avon Books, 1978).
9. *Ungame* can be ordered from Au-Vid, Inc., P.O. Box 964, Garden Grove, CA 92642. *Family Happenings* and *Conversations* are available from Kids in Progress, Inc., 2749 Third Street, Eau Claire, WI 54703. *The Changing Family Game: A Communication and Problem Solving Game for Children of Divorce* is available from Berg, Allik & Associates, 2305 Far Hills Avenue, Dayton, OH 45419.

Chapter 8

The School and
Single-Parent
Families

The number of single parent families has doubled over the past fifteen years. In 1984, 25.7 percent of families with children under eighteen were headed by a single parent, nearly 90 percent of whom were mothers.[1] Most single-parent homes result from divorce or the death of a parent, but there are also single parents who have never married. About a quarter of all single parents have never been married. Technically speaking, single parent is a misnomer for divorced mothers because, in most instances, the children have a second parent involved with them to some extent. Although we use the term single parent pragmatically, to refer to the unit of custodial parent and children who live together, we should continually remind ourselves that these children have two parents. We should involve the noncustodial parent whenever it is possible.

We should also not forget the many temporary one-parent situations caused by a parent being away on military duty, confined to a hospital, or incarcerated. Although, in many of these cases the parent may only be absent for a period of a few months, the needs and stresses of the parent who must rear the family alone during that time are similar to those faced by true single parents heading a household.

School policies, programs, and traditions have generally assumed that children live in two-parent families. This chapter will examine the kinds of changes that schools need to make in order to accommodate one-parent families.

ISSUES OF SINGLE PARENTS

The National Committee for Citizens in Education (NCCE) conducted a study, from 1979-1981, of single parents' views of school programs and policies. The following suggestions (adapted here with permission) emerged from that study. In reviewing these, you can assess how well your school is responding to the unique needs of single-parent families.[2]

School Policies and the Noncustodial Parent

The Federal law, the Family Educational Rights and Privacy Act, and the regulations arising out of it, accord the noncustodial parent the right to free access to the school records of his or her children. Any exception to this must be backed by a court order or legally binding instrument that has been presented to the school. Teachers, counselors, and administrators do not need the permission of the custodial parent to discuss a child with the noncustodial parent, to give him or her written reports, and so on. However, to maintain rapport with the custodial parent, it is wise to inform him or her that you are involving the ex-spouse.

In order for everyone to be clear about this, the school board should include it in its statement of policies: that natural parents, regardless of who has custody, have equal rights and privileges regarding their children's school activities and records. Specific rights can be spelled out. For example, the rights to visit school for special events and to attend conferences; the rights to be notified of serious problems; the privileges of receiving a school calendar, special events announcements, invitations to class performances, and copies of class pictures could all be included on the board's list.

In securing these rights, individual schools obviously have a choice of being passive and giving noncustodial parents information only when they specifically ask for it, or of taking the initiative and providing them with information as a routine procedure. The value of the latter is that it is a way of showing the children that the school believes both parents' involvement is important.

New Record Forms Needed

To facilitate smooth handling of the variety of situations that may arise with any given child, the school needs more information than has been traditionally requested on registration forms. Isolina Ricci has proposed a form that has spaces for names and phone numbers of natural parents, stepparents, an adult family friend, relatives, or a guardian. The form also asks for a listing of adults who have rights and responsibilities for the child: for parent-teacher conferences, classroom visits, emergency release; in regard to discipline, school placement and education decisions. The form contains statements regarding legal status or relationship to the child, and the adult registering the child is asked to mark the ones that apply. Further, there are questions regarding specific steps to take in an emergency: whom to call first, second, and third; to whom the child can be released, and so on.[3]

It is also important to have addresses and work telephone numbers for all adults listed, and a statement about whether a copy of the legal custody papers are on file at school. Ready access to proof of custody is needed in the event of kidnapping by a noncustodial parent, or as proof for restricting access to the child and his or her records by the noncustodial parent. Provide a file to contain copies of custody papers, and be sure that office staff and faculty know where it is located and have ready access to it.

Parent Participation

The vast majority of single parents work, and fifty-four percent live below the poverty level. They cannot afford to take time from work to attend parent conferences or other school events. Schools need to change their habit of scheduling conferences exclusively during the day. Scheduling conferences between noon and 7:30 P.M. accommodates a variety of work patterns.

Single parents would like the school to provide child care during parent conferences, school programs, and parent organization meetings. Junior and senior high school students enrolled in babysitting or child development classes could be recruited to tend the children, getting "field experience" by doing so.[4] There are other possibilities: show rented movies on the school's videocassette recorder; provide books, blocks, and drawing materials for a child to amuse him- or herself with in the hall outside the conference room; or include the children in the event. School-age children should definitely be allowed to attend parent conferences.

A high eighty-three percent of those answering the NCCE questionnaire indicated a desire for a parenting course specifically for single parents.[5] Obviously the respondents were a motivated group; implementing their request could be a challenge to one or another of the school's psychologists or social workers. Alternative options would be to arrange with a nearby university, community mental health agency, or a person in private practice to give such a course at school.

Adapting Curriculum Materials and Activities

Single parents are sensitive about the fact that in textbooks the two-parent family is the only one considered "normal." They would like library books, audiovisual materials, and textbooks to depict a variety of family styles. They would also like to see books in the school library that contain stories about children dealing with death and divorce.[6]

Single parents also believe that teachers assume two-parent families in the assignments and activities they plan. Making mother/father cards and presents, asking children to interview both parents, asking children to get both their parents to attend a parent meeting and so on all ignore the fact that alternate family units are common. In planning the making of cards or presents, teachers should consult the children who have only one parent, parents in two locations, no parents, stepparents and so on, as well as natural parents, about their preferences. If there are many children in these categories, perhaps it would be best not to focus on presents or cards for Mother's Day and Father's Day, but to talk about what the day means and perhaps make gifts for nursing home residents.[7]

Special Events

School social events that bring parents and children (and even grandparents) together are important occasions. They should be scheduled at times that will allow as many families as possible to attend. Showing awareness and sensitivity toward single parents and their children means that care will be taken to make these *family* events rather than events for specific parent-child pairs (Dad-Son, Mother-Daughter) and they will be held at times other than normal working hours, such as early in the morning, in the evening, or on weekends.

Field trips as well as plays and musical performances by the children are other events that parents are generally invited to attend. Single parents usually cannot take time from work to go on field trips, but they would like to be asked anyway.[8] If it is possible for plays and skits to be given in the evening, more parents could attend. There are so many two-parent families in which both parents work, that accommodating single parents automatically favors *all* working parents as well.

Attitude and Language

Attitude problems have to do with patronizing sympathy ("poor little thing") or being judgmental of the mother. In order to survive while getting their own as well as their children's needs met, single mothers must make many choices and decisions even *they* would prefer not having to make. We must have respect for the effort they make and try not to judge. This may be difficult in the case of a parent who continues to be embroiled in hostilities with the ex-mate that have a deleterious effect on the children. I think it is unwise to sit in silent judgment; instead, confront such a mother with an I-statement: "I can see you are bitter and hurt by the action of your ex-spouse, but I believe what you are doing is harmful to Jamie."

Nearly half of the parents answering the NCCE questionnaire indicatd that whenever their child had a problem, the school believed it was related to being from a single-parent home.[9] It is natural that parents would feel sensitive about this kind of bias. It is never wise to act as if we know the basis of a problem unless a diagnostic study has informed us, or unless believable statements from a child indicate the cause. On the other hand, we do know that children struggle with emotional dilemmas created by divorce for many years to come, and they also have difficulties that a parent may not wish to have pointed out relative to the changed structure and status of the family. It is, however, an oversimplification to say that the complex nature of children's post-divorce problems are the result of single parenting.

We must also remember that children who have grown up knowing only one parent are not in the same emotional quagmire as children whose parents divorce after many years of living as a two-parent family. For these children it is probably *always* incorrect to assume that problems relate to being in a one-parent family.

The term "broken home" is negative and offensive, and does not even describe the significant proportion of one-parent families where the mother has never married. This term and other similar ones seem to connote pathology, unhealthiness, or lack of normalcy and should therefore be avoided. Because we all have a tendency to slip into using negative stereotypes at times, administrative memos to remind us not to use these terms are helpful. Also, if friends and colleagues bring our "slips" to our attention, we may quickly get out of the habit of using these terms entirely.[10]

Services Needed by Single-Parent Families

Nearly two-thirds of the single parents surveyed feel that the school should provide before- and after-school child care. (See Chapter 1.) An overwhelming majority (87.5 percent) of the parents surveyed also expressed a wish for their children to have access to group counseling at school, to help them deal with the issues of divorce and death.[11] This is obviously a green light for those schools that have thought about offering counseling groups but have been ambivalent about proceeding. Follow the guidelines given in Chapter 7.

It is important to remember that these families have very limited time, money, and other resources. If their children are to be able to participate in intermural sports or other events not held at school, transportation and underwriting may be needed for the costs of the activity and the equipment that are required. When the school provides a special fund for this and sponsors car pooling, these families can accept help without losing their dignity.

SCHOOL COUNSELING WITH DIVORCED PARENTS

Many women and men need counseling help to successfully deal with the many adjustments necessary in divorce. We can be helpful in referring them to the appropriate resources or services. The direct involvement of the school counselor with the divorcing parent must generally be limited to those issues that affect the children. The following are areas where it is appropriate for the school social worker or counselor to offer guidance.

Economic Issues: Child Support

In 1981, fifty-three percent of women who had been awarded support by the court did not receive the full amount from the fathers of their children, and twenty-eight percent received no money at all. Is it any wonder so many divorce families are economically strapped?

A federal law was passed in 1985 that aims to remedy the situation regarding support payments. It provides for income withholding by the father's employer if he reneges on support payments. To qualify, a mother must have a support order, and it must be registered with her state's child support agency. Mothers should immediately file for income withholding when the father is one month behind. For mothers who continue to have difficulty, recommend that they contact one of the following organizations. When writing to either of the first two organizations, a stamped, self-addressed legal size envelope should be enclosed:[12]

The Children's Foundation
Child Support Enforcement Program
815-15th Street, N.W. Suite 928
Washington, D.C. 20005

The Organization for the Enforcement
of Child Support
119 Nicodemus Road
Reisterstown, MD 21136

Federal Office of Child Support Enforcement
Department 36
Pueblo, CO 81009

It is always appropriate to direct needy unmarried mothers and others without a financial support order to sources of economic help. Young unmarried mothers who had previously been living with parents may not know how to negotiate the welfare system, or may feel too proud to use this source of support. Counseling directed at improving a family's economic and living situations is always clearly indicated.

Organizing the Family

Women who are having trouble managing their daily lives may need help in setting priorities, learning to balance needs and resources, assigning chores and holding children accountable for performing them, and in understanding and managing children's behavioral responses to the divorce. Increased tardiness and absences, children without lunches, and children whose grooming has deteriorated are indicators that their mother needs help to organize the family and get a structure established that will allow the children to meet their school obligations and expectations. Offering counseling to achieve these goals is an indirect service to the children.

Keeping Communication Open

Following divorce, parents as well as children must mourn their losses. As they pull into themselves in their depression, it is all too easy for emotional distance to develop and for communication to break down. Mothers may need to be told to set aside special times to do something mutually enjoyable with their children, and to form new habits of communicating. Phone contact becomes important if the mother is working for the first time. Instruct such a mother to establish a regular time to call her children, and to set rules for the children about calling her.

Written messages are another way to keep in contact that may not have been used before. Notes are particularly helpful in remedying hurts because apologizing is harder to do orally; and they serve as reminders for chores that haven't been done, thereby avoiding defensiveness. They are also very useful for giving compliments and telling the child that the parent is pleased. Children may want to give a parent a message through a drawing or poem, and a parent who sends a message in this form will be adding variety and novelty and conveying that extra effort has gone into communicating with the child.

The use of a tape recorder is another new way to communicate and is particularly appropriate when a mother or father must be away from home overnight or longer. Hearing his or her mother's or father's voice during separations can be very reassuring to the child. For long absences of a week or longer, tape recordings can be sent home telling about the trip, describing where the mother or father is, what is going on, and so on. This should be used in addition to phone contact, which is more likely to involve listening to the children or giving them directions.

When we are thinking about keeping communication open, it is so easy to forget that there are other ways to communicate besides talking and listening. There is time for reflecting about our emotional reactivity when we send and receive notes. So writing and reading, the less-used forms of communication, are especially valuable when tension exists in relationships.

Defusing Hostile Games with Noncustodial Fathers or Mothers

Not only is it important to keep the noncustodial father or mother actively involved with the children, it is also imperative that hostile interactions that have become chronic "games" be identified and defused. We often know about these destructive processes through a child's disclosures at school, and the custodial parent is also apt to ventilate feelings about them. Point out in a matter-of-fact manner the harmful effect for the child, and suggest alternative ways to deal with situations. Custodial mothers can be advised not to probe their children about visits with fathers and not to make the children ask fathers for things their mothers want them to have. Custodial fathers can be coached about how to negotiate with their ex-spouses in ways that are assertive rather than aggressive. They should be told that their children will have the best chance for resolving all the tasks divorce imposes if they can have a close relationship with mother as well as father— separate relationships that do not make the children feel disloyal to one or the other.

Ask parents to buy and read *Mom's House, Dad's House: Making Shared Custody Work* by Isolene Ricci (New York: Collier Books, a division of MacMillan, 1982). This inexpensive paperback is a practical guide for parents that covers the issues that commonly perpetuate hostilities between parents. If parents can follow the author's advice, children have a good chance of adjusting well.

The Issue of Kidnapping

It is illegal to keep a child from talking to or going with a noncustodial parent unless you have a court restraining order. However, kidnapping by the noncustodial parent is a very real threat to many families, and some tragic consequences of parental kidnapping have been reported. Mothers who fear that a child may be kidnapped by fathers should be advised to have a copy of their custody papers on file at school. The police cannot take any action to find and return a child taken by the noncustodial parent until they verify who has legal custody. Time will be saved and immediate action possible if the school has a copy of the legal papers.

When a mother has alerted the school to the possibility of kidnapping, extra care should be taken in regard to the child's whereabouts. A mother should be called immediately if the child fails to arrive or return to school after being with his or her father.

Figure 8-1 offers a checklist/information sheet that custodial parents might be given to help them deal with the issue of kidnapping.

Each principal should have a copy of *Protect Your Child* by Laura M. Huchton (Englewood Cliffs, New Jersey: Prentice-Hall, 1985) on his or her bookshelf, for immediate reference in the event that a kidnapping does occur. The book has all kinds of useful information, including steps that parents should take, organizations to contact for help, and so on.

Time Off from Parenting

Single parents need time for themselves and opportunities to enjoy adult relationships, but it is not always easy to arrange time off from parenting, especially if the noncustodial parent cannot be counted on to take the children for a day or weekend. In this case, the custodial parent can arrange a respite from parenting by exchanging live-in overnights with other single parents. For example, Judy has Sharon's children for the weekend, then Sharon reciprocates by taking care of Judy's children for an equivalent amount of time. As simple and logical as this kind of arrangement seems, some parents will need encouragement and help to enter into relationships that allow such

KIDNAPPING PREVENTION CHECKLIST
FOR CUSTODIAL PARENT

Child's name _____

Date of birth _____   Sex _____

Hair color _____   Eye color _____

A. Assemble a personal file for each child that contains:

_____ recent photographs with child's height and weight on back

_____ fingerprints

_____ dental and medical records

B. Keep this checklist in the child's file:

PHYSICAL DESCRIPTION

_____

_____

_____

_____

_____

ANY SCARS AND/OR BIRTHMARKS (INCLUDE PHOTOGRAPHS)

_____

_____

_____

_____

HABITS, SPECIAL EXPRESSIONS, NICKNAMES OF FAMILY
MEMBERS, AND SO ON

_____

_____

_____

_____

STRONG INTERESTS, LIKES, AND DISLIKES

_____

_____

_____

_____

C. During a perceived "danger period" (expressed threat of intent to
kidnap by ex-spouse), be aware of what clothes the child wears each
day.

Figure 8-1

exchanging of children and sharing of parenting. Shy women, as well
as those who are reluctant to "impose" on others and who have an
ingrained belief that they should be able to manage without asking for
help, must overcome the tendency to neglect their own needs. This is
why it is so important for them to join groups and to avoid becoming
isolates.

A FINAL WORD

We are bound to disapprove of the ways some single parents go
about getting their needs met. I am thinking of parents who stay out all
night without informing their children, those who have live-in lovers,
those who take their children to bars or leave young ones alone at night.
We face the dilemma of not wanting to lose rapport with the single

parent by blatantly criticizing, but at the same time trying to be an advocate for the children. I think we will be less inclined to judge these people harshly if we view them as being unable to consider their own needs and those of the children simultaneously.

Our task is to try to help them become aware of the potential harm to their children when they are taking unwise risks in attempting to satisfy their own needs. The technique of asking questions to help them see the impact of their behavior on the children is far preferable to *telling* them, because the latter is always felt as criticism, and often also perceived as rejection. One approach is to ask such questions as "Have you thought about (or considered) what the children think or feel about that?" Making an I-statement followed by a question is another, such as "I've heard that live-in boyfriends often abuse a woman's children. Do you think that might happen in your situation?"

It is natural that single parents will ultimately want to begin dating. This is a transition that is frequently not handled well by either divorced parents or the children. When children share upset feelings about this with us, we can help most by encouraging a dialogue between them and their parents.

Endnotes

1. 1984 U.S. Census Bureau statistics (quoted from "Playing Both Mother and Father," *Newsweek* Magazine, July 15, 1985).
2. Phyllis L. Clay, *Single Parents and the Public Schools: How Does the Partnership Work?* (Columbia, MD: National Committee for Citizens in Education, 1981).
3. Isolina Ricci, *Mom's House, Dad's House: Making Shared Custody Work* (New York: Collier Books, division of Macmillan, 1980), p. 248.
4. Clay, p. 32.
5. Ibid,. p. 32.
6. Ibid., pp. 40-41.
7. Ibid., p. 51.
8. Ibid., p. 31.
9. Ibid., p. 50.
10. Ibid., p. 55.
11. Ibid., p. 42.
12. Jeannie Ralston, "Child Support: Getting Tough with Fathers Who Don't Pay," *McCalls Magazine*, February 1985, pp. 69-70.

PART IV

CRISIS IMPOSED BY DEATH

The death of a parent or sibling causes a crisis for a child. Student suicides, murder, and tragic accidents that occur either in school, or near school property create a crisis for a school system. Children will be traumatized, and adults will be upset unless they receive the cognitive and emotional help they need to master the anxiety, guilt, and fear aroused by the event.

Until recently, nearly everyone was conditioned to avoid talking about death with children, to ignore children's interest in the subject, to "protect" children by not having them participate in death rituals, and to shield them from witnessing expressions of grief by their elders. It is a sign of progress that these attitudes and practices have been challenged, and the need to deal openly with children about death has been acknowledged.

The chapters in this section are aimed at helping you understand your own reactions to death, know what to consider, and know what actions to take when a death (or threatened death) affects one or more members of the school community.

Chapter 9

Helping Children Cope with Death

I recently visited the director of a hospice in a small city. (*Hospice* is a program that helps a terminally ill person live at home as fully and comfortably as possible until death intervenes.) During my conversation with the hospice director, I asked about the relationship between the program and the community schools. I was startled by her response. She perceived teachers as being ignorant about the impact of death on children, insensitive to their grieving, and afraid to talk about death. Teachers, she felt, ignored the subject whenever possible, doing little or nothing to educate about death or to help a child or family handle bereavement.

DEATH ANXIETY IN ADULTS

My own view differs. I see adults as having a fairly high degree of "death anxiety" that causes discomfort in dealing with the subject. Few teachers are prepared for the emotional reactivity the subject can arouse, in themselves and in their students. The first step in teaching about death or being prepared to help a bereaved child is to become aware of how we defend ourselves against death anxiety.

Becoming Aware of Death Anxiety

Death is an emotional event of high intensity. Just hearing about the death of a child or of an adult in the prime of life makes most of us feel anxious, even if we are not close to the deceased. Because death anxiety is so pervasive and creates so much bodily and emotional discomfort, we look for ways to bind the anxiety. In the past, we have avoided the subject and denied the need to talk about death or share feelings experienced during the grieving period. We have tried to hide our tears, and have worried in silence about the "crazy" thoughts, feelings, and perceptions that occur during bereavement. Now that we know the cost, in terms of physical and mental health, of these repressive/suppressive psychological defenses, the attempt is being made to confront death openly and honestly. However, this is easier said than done.

Earl Grollman, who has written and taught about death quite extensively, says that we have been so strongly conditioned *not* to say the words *dead, die,* and *died,* that in order to deal with death more openly, we must first get used to hearing ourselves say these words. In his workshop, Grollman asks the audience to say the words aloud, as a group, many times over. It is an unusual experience, but it helps us realize that indeed we are quite inhibited about saying *dead, die,* and *died.* Avoiding the use of euphemisms is particularly important in talking about death with children; using explicit words seems to become easier as death anxiety is mastered.

Mastering Death Anxiety

Reading books and articles, attending workshops and courses, and watching movies and television shows about death all give us opportunities to identify with characters experiencing anticipatory grief and bereavement. Learning about the emotional reconstitution that friends experience in bereavement groups, becoming volunteers in the hospice movement,* and reaching out to others who have had a loved one die are other ways to become more comfortable in the face of death. These are all part of the process through which we master death anxiety. The process involves becoming aware of the intensity of feeling aroused when discussing death and dying, along with the bodily manifestations of anxiety; it also includes recognizing what mechanisms we use to ease our own discomfort.

We must also recognize that discussions of death, as well as actual occurrences of death, are likely to stimulate memories of our own dead loved ones, and to evoke the sensory and physical reactions we experienced at the time of death. This may be painful, but by such recapitulation we are better prepared to appreciate what a bereaved

---

*Support, education and counseling are provided to the dying person and his or her family. During the year following the death, bereavement counseling, support groups and arts therapy help adult and child survivors cope constructively with the emotional upheaval and grief that the death of a loved one produces.

child is going through. Those who have successfully grieved in the past will not be seriously troubled by briefly reexperiencing old feelings of pain. If the death of a student, his or her sibling or parent, or that of a friend or colleague causes you to become depressed, to have somatic difficulties, disturbed sleep, or problems in interpersonal relationships that do not lessen within a short time, it may be that you have not completed healthy mourning of past losses. It is difficult for you to help others through their grief when your own conflicts and anger about past losses become reactivated.

DEATH ANXIETY IN CHILDREN

Children's understanding of death, like other abstract concepts, develops in a gradual, orderly fashion that parallels general cognitive development. This means that we need to have a cognitive stage framework, rather than age, as the basis for understanding children's responses to death. Another phenomenon is relevant: Under stress, children may regress in their thinking to a less logical level of reasoning. It has been shown that children can simultaneously hold both magical and scientific views of illness and death. It should not surprise us, then, if an older child asks questions, makes comments, or behaves in a manner that we would usually attribute to a child several years younger, when placed in a death context.

Developmental texts describing children's thoughts, ideas, and behavioral responses about death do not mention death anxiety as existing before ages five or six. Perhaps this is because it does not become clearly manifest until school age. I suggest that death anxiety is an inherent aspect of learning about death, no matter how limited a child's understanding of death is. Preschool children incorporate death themes in their play on a regular basis. Through their play, they attempt to gain greater understanding of death, but this play also serves as a way to deal with the implicit anxiety associated with their growing knowledge.

Children who are seriously ill understand death at much earlier ages than normal children because of the many unusual experiences accompanying their illness, including the discovery that children who are seriously ill actually die. When chronically ill children are dying, they are always aware of their own impending death (even as early as age two), and they develop strategies to handle the associated anxiety.[1]

Young children believe that dead people have only temporarily departed, and expect them to return. This is at once evidence of their limited understanding of death, but also reflects their experience. Their mothers and fathers leave and return, and in playing games, children hide and are found, disappear and reappear. Their games and experiences with separation serve to "bind" their anxiety. This means the anxiety is not manifest as long as the children feel secure that those on whom they depend will be there for them, even if they leave for a while. Children who do not have this kind of security manifest anxiety, based in the primitive fear of abandonment (fear of the loss of someone to take care of them).

Children's Normal Responses to Death Anxiety

Even when young children know that a dead person will not return, they think of him or her as still needing to be fed, clothed, comforted, and kept warm because these are their own needs and they are not yet able to view things from another's perspective. At this stage, children usually believe that only old people die, not children. They can thus worry that their parents will die if they view them as old, but are protected from fearing their own death. Seriously ill children are not so protected because they do their own detective work, and find out about their chances of living or dying. However, most do not become overwhelmed by death anxiety because they construct their own psychological defenses and hold fast to even the slimmest glimmer of hope.

As children come to believe that death is permanent, they begin to manifest considerable anxiety about it. For a majority of children this happens in the six- to- seven-year range, and may explain why separation anxiety peaks in first and second graders, when it had seemingly been conquered by age three or four. When my youngest son was in first grade, he suddenly started clinging to me when I tucked him in at night, and would get up many times before falling asleep. When I asked him for an explanation he said, "I'm afraid you're going to die." When I wondered aloud what on earth could make him think that, he said, "Because you're old (my hair had turned prematurely white) and people who are old die." After his anxiety was verbalized, I could readily reassure him that I was not old, was in excellent health, and was not going to die.

Emerging from thinking that death can only happen to old people, children begin to understand that they also can die. This insight is accompanied by an almost obsessive interest in death that possibly reflects an attempt at mastery through information and cognitive understanding. However, as understanding increases, so also does anxiety, and more elaborate means of managing the anxiety are developed.

1. Preadolescents use the counter-phobic device of joking about death and making fun of it. They mock death through the creation of jokes, poems, and macabre ghost stories at which they laugh up-roariously. They take pleasure in scaring younger children with such stories, and laugh at the innocence of the young when they believe the stories.

2. More serious children who have moral objections to joking about death, or who have been firmly reprimanded for this kind of behavior, make up stories about encounters with death wherein the characters miraculously thwart death, expressing these in writing at school, during play, or in talk.

3. Adolescents continue to joke and make fun of death, but also develop a "defiance of death" kind of stance. Risk-taking challenges of one adolescent to another become common, as they test out their courage to stand on their own in a world filled with danger. Those who manifest the most extreme form of risk-taking may have an underlying suicidal impulse, or may be extremely anxious that they will die. These adolescents seem to be either inviting death or warding off intense fears by their unusual degree of daring.

Several conclusions may be drawn from reflecting on children's death anxiety. The most obvious is that any death curriculum must take into account, and be prepared to incorporate, the idea that the subject matter produces anxiety. Almost any kind of inexplicable behavior that develops in any activity related to death may be an expression of anxiety. An eighth-grade teacher wrote about behavioral reactions she observed in students after they had attended the funeral of a classmate who had died in a house fire. A boy who had cried at the funeral subsequently stole a dollar from a memorial fund being collected; the other students reacted verbally by threatening to kill him or registering angry disgust. Students also expressed disgust toward each other by claiming that attendance at the funeral was out of curiosity rather than out of friendship for the dead girl.[2] Unless children's unseemly or callow, unfeeling behaviors following a death are viewed as death anxiety (which these youngsters don't know how to handle in any other way), adults will interpret the behaviors as cruel, uncaring, and obscene, and judge the children harshly at a time when they most need support and understanding.

DEATH AND THE SCHOOL

One child out of twenty will lose a parent during childhood, and others will experience the death of a sibling through accident, illness, suicide or murder.* Murder is exceedingly traumatic when it occurs in the school, on the streets where children walk to school, and in places where children gather, such as at fast food restaurants.

Each year, it is probable that the children, parents, and professional staff of some schools will witness or be affected by a violent death. We can no longer be sure "it won't happen here" because if it is not murder, it may be a bizarre accident or sudden, unexpected death in school, on school property, or involving a school bus.

- In a Boston high school, a student took a gun from a paper bag and killed himself in front of his classmates.
- In a Detroit first-grade classroom, an estranged husband killed his wife, the teacher, as the class watched in horror.
- In Los Angeles, a gunman shot randomly at a crowded school playground and several children were slain.
- In a Chicago suburb, a five-year-old kindergarten student who had disembarked from a school bus was crushed under its wheels when he unexpectedly darted back to retrieve something he had dropped.

All the children who witnessed these deaths were affected by them, as were their families and teachers. It can happen anywhere.

DEATH: A FINAL AND PERMANENT SEPARATION

Death, whether one's own or a friend's, a parent's, or a sibling's, is a separation that is final and permanent; there can be no realistic hope of reunion with the loved one. In contrast to other separations, it is further complicated by its mystery and varying beliefs about what happens after death.

Because the issues are not the same with all deaths, the following sections will deal with the dying child, the death of a parent, the death of a sibling, and violent death that children witness.

---

*Murder has become a "deadly epidemic" in the United States and is being studied as a public health issue because other approaches to stemming its spread have failed.[3]

Children Facing Their Own Death

It seems that each generation is plagued by one or more deadly diseases that strike children. As one deadly disease is conquered, another comes along to take its place. Even when there are successful treatments for a disease, there are still so many hazards connected with chronic illness that the threat of death cannot be eliminated. Chemotherapeutic agents lower resistance and make a child susceptible to infections for which the disease-fighting mechanisms have been rendered ineffective, either by the primary illness or by the side effects of treatments. Death may thus be caused by a secondary infection rather than by the primary illness.

Currently, children with hemophilia present an example of the continuing threat to a chronically ill child after effective and readily available treatments have been developed. As we all know, many hemophiliacs have contracted AIDS through contaminated blood products. Acquired Immune Deficiency Syndrome (AIDS) is a new disease that is always fatal.

Phobic Hysteria About Fatal Illness. Whether it is cancer, AIDS, or some other as yet unheard of disease, people tend to develop a phobia about fatal illnesses; they fear it will happen to them or their children. This phobia causes a kind of hysteria that makes people want to stay away from anyone who has the illness. Even when we have a scientific explanation of an illness and know that it is not contagious, our fears make us act as if the illness can be caught. Most people are past the phobic stage regarding children with cancer, but phobic hysteria has been reactivated by AIDS. However, it is important for seriously ill children to attend school in order to have as normal a life as possible.

There is evidence that AIDS is not transmitted by casual contact; siblings of children who have the disease have not contracted it,[4] and in a boarding school in France for sick and handicapped students, where twenty-five hemophiliacs have AIDS, no one else has developed it after three years of living together.[5] In both instances, children had more intimate contact with each other than did children in public school.

There is no doubt that phobic hysteria has an impact on the child with the illness who attends school, and some parents will choose to have their children remain at home rather than subject them to harassment and rejection. Until this hysteria abates, the Centers for Disease Control recommends that only school staff who need to know should be told that a child has AIDS.[6] This is contrary to recommended policy for dealing with chronically ill children in general; in this case, all school staff should know which children have serious conditions so that everyone can be sensitive to their special needs.

Chronically ill children need special understanding and support, which I have written about in detail in my book *Helping Chronically Ill Children in School: A Practical Guide for Teachers, Counselors, and Administrators* (West Nyack, New York: Parker Publishing Company, 1985). Most chronically ill children do not die, but for those who do, classmates will be affected. The death of a classmate may be the first grief experience involving human death for many of the children. (The death of a pet is a common early grief experience.)

The Dying Child in the Classroom. Dealing with the death of a child who has been ill over an extended period of time begins with sensitive response to the child from the time he or she enters the class, and includes continued involvement with the child during the periods when he or she is hospitalized or too ill at home to attend school. Teachers will want to establish a special relationship with the family because both the parents and the child will need to be consulted on matters pertaining to what the class should be told at different points in time. The teachers of the child's siblings will also need to be helped to understand the situation. This will spare the family from having to tell their story to several teachers if the ill child's teacher takes the role of a liaison with the other involved teachers.

If at all uncertain about what to do or how to handle questions that may arise about a seriously ill child, ask a medical person who is involved in the child's care to come to school to talk to the staff. This need not be the child's primary doctor; a nurse or resident physician may better be able to spare the time to come. The child's mother will probably be able to tell you whom to contact, as she will be well acquainted with hospital and clinic nurses and doctors.

Keeping in Contact. When a child is hospitalized or at home for lengthy periods, keep in contact through phone calls and cards, and visits if possible. Tell the class how to act when visiting a sick person, and encourage those who are friends of the ill child to visit him or her. When you are making a planned visit, take one or two classmates along if the child is not too ill to have this much company, and if such a visit is welcomed by the child and family. Always make appointments for visits before going, and if the ill child does not feel like having company, tell the class how important it is to respect such feelings. You can bring the point home by asking them how they feel about having company when they are sick.

Before a child's return to school, consult with him or her and the parents about what they want the class to know. If there are changes in the child's appearance, personality, physical energy level, or in what he or she is allowed to do, the class will need to be prepared. Ask for a picture to show the class if there are dramatic changes in appearance. This will avoid having the child witness shocked reactions from the class. Others in the school, as well as the child's class, will need to be made aware if the child is to return in a wheelchair, on crutches with an amputation, wearing a hat or wig because of baldness, and so on. Ill children who are changed in these ways are extremely fearful of being teased or made fun of, often to the point of begging to be allowed to stay home. The affected child should participate in planning for his return to school and in how the people he will encounter there are being prepared for his altered appearance or condition.

Classmates' Responses to Impending Death. Children will notice the changes in the ill classmate whose condition becomes terminal, and will suspect that he or she might be dying. If the class has been properly conditioned they will not ask, "Is he or she going to die?" in the child's presence. Still, you must anticipate that such a question will be in some of the children's minds, and sooner or later someone will ask it. Be prepared to answer honestly, and be ready to accept and comfort when the children react. The children's reactions will be extremely varied; some will cry, some will fight, some will withdraw into silence, and someone may even laugh. Remember that children have had few experiences with extreme sadness, and that death anxiety is also an aspect of their response. Do not label responses to death as inappropriate, no matter how unusual or unexpected they may seem.

Some activities to help students cope with grief are suggested here.

1. When a student dies, do not expect to pursue the usual lesson plan for the day. Instead, provide a chance for the children to talk about the classmate; to ask questions and receive honest answers; to talk about death; and to discover an outlet for saying goodbye.

2. Writing in a personal journal or diary, or writing a poem or letter to the deceased provides an opportunity to express feelings and confront conflicts that the death precipitates, as well as providing a means of saying goodbye.

3. Feelings and expressions can also be channeled into sympathy notes to the family.

Some of the class may want to attend the funeral, and they may need instruction in what is proper behavior for such an occasion. They may want no one to be assigned to take the dead child's desk or locker, wanting to maintain those spaces to symbolize their classmate's continued presence. This desire should be respected in all cases. However, the child's possessions should be removed and given to the family. Small but significant details, such as removing the child's name from enrollment lists and other rosters, must also be attended to.

Questions That Need Answering. Ask the mother or father of a child who has died from a lingering illness if either one wishes to visit the class to talk with the children. Some parents will not want to do this, but mothers who have accepted such an invitation say it helps them to believe they did everything possible to show caring for their child. Having a chance to talk with the parent brings classmates into more intimate connection with the death and facilitates healthy mourning.

One question that children find hard to ask is whether they somehow caused their friend's death through their actions, thoughts, or feelings, and whether they will be punished for this. They also wonder whether they might get the illness and die. If these questions aren't asked, the teacher or counselor must mention that these are the things children usually wonder about at times like this, and a discussion should then follow to clarify facts about the death, and reassure the children that they are not to blame, won't be punished, and won't die from the disease.

The Dying Child and His Family. It is normal for parents to maintain hope until the very end. Denying that death is imminent is an important defense, and does not mean the parent is not coping. In fact, that parent will be simultaneously engaged in anticipatory grieving, a process that allows a parent to relinquish, a little at a time, some of the emotional attachment to the child so that the final parting is not so painful.

Although all children become aware of the fact that they are dying, they may want verification of the fact so they can have final wishes granted. For the most part, however, they are like their parents and strive to maintain hope; denial of their impending death is part of their psychological armor.

Dying children have two main concerns: pain and separation. They need to be told that dying itself does not hurt, and that everything possible will be done to keep them from having pain. They also need to be promised that someone will be with them when they die so that they will not be alone.[7]

Open Awareness and Mutual Pretense. Dying is an intimate matter, and the family's way of carrying this out must be respected. Some families practice *open awareness,* while others practice *mutual pretense,* and both practices have their merits. In open awareness,

eath and dying can be discussed.
nd, is a ritual in which the child and
iat the child will live, even when they
An elaborate set of rules, implicit in
ed by both the parents and the child.
its from overwhelming sadness that
between him and them, and the child
n with him as long as they don't have

Hospital? Families increasingly have
al care for a terminally ill child. At a
r where this choice is offered, eighty
iselves of the Home Care Program. A
oning of families following a child's
ere in the Home Care Program had
s whose child died in the hospital. The
parents opting for home care was
s of helplessness, including a greater
iild's terminal care. Home care also
inity for family intimacy and com-

ose home care probably sense their inability to cope with the responsibility, anxiety, and effort involved, and should not be judged for the decision they make. It is equally important to know that home care is not harmful to well siblings; rather, siblings will probably follow a more healthy pattern of grieving when terminal care is provided at home.

When a Child's Parent Dies

Grief is most intense when a strong attachment exists between the deceased and the survivor. Thus, the death of a parent will be the most deeply mourned kind of loss a child ever experiences. Later problems will result if the child fails to have a successful mourning experience, or if he or she suffers significant deprivations as a consequence of the loss. How a child copes with the death of a parent depends to a great extent on how well the adults who care for the child give support as the child struggles to come to terms with grief.[10]

The first steps to take in helping a bereaved child are:

1. Give sound advice to the surviving parent.
2. Make sure the bereaved parent is meeting the child's needs and grieving in a healthy manner.

Guiding the Surviving Parent. In guiding a surviving parent, proceed with the steps outlined in Figure 9-1, adapting them as needed depending on when you meet with the parent. For example, if the funeral has already taken place, ask "Did the children participate? How did they do?"

What Children Need to Know. Either before the death (when a parent is dying from an illness) or immediately after (when a parent dies suddenly and unexpectedly), a child needs to be told:

1. that he or she will be cared for
2. that he or she won't die of the same disease
3. that he or she wasn't responsible for the death
4. that he or she won't die when he or she is the same age as the parent who died

Without the sense of security produced by being reassured about his or her own survival, a child cannot begin to grieve. The surviving parent needs to tell the children that he or she (the parent) is healthy and well, and expects to live a very long time. Honest information

---

STEPS FOR GUIDING THE SURVIVING PARENT

1. Encourage the family to involve the children in the funeral and other rituals. It is important that children not feel pushed aside or ignored; even the youngest need to share in the expression of sadness.

2. Advise the parent not to go away on an extended trip without the children and not to send the children to stay with relatives (except for brief visits) if this can possibly be avoided. Separation anxiety in the children will be severe, and the family needs to stay together for a sense of security and to comfort one another.

3. Discuss the benefits to be derived from a bereavement group, and encourage participation.

4. Reassure the parent that it is all right for the children to stay home from school for a period of time. Ask how you can be helpful. Mention that you will be available to help the child catch up on missed work and that the child is not to worry about this.

5. Ask whether the information about the death has been given to the children; if not, indicate how important it is for children to be told these things.

Figure 9-1

about the cause of death, and the remaining parent's beliefs (if any) about an afterlife should also be discussed.[11]

When a parent's death is the result of suicide, this fact is often concealed because enormous anger, guilt, and shame are commonly experienced by the surviving spouse. However, no exception should be made to the rule of telling children the truth. Crisis intervention services, available in most communities, should be used after this kind of death because it poses special problems for the family.

What the Teacher Should Do. When you know that a student's parent has a terminal illness, begin to build a sympathetic/helping relationship with the student well in advance of the expected death. Arrange a private conference with the student and invite him or her to talk about the situation:

- "I know that your mother has been very ill. This must be a difficult time for you. I imagine you have many questions and concerns. Are you able to talk about these with your family?"
- "How is your Dad doing?"
- "Who's getting the meals prepared?"
- "Who's taking care of your little brother or sister?"

Be gentle, and take care not to be too intrusive. Your goal may be to evaluate how well the child is coping, but if he or she doesn't reveal information spontaneously, simply offer comfort and indicate your availability should the child want to talk about it later.

You can make an educated guess, based on what you learn from conversations with the child or the healthy parent, as to whether the family is practicing mutual pretense or open awareness about the impending death. If mutual pretense is being practiced, you should not initiate a discussion about the expected death with the child or healthy parent. However, you may respond frankly and honestly if either the parent or child initiates such a discussion. When a parent is open about the situation, it is possible to offer anticipatory guidance as previously discussed.

Preparing the Class. When a child's parent dies, the class should be told, but the whole school does not have to know. If the bereaved student is old enough and willing to talk with you, consult him or her about what the class should be told. Bereaved children are sensitive about returning to school; they often feel themselves to be different because they are experiencing something others have not experienced, but they do not want to be treated differently. They do not usually want to talk about their bereavement with a peer unless the peer has also lost a parent. They may seek out such a peer, even if there has not previously been much of a relationship between them.

Bereaved children say that they want their friends to talk and laugh with them and invite them to play games as if nothing happened. They may not be able to participate fully, or even at all, but they want others to keep asking them to do the usual, normal things.[12]

Before a bereaved child returns to school (an absence of one to two weeks should be expected), plan a lesson on death to sensitize the class to the feelings a parent's death might produce in a child. *How It Feels When a Parent Dies,* by Jill Krementz (New York: Alfred A. Knopf, 1981) is an excellent resource book for such a discussion. The book gives eighteen children's own accounts of what they experienced when a mother or father died, from either illness, accident, or suicide. What is striking about the narratives is that they validate what is generally known about children's fears and insecurities following parental death; but they also reveal how unique children are in the ways they come to terms with their grief. The implicit message is that we must not have stereotypes about grieving in children.

It would seem that children grieve in spurts, probably because they cannot tolerate long sustained periods of sadness and do not like friends to see them cry. Their mourning may last for years, longer than the mourning of the surviving parent. They may or may not experience anger, and may or may not want to visit the cemetery. They cherish memories of the dead parent, but do not always like to hear adults reminisce about their deceased parent.[13]

Death of a Sibling

The tragedy of sibling death is that parents are so shocked and guilt ridden when the death is a suicide or accident, and so emotionally depleted if the death follows a long illness, that they are frequently unable to offer support and understanding to their remaining children. Children need the same kind of reassurance and involvement in the family grieving that has been previously outlined for death of a parent. They may also be in greater need of psychological assistance.

For a number of reasons, children are at high risk for developing emotional and learning problems following the death of a sibling. Because of identification processes, they are afraid that the same thing will happen to them, particularly when they reach the same age when the sibling died. They are also prone to develop the idea that they don't deserve to be alive. They develop death phobias, show irrational anger towards doctors, and become fearful of hospitals.

Identity Problems. Surviving siblings also experience identity confusions, tending to either overidentify with the dead sibling's traits, or to reject aspects of the self that resemble those of the brother or sister. Identity problems stem from inner conflicts, but can be exacerbated by parental expectations that the sibling "replace" the brother or sister by becoming just like him or her.[14]

Mourning the loss of a sibling is thus complicated not only by the intense parental bereavement, but also by the parental fears and expectations that are projected onto the surviving siblings. Be persistent in recommending bereavement counseling for the parents. For the surviving sibling, art therapy at school or elsewhere is a way to open up communication that can help to resolve identity issues. If there are several siblings, plan to see them together.

Need for Professional Help. Children who are not mourning successfully will show it in their words and actions. The symptoms may first appear well after the death occurred (as much as several years), or begin following the death and persist without a sign of letting up even after a year has elapsed. The following are clues that professional help is needed:

1. denial of the death

2. distortion of the reality surrounding the death

3. persistent regressed behavior and/or school failure

4. persistent fears

5. persistent acting out

Sudden, Unexpected Death. Sometimes a sudden, unexpected death of a parent or sibling occurs while the child is in school. When the teacher, principal, or counselor must tell a child such tragic news, it is important to do so as soon as the news is received. If there are several siblings, bring them together in a private place and tell them simply and directly what has happened; then *stay with them.* The children will protest by expressing disbelief of what is being said, and at the same time may experience a physical reaction such as feeling cold and weak, or feeling as if they had received a crushing blow to the chest. The emotional shock makes the children susceptible to physical shock no matter how much they protest verbally, so have blankets or warm coats to offer. Comfort them in ways appropriate to the children's ages and your relationship to them. Physical contact may be welcomed by younger children, but resisted by older ones. Give the children permission to cry or scream, and allow them to hide themselves in the blankets if they wish. Be sure someone they are familiar with takes them home.[15]

When Children Witness Violent Death

Interpersonal violence in America is out of control. Between 1960 and 1980, the murder rate doubled, rapes quadrupled, and suicides or attempts by parents of school-aged children showed a marked acceleration. Child abuse has become a national scandal, and many believe this is not simply the result of increased reporting, but rather reflects a dramatic increase in the incidence of child abuse. There is growing concern that it is not only children who themselves are the object of violence, but also those who *witness* violence who grow up to act out violently.[16]

Studies of children who have witnessed violence indicate that they suffer from *post-traumatic stress disorder,* which produces symptoms that interfere with learning and social-emotional development. If these children are not helped to get over the trauma, they may suffer permanent personality change that has an impact on their adult adjustment. Reenactment of the violent scene in their talk, drawings, writing, and play, as well as in their dreams, is a typical response to the event. Fears of a recurrence, and intrusion in the child's thoughts and imagination, are usually pervasive and persistent. Children need a chance to explain their reactions to the event, to know that what they feel is normal and expected, to be helped to identify traumatic reminders of the event, and to be given *time* and adult support to come to terms with the horror and grief they experienced.[17]

Violent Event at School. The school has a serious responsibility towards children, parents, and staff when a violent death occurs on school property. Whether a violent death is accidental or involves use of a lethal weapon, the event is overwhelming, as well as a first of its kind for the children, and outside professional consultation should be sought. The staff will be in shock and mourning, and they must be helped if they are to model the kind of attitudes and behavior that will benefit the children and their parents.

Witnessing Accidental Violent Death. The following discussion illustrates what must be done by educators to help children following an accidental violent death that they witness. This is how my school district responded to a school bus tragedy in which a kindergarten student was run over while students aged five to twelve looked on.

The accident happened in the late afternoon when most of the school staff had gone home. As soon as the superintendent learned of the tragedy, he acted to support and protect the child's teacher. He called her husband at work and asked him to break the news to his wife in person. He informed the principals of all the schools in the district, who in their turn activated prearranged telephone "chains." In this way, every staff member and the parents of all the children enrolled in the district were informed of the tragedy as soon as possible. After performing all the necessary duties including working with the police, the superintendent called on the teacher and brought her an orchid. Later, he would telephone her and visit at important moments. The teacher was greatly moved by the caring that her superintendent showed. She said it gave her the courage and strength she needed to carry out her teaching responsibilities as she simultaneously dealt with her own grief and reached out to the family of her deceased student.

As a member of the special services staff, I was called by the school counselor, and soon after by the pupil services director. Together with the building principal, it was to be our joint responsibility to devise a plan for dealing with the traumatic impact on the children, as well as to help them deal with their grief reactions.

A book in my private library contained a section on *The School as a Community of Grief.*[18] As we intended to follow the guidelines set forth there, we made copies of the few relevant pages and distributed them to the staff of the involved school. In response to my request, the pupil services director sought outside consultation; he did not arrange for a consultant to meet with the staff because he was assured that our plan was appropriate, that there was sufficient in-district support for the staff, and the staff were showing the kind of emotional fortitude needed to meet the requirements of the task. Under most instances, it would be important to have on-site consultation.

The morning following the accident, the sad news was announced by the principal over the school's intercom system, and a moment of silence was observed. If the death had been of an older child, it would have been important for the class, and perhaps the whole school, to have had a memorial ceremony of some kind. The school counselor then visited each class to answer questions, listen to feelings, and give reassurance wherever possible. The principal, pupil services director, and I were the counselor's support system. During the following weeks, the counselor met with groups of children from each grade who had witnessed the accident, and talked to anyone individually who requested it or was showing signs of being excessively upset.

Teachers were instructed to watch for symptoms that might occur as belated reactions. The kindergarten classmates of the dead child were monitored for signs of distress, and the counselor was a ready consultant to any teacher.

When the morning kindergarten class arrived at school on the day following the accident, they were met by a weeping teacher. Mrs. M shared her grief openly with the morning class, who did not know the child who had died. In this way she prepared herself to show strength in the afternoon for the children who were the boy's classmates. It was not that she wanted to suppress her grief with the afternoon class: instead she wanted to be able to meet their emotional needs.

As the shock of the accident subsided, the parents of the larger school community formed a memorial committee and collected money. They consulted with the child's parents about a suitable memorial. It was mutually agreed upon that a piece of art was to be placed in the school, and an original sculpture was commissioned. Sufficient money had been collected for two pieces of durable equipment to be placed in the kindergarten room as well. The tragic event was brought to an end with the dedication of the school's spring musical to the memory of the child.

Witnessing Murder. If the traumatic event observed is murder, children will be faced with the necessity of appearing in court as witnesses to tell what happened, and to identify the murderer. Further, the event will attract the attention of the media and children and their families may be contacted by reporters. The staff will be doubly shocked and frightened, and mass chaos could ensue unless an outside expert is brought in to stabilize the situation. Bruce Danto was the school's consultant when a first-grade teacher in Detroit was shot by her husband as the children were preparing for lunch.[19]

Dr. Danto stresses the importance of using a competent outside consultant who is skilled in the art and application of crisis intervention techniques, thanatologic (study of death of the body) principles, and forensic psychiatry or psychology in this kind of situation. The consultant must be available as needed over a period of months. The school should not take an authoritarian stance with parents. Rather, it is important that parents be involved in the decision-making process concerning the treatment of their children, what information will be shared with the press, and so on. Making sure that parents are listened to, and helping the children and their families through the court process, are important functions of the consultant.[20]

DEATH EDUCATION

Learning about death is *basic* in the education of children, but how and when this is to be done are open to debate. Certainly, when children have witnessed a violent death, you cannot put off until another time having them do some critical learning about death.

Those who have studied children's ideas about death have found that children are vitally interested in the subject. Given the chance, they express these ideas freely. We must, of course, be very sensitive to children who have suffered a loss or who are facing the threat of a loss through death when we discuss the subject in class, but we do not have to fear that children can't emotionally handle information about death. Rather than waiting until junior or senior high school to present a mini-course on the subject, it is preferable to incorporate death education in the curriculum beginning with kindergarten, with well-defined goals for each grade level. Too much discussion of death within a protracted period can intensify anxiety to a point that the hoped-for learning will be undermined. Indeed, students may learn something other than what was intended.

Teachers must be educated and as *prepared* to teach the subject of death as they are for teaching other basic subject matter. It is better to deal with the subject informally as it comes up, in a natural way, unless we can be sure we know what we're doing in presenting a formal death education program. Your school is ready for a death curriculum only after these steps have been taken.

1. Most of the staff has participated in a workshop that considers personal reactions to death.

2. All have participated in discussion groups pertaining to a proposed curriculum guide and evaluated resource material for implementing it.

3. A parents' advisory committee has been consulted, given suggestions, and approved the proposed curriculum.

BEING PREPARED TO HELP BEREAVED CHILDREN

Grief, successfully handled, can be a stimulus for new growth. Those who have mastered traumatic events develop attitudes and problem-solving skills that prepare them to cope with other stressful events that occur in the future. Your school will be prepared to help bereaved children and their families if you follow the checklist given in Figure 9-2.

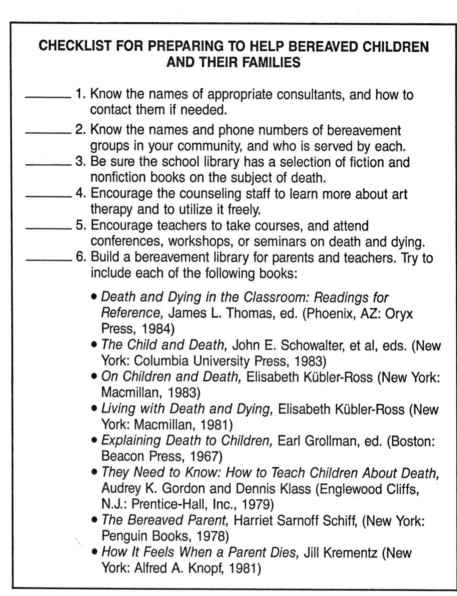

CHECKLIST FOR PREPARING TO HELP BEREAVED CHILDREN AND THEIR FAMILIES

_____ 1. Know the names of appropriate consultants, and how to contact them if needed.

_____ 2. Know the names and phone numbers of bereavement groups in your community, and who is served by each.

_____ 3. Be sure the school library has a selection of fiction and nonfiction books on the subject of death.

_____ 4. Encourage the counseling staff to learn more about art therapy and to utilize it freely.

_____ 5. Encourage teachers to take courses, and attend conferences, workshops, or seminars on death and dying.

_____ 6. Build a bereavement library for parents and teachers. Try to include each of the following books:

- *Death and Dying in the Classroom: Readings for Reference,* James L. Thomas, ed. (Phoenix, AZ: Oryx Press, 1984)
- *The Child and Death,* John E. Schowalter, et al, eds. (New York: Columbia University Press, 1983)
- *On Children and Death,* Elisabeth Kübler-Ross (New York: Macmillan, 1983)
- *Living with Death and Dying,* Elisabeth Kübler-Ross (New York: Macmillan, 1981)
- *Explaining Death to Children,* Earl Grollman, ed. (Boston: Beacon Press, 1967)
- *They Need to Know: How to Teach Children About Death,* Audrey K. Gordon and Dennis Klass (Englewood Cliffs, N.J.: Prentice-Hall, Inc., 1979)
- *The Bereaved Parent,* Harriet Sarnoff Schiff, (New York: Penguin Books, 1978)
- *How It Feels When a Parent Dies,* Jill Krementz (New York: Alfred A. Knopf, 1981)

Figure 9-2

Endnotes

1. Elisabeth Kübler-Ross, *On Children and Death* (New York: Macmillan, 1983), pp. 126-144.
2. Frances Scott, "When a Student Dies" in *Death and Dying in the Classroom: Readings for Reference*, James L. Thomas, ed. (Phoenix, AZ: The Oryx Press, 1984), pp. 67-68.
3. Nikki Meredith, "The Deadly Epidemic: Murder," *Chicago Tribune*, December 30,1984.
4. *Network* (Columbia, MD: National Committee for Citizens in Education), November 1985.
5. *Record-Eagle* (Associated Press release), Traverse City, MI, November 25, 1985.
6. *Network*, November 1985.
7. Gertrude Morrow, *Helping Chronically Ill Children in School: A Practical Guide for Teachers, Counselors and Administrators* (West Nyack, NY: Parker Publishing Company, 1985), pp. 135 and 137.
8. Myra Bluebond-Langner, *The Private Worlds of Dying Children* (Princeton, NJ: Princeton University Press, 1978), pp. 210-230.
9. Raymond K. Mulhern, Mary E. Lauer and Raymond G. Hoffman, "Death of a Child at Home or in the Hospital: Subsequent Psychological Adjustment of the Family," *Pediatrics*, vol. 71, no. 5, 743-747, May 1983.
10. Morris A. Wessel, "Children, When Parents Die" in *The Child and Death*, John E. Schowalter et al, eds. (New York: Columbia University Press, 1983), p. 125.
11. Richard A. Gardner, "Children's Reactions to Parental Death" in *The Child and Death*, Schowalter et al, eds., 1983, pp. 108-109.
12. Jill Krementz, *How It Feels When a Parent Dies* (New York: Alfred A. Knopf, 1981).
13. Ibid.
14. Albert C. Cain, Irene Fast and Mary E. Erickson, "Children's Disturbed Reactions to the Death of a Sibling," *American Journal of Orthopsychiatry*, 34 (4), 741-752, 1964.
15. Audrey K. Gordon and Dennis Klass, *They Need to Know: How to Teach Children About Death* (Englewood Cliffs, NJ: Prentice-Hall, Inc., 1979), pp. 87-89.
16. "Medical News," *Journal American Medical Association*, vol. 254, no. 6, August 9, 1985.
17. Ibid.
18. Gordon and Klass, *They Need to Know: How to Teach Children About Death*, pp. 90-93.
19. Bruce L. Danto, "A Man Came and Killed Our Teacher" in *The Child and Death*, Schowalter et al, eds., 1983, pp. 49-78.
20. Ibid., pp. 72-74.

Chapter 10

Child and Adolescent Suicide

Suicide is unacceptable and shocking; yet it is a fact that young people are taking their lives in increasingly greater numbers. Suicide is currently listed as the third leading cause of death among fifteen-to-nineteen-year olds, just behind accidents and homicides. The suicide rate among youth has doubled in the past two decades, but the statistics do not tell the whole story. Many suicides are disguised as accidents, and many homicides have been provoked by the one who is killed, leading some psychiatrists to believe that suicides are also embedded in the homicide statistics. Suicide may actually be the number one killer of youth.[1] Suicides are camouflaged as accidents by families to avoid the shame and guilt they feel, and in this deception they receive collaborative support from physicians and law enforcement officials.

Preschool children and prepubertal children also commit suicide, but their deaths are rarely counted in suicide statistics. Young children make many attempts to end their lives, but few succeed, possibly because they do not have access to more lethal means. However, it is thought that many of the accidental deaths among young children from fire and burns, drowning, being hit by motor vehicles, falls, and from ingesting toxic substances, are in reality suicides. Prepubertal children who have been rescued from such accidents often report suicidal thoughts or intent if they are carefully interviewed.[2] The fact is, we don't know the rate of suicidal behavior among children under fourteen, but we know that it is not as rare as we are often led to believe.

Most of us like to think of childhood as a time for joy and light-hearted frolicking, so being forced to think about childhood depression and suicide is like pricking the balloon of a pleasant illusion. As I have indicated in previous chapters, abuse and neglect, as well as separations from attachment figures (through death, divorce, and abandonment) result in depressed children, and depressed children have a potential for suicide. One study of abused children revealed that forty percent of the sample manifested self-destructive suicidal behavior.[3]

IS SUICIDE PREVENTABLE?

Experts believe that in the majority of cases, suicide is a ⊦ ble tragedy. Therapy and a favorable turn of events can reverse the trend toward a suicidal future for depressed children.

The school has a crucial role in changing the course of events that ultimately leads to the suicide decision. Suicide decisions are generally preceded by emotional stress that has been building up for a long time, probably years. Children send out many distress signals that are more observable and identifiable by teachers and peers than by parents. You can learn to recognize and respond to the messages that children and adolescents convey in their behavior, moods, conversations, drawings, journal entries, essays, and personal notes that constitute a plea for help.

My focus will be on preventing suicide, recognizing that this is not always possible. Major depression can emerge in children and adolescents *without evidence of previous emotional or behavioral disorder*. Although these young people may be responding to pressures to grow up before they are ready, or to their perceived inability to live up to their own (or parents') perfectionistic standards, they most likely also have a genetic (biologic) predisposition to depression. These children are less likely than other depressed children to be recognized as being in need of help.

The School's Role in Prevention

The school staff must be ready to deal with the reactions of students and faculty if a youngster takes his or her life. This is no ordinary kind of death; a student suicide often triggers similar action by other suicide-prone young people. Thus, a plan of action for dealing with the crisis created by a student suicide must be carefully prepared in advance to prevent suicide contagion.

Schools hold an important key to the prevention of suicide because they have the potential to create a mentally healthy atmosphere that can be an antidote for depression. Furthermore, schools have more psychological services available for helping children than do any other social institutions. It is a sad fact that, except for schools, our society has created few mental health resources for children and youth. Suicide awareness programs in the schools are now being viewed as a needed major thrust in suicide prevention.

Limitations of Schools

Regardless of the critical position of schools in suicide prevention, they also have limitations. Seriously depressed youngsters cannot be adequately treated by school psychologists and social workers, yet efforts to get psychiatric help for a student requires the cooperation of the parents. Often, the parents' denial of the seriousness of the symptoms causes them to resist seeking help or to undermine the therapist once improvement is apparent. What school professionals can do is identify depressed children, persist in trying to get them medical/psychiatric help, monitor their symptoms over time, and offer supportive counseling if the parents will permit it. If the parents refuse counseling, the counselor can still guide a teacher who is willing to make the extra effort to relate personally to the youngster.

SCOPE OF THE PROBLEM

Of all the depressed children in our schools,* only a fraction will complete an act of suicide, but many will make one or more attempts. All seriously depressed children and adolescents are at risk of attempting suicide. Several surveys have found that more than ten percent of high school students have *attempted* suicide, and fifty to sixty percent have seriously thought about suicide as a solution to their problems.[4]

If a person is determined to take his or her own life, he or she will find the means to do so. However, most suicidal young people are ambivalent and want to be saved. If they did not have access to the most lethal means for ending life, they would probably be rescued more often. Two to three times as many girls as boys *attempt* suicide, while boys outnumber girls four to one in actually killing themselves.[5] One factor that is believed to account for the difference is that girls tend to choose methods that are less lethal (slashing wrists and ingesting pills),

---

*Researchers for the National Institute of Mental Health estimate that one in five children may suffer from depression. A variety of studies indicate that two to thirty percent of five- to eighteen-year-olds become depressed. There is no doubt that the incidence of depression increases with age; a study of 5,600 high school students concluded that depression in adolescents is second only to colds in commonness.

while boys usually use violent methods (handguns, jumping from high places, and smashing vehicles at high speeds).

Experts suggest that suicides in the young would automatically be drastically reduced if society would control accessibility to handguns, drugs, and alcohol. Young people try to self-treat their depressions with drugs and alcohol, both of which only deepen the depression. Although other means of self-destruction would remain, those with suicidal intent might not be as willing to consider them. Many suicidal gestures depend on the immediate availability of the means to carry them out. When only less lethal means are present, the suicide attempt will usually be unsuccessful, and the young person will be rescued and offered help.

ROOTS OF SUICIDE IN THE YOUNG

Brenda Rabkin, author of *Growing Up Dead,* says in her introduction: "…young people commit suicide because of unbearable pain and a conviction that life is without hope, that new tomorrows are just miserable repeats of old yesterdays; so to continue living is pointless."[6] There seems little doubt that most suicidal young people are depressed to the point where they cannot consider options other than suicide for the relief of their misery. To understand suicide and its prevention, we must understand depression and the three main contributory factors in youth suicide.

Psychological Roots of Suicide in Young People

Failed bonding or disturbed or disrupted attachment during the early years of a child's development may plant the suicidal impulse. It is true that social isolation, poor school performance (possibly based in unidentified learning disabilities), and family disruption that involves divorce, desertion, abuse, alcoholism, or all of these, are common findings in the case histories of the majority of young people who attempt suicide.[7] Disturbances in the parent-child relationship are usually evident, and attachment difficulties dating from the earliest years can often be identified.

Other psychological phenomena noted by clinicians and researchers include:

1. "reunion with a dead parent fantasy" that is acted out
2. imitation of a suicide act carried out by someone with whom a youngster is closely identified

3. acting out of a parent's perceived wish to be rid of the child or adolescent

4. acting out revenge against a parent

5. belief in reincarnation as a means of obtaining a better life

6. belief that Heaven, which is achieved through death, is a desirable place to be because there everything is beautiful, peaceful, and serene

Perhaps the most inexplicable of all psychological phenomena is the very talented person's seeming inability to accept less than superlative performance at all times, in all things, no matter how select the competition is. Dr. Jerome Motto, a professor of psychiatry at the University of California, Irvine, Medical School believes we must confront our bright and very talented children very early in life with problems that they cannot solve so they will experience failure. He has said, "Very bright children know they will be loved if they always bring home 'A's, but they do not learn that they will also be loved if they do not achieve top honors in all that they do."

Societal Roots of Youth Suicide

David Gil believes societal factors to be important in youth suicide. These include:

1. the dehumanizing aspects of our societal institutions and workplaces that inhibit the full development of human potential;

2. our value system that emphasizes competition rather than cooperation; domination and exploitation rather than freedom and self-direction; inequality rather than equality; and selfishness rather than concern for others.

He says, "Suicidal urges, thoughts, desires, and acts seem to be one response of individuals who feel irreversibly trapped by societal conditions that violate the unfolding of their life process and the development of their innate potential."[8]

This point of view implicates schools along with other social institutions because they reflect the dominant cultural attitude that places a high value on the acquisition of material possessions and defines success in terms of wealth, position, and status. The pervasive isolation, disruptiveness, and violence that characterize American families exist because society has failed to provide the supports needed for adequate development of families and their individual members, and has failed to emphasize quality of life and compassion for others as the basis for a meaningful existence.

Biological Roots of Adolescent Suicide

The precursor to suicide during adolescence is depression. Whether or not their condition has been diagnosed, young people who attempt suicide are usually depressed, although suicide does also occur in the context of other psychiatric disorders.

Dr. William Beardslee, a Harvard University psychiatrist, has stated, "There is conclusive evidence for clustering of individuals with the diagnosis of depression within families."[9] There is mounting evidence that the most severely depressed youngsters have a parent, sibling, or close relative who has a major depressive illness. Childhood depression is most responsive *initially* to drug therapy, supporting the idea that chemical imbalance is a major consideration in childhood depression, with genetic predisposition a significant factor.

Is it possible that emotional and physical neglect during infancy by a depressed mother can alter the child's body physiology to the extent that a biological basis for depression results? This idea would support Mary Giffin's ideas about bonding failure implanting the suicidal impulse, but implicates body physiology as well as psychological factors in the process.

Genetically transmitted depression may occur in a child or adolescent "out of the blue," accounting for the sudden appearance of depression in a previously well-functioning young person. Psychological factors, such as the stress of a major transition, a move to a new city, or going from junior to senior high school or from high school to college, may also contribute. There is speculation, too, that the hormonal changes of adolescence may trigger depression in a person who is genetically predisposed to it. The combination of a stressful transition and a hormonal trigger could explain the drastic increase of depression after the onset of puberty.

CHILDHOOD DEPRESSION

The facts outlined in earlier chapters also pertain to the topic of childhood depression, out of which suicide evolves. The warning signs of depression are basically the same as the warning signs of suicide.[10]

Although some psychiatrists believe that depression as a clinical syndrome does not occur in prepubertal children, the bulk of the evidence is to the contrary. It is clear that depression in children *does* exist, and that it can be diagnosed using the same criteria as for diagnosing it in adults.[11]

One clinician describes depressed children as follows: "Their eyes look like burnt sockets. Their faces seem immobile, static; their expressions don't change. They're often skinny and ashen colored; their voices sound flat and their words don't jibe with their tone. Their speech seems colorless, as if they're deliberately deleting all adjectives."[12]

Masked Depression

Some say we fail to recognize when a child is depressed because the depression does not present itself in the same form as in adults. For example, in contrast to adult depressives who tend to become immobilized, adolescents may become reckless; while depressed adults act sad and lethargic, depressed teens often act angry, unreasonable, rebellious, or incorrigible. Depressed adolescents tend to manifest their depressed feelings in dangerous driving, drug and alcohol abuse, running away from home, stealing, and sexual promiscuity.[13]

Children who are depressed often exhibit conduct disorders, hyperactivity, enuresis, learning disabilities, and somatic complaints of varying severity. Because the underlying depression is not readily perceived, some professionals call it "masked depression." These symptoms apparently only mask the depression to the casual observer.

Perhaps the term "masked depression" came into being because teachers, parents, and sometimes even mental health professionals, unfamiliar with the diagnostic criteria for depression, tend to focus on a particular symptom and its removal rather than attending to the *constellation* of symptoms that point to depression. There is no doubt that a child's significant depression is often overshadowed by a morass of other symptoms that are quite bothersome to all concerned. This is why it is important to consider depression when a child is relatively nonfunctional and has a list of diverse symptoms.

Psychiatric Diagnosis

Major depression is a psychiatric diagnosis, and children suspected of being depressed should be referred for psychiatric evaluation. Diagnosis of depression is arrived at through careful, structured interviewing of the parents and the child, combined with data supplied by the school and the primary physician. Teachers and other school staff will be asked for information about the child's social and academic functioning, energy level, concentration, self-esteem and mood, and may be asked to fill out rating scales.

Criteria for a Diagnosis of Depression

The persistence of depressive mood, or the disinterest in or inability to derive pleasure from the usual activities, are at the core of a depressive state. In addition, a child will have characteristic symptoms in several of the categories given in Figure 10-1.

Psychiatrists diagnose major depression when four of the eight symptom clusters in Figure 10-1 are present with a general feeling of ill-being that has lasted two weeks or longer. This rule does not apply if there is a known organic mental disorder, if the child is recently bereaved, or if symptoms are superimposed on a preexisting non-organic psychotic disorder.

IDENTIFYING DEPRESSED CHILDREN IN SCHOOL

Teachers, counselors, and school psychologists can identify depression in children by being aware of the criteria for making such a diagnosis, and by conducting a structured interview that elicits a child's perception of his or her *inner state*. Affective states are internally experienced, so a child's report of his or her own emotions, what the behavior means, and how he or she thinks and feels about relationships or school problems is crucial in determining whether or not the child should be evaluated by a psychiatrist. The opportunity to conduct such an interview is usually available, either because a child seeks out a teacher or counselor to talk with, or because the parents have given permission for counseling or psychological evaluation at school.

Categorizing Symptoms

Teachers and counselors usually have a lot of observations and information about a youngster who has problems. Many of these, if properly categorized, would fit under one or another of the eight symptom clusters of depression. The first step in the identification of a depressed child is to arrange symptoms or behavioral observations into the eight clusters.

Interviewing Children

Most educators are comfortable interviewing children and are familiar with the need to be concrete and talk with a youngster "on his or her level." However, most are not in the habit of talking with students on a personal, intimate level. We must not be too intrusive with young people, yet troubled children and adolescents *need* someone to help them talk about their deep concerns. It is not easy for them to initiate an intimate conversation with an adult, so we must be willing to approach them.

Use a structured interview that covers four major areas: school; outside activities including peer relationships; home life; and thoughts

SYMPTOMS OF DEPRESSION

Energy Level

The child lacks energy, manifested by apathy, fatigue, or tiredness.

Self-Appraisal

The child has low self-esteem, manifested by negative attitudes toward him- or herself; makes self-deprecatory remarks, shows excessive or inappropriate guilt (i.e., blaming self), feelings of being bad. Evidence of poor self-esteem may be readily apparent or come to light in projective data gathered during psychological evaluation.

Thought Processes

The child has difficulty concentrating, showed by forgetfulness or slowed thinking. In school, the child may exhibit scrambled, rambling thoughts, be unable to recall what has been learned, forget to bring materials to class, or persistently misplace things.

Attitude

The child shows pervasive pessimism, manifested by a lack of interest in usual activities and a sense that "nothing will ever be right," that "nobody cares about me," or "I can't do anything without lousing it up."

Psychomotor Functioning

The child's activity level may be agitated or slowed down. Deterioration in visual-motor tasks may be evident in school. The child's handwriting becomes illegible, drawings become qualitatively poorer, and/or the child may be less coordinated than previously (e.g., doing less well in sports).

Sleep Disorders

The child may have difficulty falling asleep, wake frequently, or waken early in the morning and not be able to go back to sleep. The child may be sleepy in school after reportedly being up until "all hours" at home; or, in school the child may fall asleep often but also have slept long hours during the night, resulting in too much sleep.

Eating Disorders

The child may eat too little or too much, have no appetite or a voracious one. Abnormal weight change for a child's age is an accurate measure of the significance of this problem.

<u>Morbid Preoccupations</u>

The child may be unusually preoccupied with illness and death (own or that of close family member), may verbally express suicidal ideas ("I feel like I want to kill myself") or exhibit them symbolically in poems, stories, or artwork. The psychosomatic child should always be questioned about fears or thoughts of dying ("Do you ever think your headache is so bad you might die from it?"). Suicidal adolescents are often convinced and continue to believe that they have a rare terminal illness of unknown name and origin, even after they have been thoroughly checked medically and told that no organic basis can be found for their physical symptoms, which are of psychosomatic origin.

Figure 10-1

or feelings about the self, the world, and the future. Start with talking about school and peers.

1. Ask questions that will elicit both positive and negative thoughts and feelings, such as "What do you like best about (school, your friends, family, yourself)?" and "What do you *not* like (or hate) about...?"
2. Always ask if there are times the student would wish not to have to go to school.
3. Ask "What are the best things that ever happened (at school, with family, with friends) and what were the worst?"
4. In pursuing feelings about the self, ask, "If you had a magic wand and could change anything about yourself, how would you want to be different?"
5. Ask the same question about the world. Questions about the world and the student's own future in it are important because suicidal youth are not able to see anything good for themselves in the future. The total lack of any future orientation is significant and should be probed.

By picking up on cues offered in response to questions of this kind, you encourage and allow the student to give you an intimate, personal view of his or her inner self.

AWARENESS OF SUICIDAL RISK

Not all depressed children are suicidal, but seriously depressed young people should be under the care of a psychiatrist. Having a psychiatric disorder is still considered a shameful thing, despite the frequency with which depression occurs in the general population. For this reason, referral to a psychiatrist should never be made impulsively, nor should it be a unilateral decision. The staff member who feels that such a referral is indicated should confer with the principal, teacher, and special services staff, before presenting such a recommendation to parents.

Considering the prevalence of depression in children and adolescents, it is obvious that we must not get panicky and assume that every depressed child is at suicidal risk. However, the schools can monitor depressed children *over time,* and keep a watchful eye on symptom development. This requires that someone in the school (counselor, psychologist, nurse or principal) keep an updated file on the changes, both positive and negative, that these youngsters show over the years, once they have been identified as depressed. Even if they have not been officially diagnosed by a psychiatrist, these children should be monitored on the basis of your own diagnosis. Watchfulness also requires that a coordinated effort be made between the elementary school staff and junior and senior high school principals and counselors.

Evaluating Distress Signals

No one has yet developed a way to accurately predict whether a troubled child will become suicidal, but Mary Giffin offers a schema that can help us know when a youngster is moving in the direction of a suicidal future. Troubled children experience a constant erosion of self-esteem when the distress signals they send out (in their behaviors) are not responded to with appropriate kinds of help. As their self-esteem slips away, so also does their ability to maintain a sense of balance and control, and they slide into a state of hopelessness in which they can think only about wanting to die.[14]

The symptom phases that reflect this movement toward hopelessness are given in Figure 10-2.

Learning Disabilities/School Failure

Some researchers who have assembled psychological profiles of youth suicides have been impressed by how often they discover a history of learning disability.[15] Even when there was no diagnosis of

---

TROUBLED CHILD'S DISTRESS SIGNALS*

Phase One Symptoms

_____ Acting out with aggressive, hostile behavior

_____ Alcohol and drug abuse

_____ Passive behavior

_____ Changes in eating habits

_____ Changes in sleeping habits

_____ Fear of separation

Phase Two Symptoms

_____ Abrupt changes in personality

_____ Sudden mood swings

_____ Impulsiveness

_____ Decreased interest in school work and decline in grades

_____ Inability to concentrate

_____ Loss or lack of friends

Phase Three Symptoms

_____ Loss of an important person or thing

_____ Hopelessness

_____ Obsession with death or a death wish

_____ Evidence that the child is making a will

*Excerpts from *A Cry for Help* by Mary Giffin, M.D., and Carol Felsenthal. Copyright © 1983 by Mary Giffin, M.D., and Carol Felsenthal. Reprinted by permission of Doubleday & Company, Inc.

Figure 10-2

learning disability, chronic school failure since beginning school may indicate that there was an unidentified learning disability. Learning failure is one cause of low esteem; children who fail in school tend to have trouble making friends and pleasing their parents, and learning-disabled children are vulnerable to becoming depressed.

When a learning-disabled student shows changes in attitude, motivation, or usual performance, or else begins forgetting to come to L.D. sessions, always investigate. The changes could indicate that the

student is giving up hope, even when you are satisfied with his or her
progress. If you suspect that a student has become discouraged or
depressed, it would be wise to have the psychologist interview the
youngster.

Even when learning-disabled children are making what we consider good progress and have a warm, supportive family, they must be
carefully evaluated psychologically at every follow-up assessment.

Symbolic Messages of Anguish and Hopelessness

Suicide-prone youngsters often make their morbid mood manifest
in symbolic form, in either writings or artwork. When children and
adolescents have no close friends, no one to share their feelings and
innermost thoughts with, they may take the opportunity offered
through poetry, essay, or story writing, or in what they paint or draw to
express their sense of loneliness, nothingness, grief, anger, or
hopelessness.

Teachers who are on the alert to receive messages that reflect
despair, desperation, despondency, or futility, will not overlook the
metaphors contained in students' writings; nor will the art teacher miss
the point that the product reflects a preoccupation with death when a
young person draws or paints graveyards, coffins, ghosts, skeletons,
executions, or depicts massive destructive forces bringing death in their
wake.*

It is true that most adolescents think about death and suicide, as
well as the fate of mankind and the world, and these subjects may be
debated in their writings or explored in their artwork. Writing and art
can be constructive outlets that reflect good use of coping resources.
Intuition is important in distinguishing the mentally healthy student
from a suicide-prone student. A hopeful or constructive outcome of the
conflicts and fears about death and fate depicted would not be found in
the work of a suicide-prone student. However, if you have any doubts
about a student's state of mind, especially where marked ambivalence
about living and dying is expressed, proceed as you would if your
"suicide alert" mental buzzer had gone off.

When morbid ideas or messages of futility are detected in a
student's work, do not grade, offer criticism or pass judgment on the
content or quality of the product. Rather, treat it as a serious attempt by

---

*Terminally ill children (or chronically ill children who are afraid they might die)
also use death themes in their writings or artwork; and children trying to come to terms
with tragic natural disasters that are in the current news may draw pictures of these
events. Always investigate.

the student to communicate his need for help. Someone must talk with the student about the written or artistic product promptly, and this does not necessarily have to be the teacher for whom the work was done. Schedule a meeting to include the principal, nurse, counselor, all the student's teachers, and the school psychologist in order to share information, exchange ideas and suggestions and decide who should talk with the student. There may be some indication that the student has been trying to get close to one or another of the staff, or perhaps one of you already has such a relationship. Generally speaking, the staff member who has the greatest rapport with the student should probably be the one chosen as spokesperson.

When a Student Tells You About a Friend

Young people do not usually disclose their suicidal feelings and thoughts to adults, but they often tell a friend. They usually pledge the friend to secrecy first, and the friend, although upset, is reluctant to tell an adult who could help. An important thrust of the many suicide prevention programs that are springing up across the country is to instruct teens in how to respond when a friend starts talking about suicide. Teens are being told, "Don't keep *that* information a secret!" Brochures that are being distributed to teens give brief facts and myths about suicide, the warning signs of suicide, whom to tell, where help is available, and what to do.[16] This advice is summed up in the following list:

1. Take the signs seriously.
2. Stay calm.
3. Talk with the person.
4. Tell a parent or another adult immediately.

You, as a teacher, principal, nurse, or counselor may be the person the friend tells. You must be ready to meet the challenge of getting help for the suicidal student. The first step is to talk frankly and openly with the suicidal person, whether it is the student or a friend who alerts you. If a youngster refuses to disclose the identity of the "friend," he or she may be talking about him- or herself.

Discussing Suicide with a Student

What teens are being taught to do in response to a friend who is suicidal also applies to the adult who is sought out to help.

1. Take the matter seriously, stay calm, show concern, and talk with the young person in a direct manner.

2. Find out how serious the suicidal intent is; what prompted this kind of thinking; what is going on with schoolwork, friends, and family; whether any consideration has been given to the means of suicide, and if so, have any steps been taken to procure those means (for example, obtaining a gun or drugs).

3. Ask the student if he or she would be willing to talk confidentially with someone who is more of an expert with such problems.

The more specific the suicide plan and availability of means, the more immediate the danger. In such a case, don't leave the student alone.[17]

Suicidal youth feel that they have no future, that there is no way out of their problems, and that no one cares whether they are alive or dead. These youth need to know that:

1. Someone cares. ("I don't want you to die.")

2. They are not crazy and their suicidal feelings will abate. ("Anyone feeling as down as you is going to think he should kill himself. But these ideas do go away, because life can be better for you than it is now.")

3. Problems can be solved. The way this can happen is to get help to relieve depression, get off drugs and alcohol (if these are being used) because they make depression worse, and explore how problems can be solved. It is important not to judge the use of alcohol and drugs, but to be factual in stating that they *do* deepen depression and make problems seem impossible to solve.

Clinicians who treat depressed and suicidal young people agree that you should not be afraid to discuss suicide in this kind of detail. Talking about suicide with depressed people will not give them the idea to kill themselves; rather it will offer relief. Fears or obsessions about killing themselves are already in the minds of suicide-prone depressives. Most suicidal adolescents are not psychotic, but typically they think they must be going crazy because of their pervasive suicidal preoccupations.

Get the Student Help

When parents deny a young person's problems, refuse to take suicidal gestures seriously, or will not cooperate in getting help for a son or daughter, *don't give up*. With younger children, report the case to

Protective Services (see Chapter 3), and with adolescents, get them to seek help on their own. In order to do this you must know your community's resources: crisis intervention services are available through hospitals; mental health associations may have a suicide prevention program, or be able to tell you where a teen can get help; youth centers may offer individual therapy or peer counseling groups and have a psychiatric consultant available; there may be a Samaritan program in your community.

Adolescents, we know, are inclined to deprecate psychiatry and to refer to any mental health therapist as a "shrink." They can be resistant to admitting a need for help, particularly if parents deny the problem, and in availing themselves of help that is offered. Be supportive and persistent in leading a young person to help. Be willing to go to the crisis center with the student, or engage the student's friends as helpers. Ask a friend of the student to help you persuade the youngster to go for the appointment you have arranged, and to accompany you when you take the adolescent to the appointment. You may find that suicidal youth are more open to help than other adolescents. Your persistence may be what is needed to make the youngster feel that someone cares.

SUICIDE PREVENTION

Suicide, and particularly youth suicide, is not well understood by anyone. None of the approaches taken so far has slowed the alarming rate at which young people are taking their lives. Suicide is now being studied by the National Centers for Disease Control as a public health issue.

There is growing concern that suicide prevention programs must proliferate, and that schools must be the locus of such programs. The trend is toward enactment of state laws that encourage the development of prevention programs and provide funds for their implementation. California, New Jersey, and Florida have passed such laws. In each instance, a great deal of preparatory work preceded the writing of the laws. Parents of adolescents who had attempted or completed acts of suicide joined therapists, researchers, educators, and P.T.A. representatives to offer input to those drafting the suicide prevention program laws.

No one is yet urging that prevention programs in schools be mandated, but some people clearly fear that this will happen. At the first National Conference on Youth Suicide held in Washington, D.C. on June 19-20, 1985, a heated debate took place in the workshop "The

School and Youth Suicide." The degree of emotionalism that was sparked between those for and those against suicide prevention programs in schools shows the importance of the issue. Suicide prevention education *is* a serious matter, and the debate was warranted.

As long as legislation is permissive rather than mandatory, individual communities cooperating with mental health agencies, educators, and parents can decide what is most feasible for them. Everyone who believes in prevention programs agrees that educational programs and training workshops must be conducted by professionals who are experienced and knowledgeable about youth suicide. Parents, educators, and young people must *all* learn to recognize the warning signs and know what to do when a child or adolescent is suicidal.

Educational Programs

Even in the absence of legislation, suicide prevention is being taught all over the country. In some instances, courses on suicide are being taught in junior and senior high schools. More commonly, information forums are being sponsored during after-school hours. Although presented in school auditoriums, these programs are open to the public and aimed at increasing awareness. While teacher attendance may be mandatory, attendance for others is optional. Students are encouraged to attend *with their parents*.

The Controversy

The controversy about suicide prevention programs in schools concerns the question, "Should education about suicide be incorporated into the curriculum?" It is an inflammatory issue for several reasons.

1. There is evidence that both suicide and death have been inappropriately dealt with in the curriculum *in some schools*.[18]
2. There is the belief on the part of some that discussing the subject in class carries the risk of triggering suicide in vulnerable individuals.
3. Educators are ill-prepared to deal with the subject.
4. There are not enough knowledgeable mental health practitioners who are sufficiently trained to do the job of teaching the subject.
5. Emphasizing suicide by devoting a course to it opposes the value of living.

6. Because the thrust of suicide education is to teach teens how to reach out to a suicidal friend, there is the fear that the teen will feel terribly responsible if he or she is not successful in preventing a suicide.

Training Programs for School Staff

The most effective approach to suicide prevention is to train at least one staff member, but preferably all key staff (principal, nurse, counselor, and psychologist) in every school as suicide "experts." If key staff are thoroughly trained, not only in how to identify depressed and suicidal children and adolescents, but also in the skills of talking with them and their parents, and in dealing with a suicide crisis, the need for student courses about suicide will be lessened.

The Rutgers Model

A team of professionals from the Mental Health Center of the Rutgers University Medical School has developed a comprehensive suicide prevention training program for school personnel. It is a sixteen-hour, eight-week course that offers training in both assessment and intervention skills. The program recognizes that a person intervening with a suicidal youngster must not only be in touch with his or her feelings, but also in charge of those feelings, lest they prevent him or her from being effective. Trainees explore their own personal experiences with suicide as part of the course.

Like the state laws already enacted, the Rutgers model emphasizes the necessity for collaboration between schools and mental health agencies in the community. The rationale is that there are limits and limitations to what schools can do; outside consultation is often needed in a crisis, and the help of outside mental health workers will be needed if a student suicide occurs.

THE SUICIDE CRISIS

An impending suicide is always a crisis. The student who has made a previous attempt is *always at risk* of making another, whether or not he or she is in treatment. In some cases treatment is terminated when the adolescent starts to improve; but even when treatment is not terminated, improvement may provide the youngster the energy needed to make another suicide attempt.

I have already discussed depression as a precursor to suicide, and the progression of symptom development that brings a youth to the edge of suicide. An impending suicide attempt can be predicted if a child or teen exhibits the signals listed in Figure 10-3.

Guiding Parents

There is no time to waste in a suicide crisis. The suicidal youngster typically feels out of control and uncared for, and needs someone to take control immediately. When an adult does this, whether it is the parent or someone else, the child will sense it as caring.[19]

If you are called by a parent who suspects that his or her child is suicidal, tell the parent to take charge. The parent should confront the child with whatever has created suspicion of a suicide attempt, and should not be afraid of making the son or daughter angry. The parent must talk to the child directly about suicide ideas and plans, then get the youngster to a psychiatrist without delay.[20]

Depending on the circumstances and how comfortable you are with doing so, you may want to offer to be with the parent when the matter is discussed. On the other hand, if you do not trust yourself to give the necessary guidance, direct the parent to a twenty-four-hour crisis hot line, or to a suicide or crisis-intervention center. In either case, follow up to find out what the parent has learned from her child and what action has been taken. Parents will need a lot of support in this kind of crisis, and even more so in the case of a single parent, so be prepared to make short follow-up calls over the next several months. Be sure to ask how the school can help.

When a Student Suicide Occurs

Demographers suggest that as the birth rate goes down, so also will the rate of suicide in the young. However, the birth rate *is* going down, without a reverse trend in youth suicide. Suicide is too complex and multifaceted a phenomenon to respond dramatically to a single factor. Remember, one out of ten high school students admits to having made at least one suicide attempt, so we must not kid ourselves that "It can't happen here."

News that a student has killed him- or herself spreads throughout a school by its own self-generated mechanism. Students' imaginations run wild, and fiction becomes fact as a variety of rumors circulate. There is a propensity for other students to become overtly suicidal. The staff is likely to become anxious and depressed, and frightened confusion sets in. It is important to have a psychiatric consultant come

---

WARNING SIGNALS OF IMPENDING SUICIDE ATTEMPT

_____ Makes suicidal threats

_____ Makes statements about desire to die

_____ Describes in detail various ways to commit suicide

_____ Asks others what would be a good and easy way to kill oneself

_____ Gives away prized possession, makes peace with peers and family, or makes a will (so-called "final arrangements")

_____ Takes unusual risks (including abuse of drugs or alcohol)

Figure 10-3

to school to gather facts, clarify information, and talk about the factors involved in the suicide. The consultant's role is to reduce confusion, stop rumors, stem the spread of anxiety, and prevent further suicidal behavior. He or she does this by releasing as many facts as possible about the death, and by seeing that counseling services are sufficient to handle all requests by students for someone to talk to.[21]

A student suicide is a crisis that may affect everyone in school, as well as the family and the community at large. Cluster suicides, that is, groups of several suicides that occur relatively close in time and space are particularly tragic. This is a new phenomenon, and not yet completely understood. The question to be answered is whether exposure of youngsters to the first suicide triggers others, spreading like a contagious disease, or if it is just coincidence that several suicides occur within a short period of time in a particular school or community.

Dr. Mark Rosenberg, Chief of Violence Epidemiology of the National Centers for Disease Control, and his staff are making an effort to study cluster suicides, but must first develop a way to detect clusters and get them reported.* He believes that every community or school board should develop a response and action plan for when a student suicide occurs. He thinks that having the plan, whether or not a suicide has ever occurred, will serve to keep people calm and avert a panic. His recommendations for what should be included in such a plan[22] are shown in Figure 10-4.

---

*Dr. Rosenberg would welcome voluntary reporting of any such suspected clusters. He has graciously consented to the presentation of his views here.

ROSENBERG'S POST-SUICIDE ACTION PLAN

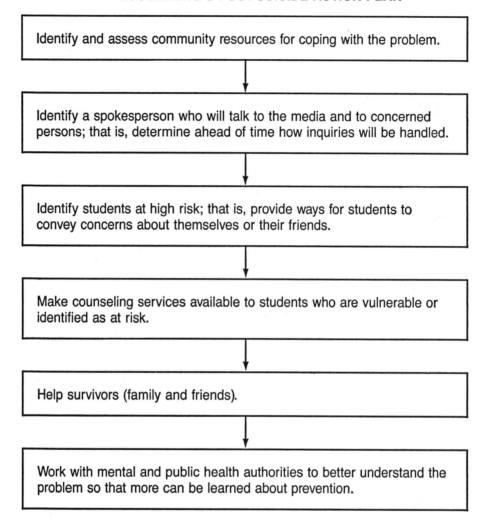

Identify and assess community resources for coping with the problem.

Identify a spokesperson who will talk to the media and to concerned persons; that is, determine ahead of time how inquiries will be handled.

Identify students at high risk; that is, provide ways for students to convey concerns about themselves or their friends.

Make counseling services available to students who are vulnerable or identified as at risk.

Help survivors (family and friends).

Work with mental and public health authorities to better understand the problem so that more can be learned about prevention.

Figure 10-4

ORGANIZATIONS DEVOTED TO SUICIDE PREVENTION

At the present time there are two organizations devoted to youth suicide prevention. They may be contacted for information about training programs, brochures for parents or students, or to answer any questions. The two organizations are:

The National Committee for Youth
  Suicide Prevention
1811 Trousdale Drive
Burlingame, CA 94010   or
(415) 877-5604

230 Park Avenue, Suite 835
New York, NY 10169
(212) 587-4998

Youth Suicide National Center
1825 Eye Street, N.W., Suite 400
Washington, D.C. 20006
(202) 429-2016

Endnotes

1. Mary Giffin and Carol Felsenthal, *A Cry for Help* (Garden City, New York: Doubleday and Co., 1983) p. 7.
2. Perihan A. Rosenthal and Stuart Rosenthal, "Suicidal Behavior by Preschool Children," *American Journal of Psychiatry*, 141:4, April 1984, pp. 520-525.
3. A. H. Green, "Psychopathology of Abused Children," *Journal of the American Academy of Child Psychiatry*, 17:92-101, 1978.
4. Francine Klagsbrun, *Too Young to Die* (Boston: Houghton Mifflin, 1976), pp. 5-17; Charlotte P. Ross, "Teaching Children the Facts of Life and Death: Suicide Prevention in the Schools" in *Youth Suicide*, Michael Peck, ed. (New York: Springer, Inc., 1985), pp. 148-149; and "63% of High School Students Surveyed Had Thought About Suicide," *Pediatric News*, vol. 18, no. 12, December 1984.
5. Leon Eisenberg, "The Epidemiology of Suicide in Adolescents," *Pediatric Annals* (Depression and Suicide in Children and Adolescents), vol. 13, no. 1, January 1984, pp. 48-49.
6. Brenda Rabkin, *Growing Up Dead* (Nashville: Abingdon Press, 1979), p. 13.
7. Reuben D. Roh et al, "Adolescents Who Attempt Suicide," *The Journal of Pediatrics*, vol. 90, no. 4, April 1977, pp. 636-637.
8. David G. Gil, "Societal Roots of Suicide" in *Child Abuse and Violence*, David G. Gil, ed. (New York: AMS Press, 1979), pp. 596-600.
9. William R. Beardslee, "Familial Influences in Childhood Depression," *Pediatric Annals* (Depression and Suicide in Children and Adolescents), vol. 13, no. 1, January 1984, p. 32.
10. Giffin and Felsenthal, *A Cry for Help*, p. 222.
11. Dennis P. Cantwell, "Depression in Childhood: Clinical Picture and Diagnostic Criteria" in *Affective Disorders in Childhood and Adolescence: An Update*, Dennis P. Cantwell and Gabrielle A. Carlson, eds. (New York: Spectrum Publications, 1983), pp. 3-18.
12. Giffin and Felsenthal, *A Cry for Help*, p. 223.
13. Ibid., p. 222.
14. Ibid., p. 43.
15. Michael L. Peck, "Crisis Intervention Treatment with Chronically and Acutely Suicidal Adolescents" in *Youth Suicide*, p. 115.
16. *Teen Suicide: Sometimes Being a Friend Means Not Keeping a Secret* (brochure) published by LINKS, North Shore Youth Health Service, 405 Central Street, Northfield, IL 60093. Phone: (312) 441-6191.
17. Charlotte P. Ross and A. Russell Lee, *Suicide in Youth and What You Can Do About It: A Guide for School Personnel* (pamphlet) prepared by the Suicide Prevention and Crisis Center of San Mateo County, 1811 Trousdale Drive, Burlingame, CA 94010.
18. Phyllis Schlafly, ed., *Child Abuse in the Classroom* (Westchester, IL: Crossway Books/ Division of Good News Publishers, 1985).
19. Giffin and Felsenthal, *A Cry for Help*, p. 247.
20. Ibid., pp. 247-263.

21. Irving H. Berkovitz, "The Role of the School in Child, Adolescent and Youth Suicide" in *Youth Suicide,* p. 182

22. Mark Rosenberg, "Cluster Suicides: Contagion or Coincidence?" presentation at the National Conference on Youth Suicide, Washington, D.C., June 19, 1985. Available on tape from Satellite Broadcasting, P.O. Box 5364, Rockville, MD 20851.

PART V

MEETING
THE
CHALLENGE

We are involved in the plight of traumatized children, whether or not we want to be, because these children do not learn in keeping with their potential. To some extent, we all share in the responsibility for their failure. Many of the traumas addressed here are the consequence of huge societal problems, but we need not feel helpless in the face of them.

One thing seems certain: if we are to successfully educate traumatized children, we must provide a nurturing and secure environment at a school where compassion prevails. Effort must be made, from the school board and superintendent all the way down the line to the classroom teacher, volunteers, and aides. What is required of the school staff cannot be delivered without a strong support system and an appropriate philosophical commitment from the school board and the community.

Chapter **11**

Establishing a
Staff Support
System

If we expect the emotionally distressed children who fill our classes to learn, we must be ready to understand and help them in a deeply personal way. Is this possible, or too much to expect?

THE NEED FOR SUPPORT

A few years ago in a suburban school district, an on-site college-level course called "Behavior Problems in the Classroom" was given over and over again at the request of groups of teachers who had heard about it from earlier enrollees. School counselors decided to take the course to find out why it was such a hit with teachers. What they discovered was that in addition to receiving sensible instruction about handling children's behavior, the teachers in the class functioned as a support group for each other. The instructor used a group process method of teaching that validated each teacher's self-worth and reinforced his or her sense of competence. The instructor described the "ideal" teacher as one who sees value in each student, who encourages the student to take risks, and who does not let the student down when he or she is vulnerable. This teacher encourages the other students in class to give suggestions and offer help and support to the one who is struggling with a seemingly unsolvable problem.

People in all kinds of endeavors, whether governing a country, running a household, or managing a classroom, need an available source of support and help on a daily basis. The behavior problems course was time-limited; it offered the kind of support teachers need, but was no longer available once the course ended. This chapter will describe how an ongoing support program, called the Teacher Assistance Team, can be established in any school, large or small, urban or rural.

GOALS FOR A SUPPORT SYSTEM

Before discussing the specifics of the Teacher Assistance Team, let's consider what a support system should do for us.

Emotional Renewal

Physical health and mental health are inextricably intertwined. Chronic illness makes us feel depressed, and unrelieved emotional conflict or distress has physical consequences. The word *burnout* is the popular way of describing emotional depletion and physical exhaustion. Obviously, we are no good to anyone if we allow ourselves to burn out. Therefore, a primary goal of a support system is to emotionally sustain and renew the staff.

Problem Solving

We are intellectual and emotional beings who can assess a difficult situation logically, but whose feelings that intrude upon thought often limit the range of ideas that come to mind to solve a problem. If we consult with someone *outside the situation,* we get help both in directing and objectifying our thinking, and in discovering alternate solutions to the ones being tried. An important purpose of a support system is the help it offers in problem solving.

Maintaining Confidence and Self-Esteem

Self-confidence is elusive; success reinforces it, failure erodes it. As you reach the frustration point with a problem child, you may sense that your self-confidence is slipping away. A support system can check this process and keep you feeling confident. A supportive person will remind you of previous or ongoing achievements and successes, and perhaps help you see that you are making much more progress with a student than you had realized.

I know a counselor who makes a chart for a frustrated teacher that lists the behaviors of a specific child that both are concerned about. After a program to help the student has been initiated by the teacher and the counselor, and the teacher is convinced there has been no progress, the counselor asks her to evaluate the behaviors on the list weekly to see whether there is no observable change, the behaviors are more pervasive, or occurring less often. Invariably, marking the chart helps the teacher see that at least a modest degree of change is occurring. Feedback that you're doing better than you realized restores self-confidence. A support group is therefore necessary to help a person maintain self-esteem and remain confident.

Knowing You're Not Alone

Desperation sets in when we feel that we are reaching the end of our rope with no help in sight. Wouldn't any one of us want to give up if there were no one to look to for help and guidance when we're feeling defeated? Emphasis on independence and self-sufficiency in our culture causes us to grow up being afraid to admit our need for help and our desire to have someone on whom to lean. With a support system firmly established, it is there to help you; you don't have to deal with difficult situations all by yourself. At the core, a support system embraces the idea of interdependency and shared responsibility: you are no longer alone.

THE TEACHER ASSISTANCE TEAM

The Teacher Assistance Team (TAT) was conceived by Dr. James Chalfant and Dr. Margaret Pysh in the early 1970s when mainstreaming of special education students began, and referrals for special education evaluation far exceeded the ability of the staff to process them.* Of those evaluated, many did not require special education services, even though they were presenting serious behavior and learning problems.

Teachers expressed disappointment and resentment when their referrals to special services brought no help, and when handicapped youngsters still in need of a lot of special help were returned to the regular classroom. There would never be enough money to employ the number of special educators needed to give direct supportive services to all the children in need of individualized help. The Teacher

---

*Dr. James Chalfant is professor of special education at the University of Arizona, Tuscon, AZ. Dr. Margaret Pysh is Director of Programs, Northern Suburban Special Education District, Highland Park IL. They have graciously given me permission to explain their model for providing support for classroom teachers.

Assistant Team concept emerged out of the recognition that teachers at the building level needed immediate available help to deal with the complex problems of today's children.

Rationale of TAT

The Teachers Assistance Team is a peer support system organized within individual school buildings. Team members are teachers of the regular faculty of that school. Elected by the faculty, the Team can be assembled whenever needed to deal with a teacher's immediate classroom concerns. The teacher seeking assistance follows a formal procedure of defining his or her problem in writing. The teacher meets with the team and together they generate alternatives for intervention. The teacher then selects the ideas that he or she wants to try to deal with the problem. The team and teacher plan a procedure for evaluating the effectiveness of the recommendations. Because the ideas are those of fellow teachers who have faced similar problems in their classrooms, they are viewed as realistic and feasible by the teacher seeking help. In contrast, ideas offered by special education or mental health "experts" are sometimes felt to be impossible to carry out.[1]

Uniqueness

The Teacher Assistance Team model is unique because of its philosophical basis. The TAT model takes advantage of the vast potential that all too often remains hidden in a teaching staff. This model helps maintain teacher esteem which is crucial in any effort to offer them support.

Unlike other models, TAT keeps the teacher in the driver's seat; all decision-making power remains with the teacher. Special services staff, parents, and even the student can be called upon to join the team as resources, but only at the teacher's invitation. Mutual respect and equality of status between teacher and team members are implicit in this model, which is based on the idea that teachers have experience, knowledge and creativity that, when shared with one another, will enhance each other's professional growth and lead to the solution of problems.

Basic Assumptions

These assumptions are basic to the TAT model: that regular education teachers have the skills and knowledge to help many students who present learning and behavior problems; that teachers can resolve more problems working together than alone; that regular education should make every effort to resolve problems at the building level before referring a child to special education; and that teachers learn best by doing; the best way for them to increase skills is to receive immediate help in solving classroom problems.

How to Establish Teacher Assistance Teams

Obviously there must be a felt need for a program such as TAT before setting about to establish it. Any interested teacher or administrator can become familiar with the program by contacting the authors of the concept,[2] by reading journal articles,[3] by watching a filmstrip,[4] or by visiting a school where TAT has already been established. To succeed, a program must have full administrative support from the top level down; superintendent, building principal, and teachers. It is crucial that administrators understand the concept and agree with its underlying assumptions and goals.

Administrative support is particularly important during the implementation and developmental process. The first step is to get the backing of the superintendent and principal. The next step is to arrange an orientation meeting, which takes one to two hours, to introduce the administration and faculty of a building to the basic ideas of the concept, and to determine interest. It is not necessary for every teacher in the building to embrace the idea initially, but at least half the faculty should be enthusiastic about it to assure success.

When sufficient administrative and faculty commitment has been obtained, arrange for a six-hour training workshop for the staff of the building. Only three elected team members will serve at a time, but it is assumed that rotations will take place, so it is desirable that all teachers, as well as the principal and other staff, attend the training workshop.

Once a team is in operation within a building, certain problems will inevitably be encountered. Although administrators do not function as team members, they have a role in helping a team work out problems that arise.

Finally, the team leader assumes the responsibility of evaluating the team's performance by collecting relevant data.

HOW TAT WORKS

The Teacher Assistance Team is comprised of three elected members, one of whom is chosen to be the team leader. These are usually regular teachers from the building, although occasionally a special education teacher is elected. Once the staff has been trained in the procedures to be followed, the team is ready to function. The process begins when a teacher who wants help contacts the team by completing a "Request for Assistance" form.

The "Request for Assistance" Form

The "Request for Assistance" form asks for the following information:

1. a description of what the teacher would like the student to do that he or she does not presently do
2. what the student's assets and deficits are
3. what the teacher had done to help the student up to now
4. what the teacher knows about the student's background, including previous test data

Completing the "Request for Assistance" form usually takes from ten to twenty minutes.

The Team Meeting

When a request for assistance is received, the team leader alerts the team and assigns a member of the team to talk with the teacher and perhaps observe the child in the classroom. Additional information is gathered when indicated; then a team meeting is scheduled. It is each team member's responsibility to be thoroughly familiar with the information submitted by the referring teacher, to have identified what the problem areas are, and to have considered recommendations *prior* to the team meeting. The meeting is planned to last no longer than thirty minutes, and the discussion must be relevant and focused on problem solving. The training session will have trained teachers to conduct thirty-minute meetings using selected principles of group dynamics.

The meeting is usually held in the morning before school begins, at the noon hour, or after school. The following points are covered during the team meeting:

1. The group reaches a consensus on what the problem is, negotiates objectives to be achieved, then brainstorms possible strategies to be used in achieving the objectives.
2. The referring teacher participates on an equal basis in each step of this process, then chooses the suggestions that he or she wants to try.

3. The team leader's job is to make sure the referring teacher is comfortable with the process, and is fully in control of decision making. Reinforcing the teacher's confidence is an implicit goal.

4. After the teacher has decided on an approach to use with the student, methods and procedures to be followed are refined.

5. A plan to evaluate the student's progress is made.

6. A follow-up meeting is scheduled.

HOW TO ASSURE TAT SUCCESS

Besides commitment to the TAT concept and full administrative support that includes training for the staff, there are additional requirements, more personal in nature, that determine whether this kind of support system will meet with success in a given school. Success is based on the following four factors:[5]

1. desire for assistance

2. willingness to ask for help

3. belief that peers can help

4. willingness to try alternatives

Support for Administrators and Special Staff

Because of their training in assessing and solving problems, and because they function as advisors and consultants in their jobs, administrators and special services staff habitually discuss their difficult situations with colleagues, with the aim of soliciting advice or getting a new slant on the problem. They tend to form informal support systems with each other, and their routinely scheduled staff meetings offer a more formal support arrangement. However, conflicts can arise within a group of administrators, or within a staff of social workers or psychologists, or between special staff and administration that threaten the integrity of the group and destroy the support function. When this happens, it is important to bring in an outside consultant; someone who understands group process and is experienced in conflict resolution, and most particularly, someone who has no vested interest in the issues involved.

Multidisciplinary teams may be in particular need of help from such an outside consultant, not only to solve problems, but to develop the kind of group cohesiveness that will allow them to be effective in coordinating their efforts. The multidisciplinary team concept was born when expertise in diagnosing handicapped persons and planning their rehabilitation became common. It was soon discovered that it was difficult to combine the recommendations of diagnosticians in medicine, education, psychology, social work, physical and occupational therapy and so on to create a coordinated plan for a handicapped child that would please everyone. Administrators must recognize that this is one kind of situation that requires outside consultation, and be ready to provide it.

Highly emotionally charged situations that involve violence, death (particularly from youth suicide), and threats from parents are other instances where the special services staff may be in need of support from an outside consultant. A supportive administration will not hesitate to make this available when the special staff request it.

Endnotes

1. James C. Chalfant, Margaret Van Dusen Pysh and Robert Moultrie, "Teacher Assistance Teams: A Model for Within-Building Problem Solving," *Learning Disability Quarterly*, vol. 2, Summer 1979, pp. 85-96; and James C. Chalfant and Margaret Van Dusen Pysh, "Teacher Assistance Teams: A Model for Within-Building Problem Solving," *Counterpoint*, November 1981, pp. 16-21.

2. The addresses and phone numbers of Dr. Chalfant and Dr. Pysh are:

   Dr. James C. Chalfant   Dr. Margaret V. Pysh
   P.O. Box 40785   Stratford Center
   Tuscon, AZ 85717   760 Red Oak Lane
   (602) 621-3214   Highland Park, IL 60035
       (312) 831-5100

3. Chalfant and Pysh, 1979 and 1981.

4. TAT filmstrip available through Goldberg-Werrenrath Productions, c/o Kate Goldberg Lechnir, 360 Vernon, Apartment 11, Glencoe, IL 60022.

5. Interview with Dr. Margaret Pysh, November 4, 1985, Highland Park, IL.

Index

Protection of Pupil Rights Amendment
(Hatch Amendment), 118, 129-130, 131
Protective Services:
child/adolescent suicide and, 221
child neglect and, 70-71, 73
physical child abuse and, 25, 46-48
psychological child abuse and, 130
reporting child abuse to, 25, 46-48, 70-71,
73, 83, 130
seeking advice from, 46
sexual child abuse and, 83, 96, 97
Protect Your Child, 177
Psychological child abuse:
consulting teachers and, 8
definitions of, 113-129
developmental progress and, 113
emotional neglect, 60-61, 73-74, 114-120,
124-129
Hatch Amendment and, 129-130
prevention of, 133-134
Protective Services and, 130
reporting, 73-74, 130
treatment of, 131-134
verbal abuse, 120-124
P.T.A *See* Parent-Teacher Association
Punishment, corporal. *See* Corporal
punishment
Pysh, Margaret, 235

R

Rabkin, Brenda, 209
Rainbows, 164
Rapist, definition of, 87-88
Regressed pedophile, definition of, 87
Remarriage, children's adjustment to
parental, 159
Reporting absent children, 72-73
Reporting child abuse:
legal obligations and, 17, 42, 70-71, 83,
97-98
neglect, 70-74
physical, 25, 44-48
Protective Services and, 25, 46-48, 70-71,
73, 83, 130
psychological, 73-74, 130
sexual, 83, 97-98
"Request for Assistance" form, 238
Ricci, Isolina, 170-171, 176-177
Rosenberg, Mark, 225
Rutgers University Medical School, Mental
Health Center of, 223

S

Safe Home/Block Parent plan, 12, 14
Salvation Army, 70, 74
Schlafly, Phyllis, 129
School-Age Child Care: An Action Manual, 15
School as a Community of Grief, The, 201
Self-Protection Week, 12-13
Separation, 139
anxiety and, 141-142
placement/foster care and, 148-152
preparing children for, 145-147
reactions to, 142-144
reasons for, 142
See also attachment
Sexual child abuse:
alcohol and, 84
child molestor defined, 86
children likely to suffer, 88-89
child sexual abuse defined, 84
consequences of, 103-104
differences between other forms of abuse
and, 82-84
disclosure phase of, 93, 94-97
educators accused of, 106
engagement phase of, 91-92
fixated pedophile defined, 86-87
incest defined, 84
incest-prone families, 89-91
men as the typical abusers, 83-84
pedophile defined, 86
pedophilia defined, 85
prevention of, 104-105, 110
progression of, 91-94
Protective Services and, 83, 96, 97
public awareness of, 81-82
rapist defined, 87-88
regressed pedophile defined, 87
reporting, 83, 97-98
secrecy phase of, 93
sexual interaction phase of, 92
suppression phase of, 94, 96-97
symptoms of, 98, 100-103
treatment of, 107-110
Sibling, death of a, 198-200
Single parent (s):
attitude and language toward, 172-173,
179-180
child support and, 174-175
curriculum materials/activities and, 172
new record forms needed for, 170-171
noncustodial, 170, 176-177
number of, 169
participation in school functions by, 171